A HISTORY OF
NORFOLK
IN 100
PLACES

A HISTORY OF
NORFOLK
IN 100
PLACES

A GUIDE TO ARCHAEOLOGICAL
SITES AND HISTORIC BUILDINGS

DAVID ROBERTSON, PETER WADE-MARTINS
AND SUSANNA WADE-MARTINS

WITH AERIAL PHOTOGRAPHS BY JOHN FIELDING AND MIKE PAGE

The
History
Press

Front cover images (clockwise, from top left):
Warham Camp. (Mike Page)
North Walsham and Dilham Canal. (Peter Wade-Martins)
St Benet's Abbey. (Mike Page)
Castle Acre Castle and Planned Town. (John Fielding)

Back cover image
Worstead (John Fielding)

First published 2022
Reprinted 2022

The History Press
97 St George's Place, Cheltenham,
Gloucestershire, GL50 3QB
www.thehistorypress.co.uk

British Library Cataloguing in Publication Data.
A catalogue record for this book is available from the British Library.

ISBN 978 0 7509 9366 1

Typesetting and origination by The History Press

Printed and bound in Great Britain by
TJ Books Limited, Padstow, Cornwall

CONTENTS

ACKNOWLEDGEMENTS

This book is based on the work of many archaeologists, historians and antiquarians, to whom the authors are indebted. The published works used by the authors are listed in the further reading sections at the end of the relevant place entry or, as some were consulted for several sites, in the introduction or period overview sections. Websites were consulted but only a couple are listed in the further reading sections, in case the others used are no longer available in the future for readers to use.

The authors would like to thank Will Bowden, Tony Bradsheet, Jonathan Hooton, Catherine Hills, David Johnstone, Susan Maddock, Robert Rickett, Elizabeth Rutledge, Clive Wilkins-Jones and Alison Yardy for commenting on various pieces of text.

Alison Barnard, Oliver Bone, Belinda Kilduff, Heather Hamilton, Chloe Phillips, Sophie Tremlett and Dayna Woolbright kindly provided images and permissions for their inclusion in this book. David Adams, James Albone, Hemali Chudasama, Julie Curl, David Dobson, Ken Hamilton, Anne Howlett, Rob Liddiard, Michael Ridge and Fred Squires supported efforts to source suitable images.

The guidance, advice and help provided by Nicola Guy, Ele Craker and Lauren Kent of The History Press is very gratefully acknowledged, along with the cover designer Martin Latham. Thanks also to the book designer, Megan Sheer.

David would like to thank Suzanne, Alex, Anna, Ian and Rosemary Robertson for their support during the three years invested in this book. All three authors would like to thank each other for their forbearance and for endlessly reading each others' texts! Peter and David are grateful to John Fielding, who took them flying over Norfolk, and to Will Fletcher who helped identify the need for this book.

MAP OF NORFOLK

KEY

Palaeolithic		*c.* 1 million to 10,000 years ago
Neolithic and Bronze Age		*c.* 4000-700 BC
Iron Age		*c.* 700 BC-AD 60./61
Roman		AD 43-*c.* 410
Anglo-Saxon		*c.* 410-1066
Medieval		1066-1485/1530s
16th to 19th centuries		
20th century		

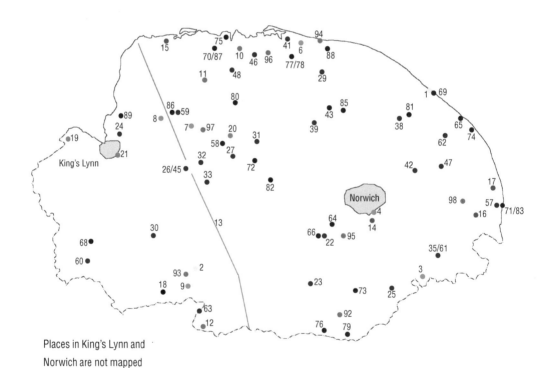

Places in King's Lynn and
Norwich are not mapped

INTRODUCTION

The three authors have greatly enjoyed writing this book, and we hope our readers will enjoy it too. Our aim has been to tell the story of Norfolk in places you can see. This starts with the location where Britain's earliest human footsteps were recently discovered preserved under the gravel left behind by glaciers as they retreated, right through to a Cold War airfield when Norfolk was very much on the front line. We close with the wonderful new Millennium Library in the Forum in Norwich, which can be a good starting point for further research. Choosing which places to illustrate has been a fascinating exercise and it has been governed by the need for each place to be clearly visible and, as far as possible, accessible. This has ruled out some earthwork monuments on private land, but for every period there is something to see, although for early prehistory and for the much of the Anglo-Saxon period the choice is limited.

There is inevitably a very uneven coverage that reflects the nature of the evidence. Most surviving prehistoric earthworks are Neolithic or Bronze Age burial mounds, leading us to describe a good selection of these funerary monuments, but there are no settlements we can include. For the Roman period there is the *civitas* capital and three forts, but no villas or farmsteads. The bias is particularly strong for the Middle Ages, where there are so many great castles, monasteries and churches, but no peasant houses.

The map references, the postcodes and the guidance at the end of each entry will help you find these places, and the Further Reading lists after each site description will allow you to follow up these sites further.

As well as places, we have covered, as far as we can, four of Norfolk's most celebrated people: Queen Boudica, who came close to pushing the Romans out of Britain in AD 60–61 and whose monument is not in Norfolk but on the Embankment in London; Robert Kett, who led a rebellion against the enclosing of the open fields and commons in 1549 and has a plaque on the Castle Museum (No. 64); Horatio Nelson, who defeated the French at Trafalgar in 1805 and has a column at Yarmouth (No. 71) as well as many pubs named after him; and nurse Edith Cavell, who was shot by the Germans for 'war treason' in the First World War in 1915 and who has a monument and a grave near Norwich Cathedral (No. 91). They all died for their efforts, but each displayed the true Norfolk character of great determination to 'do different' and to win.

★ ★ ★

For further study we recommend the Norfolk Historic Environment Record (available online as www.heritage.norfolk.gov.uk), the Norfolk Heritage Centre in the Forum, and the reference library of the Norfolk and Norwich Archaeological Society now available for study in the public search room of the Archive Centre, County Hall.

There will usually be a description of each important building we cover in the Pevsner and Wilson 1997 and 1999 Norfolk volumes of *The Buildings of England*. The two volumes of *Norfolk from the Air* (Wade-Martins, 1997 and 1999) have aerial photographs of some of the sites and buildings described in this book. A remarkably useful source is *An Historical Atlas of Norfolk* (Ashwin and Davison, 2005). For period studies the most up-to-date summary of prehistoric and Roman Norfolk is by John Davies (2008) and for the Viking period it is by Tim Pestell (2019). We are just waiting for someone to write a study of Anglo-Saxon Norfolk! For the archaeology of Norwich and for the Middle Ages there are several books listed below. The most recent general histories of the county are by Chris Barringer (2017) and John Davies (2020).

For those who wish to explore the historic landscape of Norfolk we strongly recommend the Ordnance Survey's Explorer series of maps published at a scale of 1:25,000. But there is also a remarkably detailed printed map of Norfolk surveyed in 1797 before most of the heaths and commons were enclosed that can give hours of pleasure (Faden, 1797; Tom Williamson and Andrew Macnair, 2010).

FURTHER READING

Ashwin, T. and Davison, A. (eds), 2005, *An Historical Atlas of Norfolk* (Phillimore).

Barringer, C., 2017, *A History of Norfolk* (Carnegie Publishing).

Bates, D. and Liddiard, R., 2013, *East Anglia and its North Sea World in the Middle Ages* (Boydell).

Cushion, B. and Davison, A., 2003, *Earthworks of Norfolk*, East Anglian Archaeology 104.

Davies, J., 2008, *The Land of Boudica: Prehistoric and Roman Norfolk* (Norfolk Museums and Archaeology Service).

Davies, J.A., 2020, *The Little History of Norfolk* (History Press).

Davies, J.A. and Pestell T., 2015, *A History of Norfolk in 100 Objects* (History Press).

Davison, A., 1996, *Deserted Villages in Norfolk* (Poppyland).

Faden, W., 1797, *Map of Norfolk* (republished by The Larks Press in 1989 with an Introduction by Chris Barringer).

Heaton, T. (ed.), 1999, *Norfolk Century* (Eastern Daily Press).

Margeson, S., Ayers, B. and Heywood, S. (eds), 1996, *A Festival of Norfolk Archaeology* (Norfolk and Norwich Archaeological Society).

Mortlock, D.P. and Roberts, C.V., 2017, *Norfolk Churches*, third edition (Lutterworth Press).

Pevsner, N. and Wilson, B., 1997, *The Buildings of England: Norfolk Vol. 1 Norwich and North-East* (Penguin).

Pevsner D.P. and Wilson B., 1999, *The Buildings of England: Norfolk Vol. 2 North-West and South* (Penguin).

Wade-Martins, P. (ed.), 1997, *Norfolk from the Air I* (Field Archaeology Division, Norfolk Museums Service).

Wade-Martins, P., (ed.), 1999, *Norfolk from the Air II* (Archaeology and Environment Division, Norfolk Museums Service).

Wade-Martins, P., 2018, *A Life in Norfolk's Archaeology* (Archaeopress).

Wade-Martins, S., 2015, *The Conservation Movement in Norfolk: A History* (Boydell).

Williamson, T., 1993, *The Origins of Norfolk* (Manchester University Press).

Williamson, T. and Macnair, A., 2010, *William Faden and Norfolk's 18th-Century Landscape* (WINDgather Press).

THE PALAEOLITHIC

INTRODUCTION

Humans have occupied the areas we now know as the British Isles for nearly a million years. For the great majority of this time they were incredibly mobile, responding to the need to gather and hunt food. They left little behind but their stone artefacts, and most sites associated with them are known from their tools and knapping waste alone. This makes it difficult to recommend Palaeolithic and Mesolithic places to visit, but it is impossible to leave out two of Norfolk's most significant archaeological discoveries from this book.

The period covered by the Palaeolithic (1 million to 10,000 years ago) saw considerable fluctuations in climate, with cold periods (glaciations) interspersed by warm periods (interglacials). At the turn of the twenty-first century the earliest uncontested evidence for human occupation in the British Isles was dated to around 500,000 years ago. But from the year 2000 onwards discoveries at Pakefield (Suffolk) pushed this back by around 200,000 years. The results of subsequent excavations on Happisburgh Beach recovered even earlier evidence. Tools and footprints here are dated to between 780,000 and 990,000 years ago (No. 1), providing us with the earliest evidence for human occupation in northern Europe and the earliest human footprints outside Africa. Early human footprints are incredibly rare and are only known from a handful of sites across the world.

The Happisburgh footprints and tools date to a period known as the Cromerian, which is named after the silt, sand, gravel and organic deposits identified in cliffs between Cromer in Norfolk and Kessingland in north Suffolk that are now known as the 'Cromer Forest Bed Formation'. This lasted around 500,000 years (1 million to 478,000 years ago) and saw climate alternate between glacials and interglacials. Several different human species were present in the British Isles during the Cromerian's warm periods. *Homo antecessor*, fossil remains of which have been found in Atapuerca, Spain, was more than likely the creator of the Happisburgh footprints. A shin bone and two teeth from *Homo heidelbergensis* dating to around 500,000 years ago have been found at Boxgrove in West Sussex, in association with hand-axes, other tools and bones of butchered horse, bison and rhinoceros. Hand-axes were first made in Britain around 500,000 years ago and have been found across Norfolk, including at Happisburgh.

Between 478,000 and 424,000 years ago the Anglian Glaciation saw northern, central, western and eastern Britain (including Norfolk) covered in ice.

This made it impossible for humans to survive here. The Bytham River that had flowed through the Midlands and East Anglia in the Cromerian was destroyed by the glaciers. They also pushed the River Thames, the estuary of which had possibly been at Happisburgh during the Cromerian, southwards close to its current position.

The Anglian glaciation was followed by the Hoxnian interglacial (424,000 to 374,000 years ago). The warmer climate saw humans return to Britain alongside exotic animals, including rhinoceros, giant ox, monkeys, lions and a now extinct straight-tusked elephant. Hand-axes continued to be used but new types of choppers, knives and scrapers known to archaeologists as 'Clactonian' also appeared. Swanscombe (Kent) and Clacton (Essex) are amongst the best-known sites from this period.

At the start of the Wolstonian glaciation (374,000 to 130,000 years ago) conditions were once again too harsh for human occupation, and the British Isles was again abandoned. Although cold, the climate was suitable again for colonisation around 240,000 years ago and this time it was *Homo neanderthalensis* that moved in. They brought with them new and more sophisticated ways of flint knapping that archaeologists call 'Levallois'.

Forced out again around 180,000 years ago by deteriorating climate, Neanderthals did not return to Britain until around 60,000 years ago, part-way through the Devensian glaciation (115,000 to 12,000 years ago). They lived in open grass steppe, alongside woolly mammoth, woolly rhinoceros, reindeer, horse and bear. In 2002 archaeological investigations at Lynford quarry revealed evidence from around this date. One of only a few Neanderthal sites where stone tools have been found alongside mammoth remains, it is one of the most important discovered to date in northern Europe (No. 2). Around 20,000 years later this species disappeared, close to the time modern humans (*Homo sapiens*) first arrived in Britain.

At the peak of the Devensian glaciation (18,000 years ago), the southern edge of the ice sheet reached as far as the north Norfolk coast. Evidence that people were active in Norfolk towards the end of this cold period includes distinctive flint long blades, such as those found alongside the rivers Little Ouse and Wissey and at Carrow Road, Norwich.

The Mesolithic period (10,000 to 6,000 years ago) began as the climate moved into the current interglacial (known as the Holocene). Trees spread to cover the previously open landscape and food collection methods changed. The period probably saw the first use of the hafted axe and the invention of the microlith. Microliths are tiny pieces of knapped stone that were fixed to wooden shafts to create spears and possibly arrows. Studies of ancient DNA indicate Mesolithic Britons probably had dark or black skin, dark brown or black hair, and blue or green eyes.

Until around 8,500 years ago Britain was connected to continental Europe. Norfolk was not a coastal area, instead it was on the edge of a plain stretching across where the North Sea is today (an area that has become known as 'Doggerland'). The melting of the ice sheet saw sea levels rise and the flooding of Doggerland to create the North Sea and English Channel, forming our islands as we now know them.

FURTHER READING

Dinnis, R. and Stringer. C., 2013, *Britain: One Million Years of the Human Story* (Natural History Museum).

Robinson, B., 1981, *Hunters to First Farmers* (Acorn Editions).

Wymer, J., 2005, 'Occupation Before the Last Glaciation: The Palaeolithic Period', in Ashwin, T. and Davison A. (eds), *An Historical Atlas of Norfolk*, pp. 13-14 (Phillimore).

Wymer, J., 2005, 'Late Glacial and Mesolithic Hunters (c.10,000-4000 BC)', in Ashwin, T. and Davison A. (eds), *An Historical Atlas of Norfolk*, pp. 15-16 (Phillimore).

1. HAPPISBURGH BEACH

Happisburgh Beach has long been known for its animal fossils and hand-axes, but in 2000 a chance discovery raised the site's profile and importance. While walking his dog, Mike Chambers saw a Palaeolithic hand-axe embedded in Cromer Forest Bed deposits. Little did he know that his find would turn out to be of international significance and result in the detection of the earliest evidence for humans in northern Europe, including the oldest footprints outside Africa.

Mike's hand-axe led to archaeological investigations involving many organisations, including the British Museum, Natural History Museum, Norfolk Museums Service and University of Leiden. For more than twenty years archaeologists have explored the laminated silts, sands and gravels within the Cromer Forest Bed, sediments that were deposited by a large river and are now known as the 'Hill House Formation' (after Happisburgh's pub). Over 200 flint artefacts have been recovered, including cores, flakes and flake tools. Many have sharp edges, suggesting they were found close to where they were originally dropped.

Happisburgh Beach from the east. The Hill House formation deposits have been identified between the two Xs. The location of the footprints is marked F, the car park P. (John Fielding)

Two of the Happisburgh footprints. (Martin Bates)

Over the last 5 million years the earth's magnetic field has alternated between periods of normal polarity (when the direction of field was the same as today) and reverse polarity (when the direction of field was the opposite). Samples from the laminated deposits at Happisburgh show reversed polarity, indicating a date between 2.52 million and 780,000 years ago. Analysis of plant and animal fossil assemblages recovered during excavations, which include mammoth, extinct horse, vole and elk species, and red deer, suggest a date towards the end of this time span, an interglacial between 990,000 and 780,000 years ago.

In May 2013 coastal erosion exposed over 150 hollows reminiscent of human footprints in the surface of the Hill House Formation. These were photographed from numerous positions to produce a three-dimensional photographic map before they were destroyed by the sea. Analysis confirmed forty-nine footprints, with toe impressions in one and the arch, front and/or back of foot in many. They measured 140–260mm long, 50–110mm wide and 30–50mm deep; comparing foot length to stature suggests heights between 0.93 and 1.73m. With at least five different people's feet identified, it is likely adults and children were walking together on the edge of the river. They were probably *Homo antecessor*, the only human species known to be in Europe at the time.

Plant remains (including pine cones) recovered from the sediments show the river passed through a grass floodplain with reed swamp, alder carr, marsh, pools and coniferous forest close by. Marine molluscs and barnacles indicate human activity was taking place in the upper reaches of the river's estuary. Beetles suggest average summer temperatures of 16–18°C, similar or slightly warmer than those of today.

A significant amount of non-local stone has been collected from the Hill House Formation. This includes quartz, quartzite and sandstone from Midlands, chert (possibly from southern and northern England) and Hertfordshire puddingstone. Prior to the Anglian glaciation two major rivers flowed across East Anglia from southern England and the Midlands – an ancestor of the Thames and the Bytham. The combination of stone types recovered suggests the river at Happisburgh was more likely the ancestral River Thames, perhaps at a time when the Bytham was one of its tributaries.

The periodic exposure of the Hill House Formation deposits is dependent on the impact of coastal erosion and storms. Although the footprints found in 2013 have been lost, another possible set was seen in 2019, suggesting further discoveries are possible. Parking is available on the cliff top at the eastern end of Beach Road. There is a ramp that leads from the car park to the beach – the location of the discoveries is best visited at low tide and there is a risk of becoming cut off by the incoming tide, so please carefully check tide tables before visiting. (Car park: NR12 0PR)

FURTHER READING

Ashton, N., Lewis, S.G., De Groote, I., Duffy, S.M., Bates, M., Bates, R., Hoare, P., Lewis, M., Larkin, N.R., Lewis, M.D., Karloukovski, V., Maher, B.A., Peglar, S.M., Preece, R.C., Whittaker, J.E. and Stringer C.B., 2010, 'Early Pleistocene human occupation at the edge of the boreal zone in northwest Europe', *Nature* 466, pp.229–233.

Parfitt, S.A., Peglar, S., Williams, C. and Stringer, C., 2014, 'Hominin Footprints from Early Pleistocene Deposits at Happisburgh, UK', *Plos One* 9, pp.1–13.

Parfitt, S.A., Ashton, N.M., Lewis, S.G., Abel, R.L., Coope, G.R., Field, M.H., Gale, R., Hoare, P.G., Larkin, N.R., Lewis, M.D., Karloukovski, V., Maher, B.A., Peglar, S.M., Preece, R.C., Whittaker, J.E. and Stringer C.B., 2010. 'Early Pleistocene human occupation at the edge of the boreal zone in northwest Europe', *Nature* 466, pp.229-233.

2. LYNFORD LAKES

In 2002 archaeological investigations at Lynford Quarry examined an infilled river channel containing a wealth of flint tools and animal bones. The quantity and types of tools, combined with well-preserved and palaeo-environmental remains, make Lynford the most important Neanderthal site so far discovered in Britain and one of the most important in northern Europe.

John Lord and Nigel Larkin were carrying out a watching brief during gravel quarrying when they discovered a rich organic sediment containing mammoth bones and flint tools, including three probable hand-axes, more than 2m below ground level. With the support of English Heritage and Ayton Ashphalte, a twelve-week rescue excavation was organised by the Norfolk Archaeological Unit that, due to the importance of discoveries, eventually lasted for five months.

Some 2,720 stone artefacts were recovered during the investigations, the great majority of which (83 per cent) came from the rich organic sediment that is interpreted as having developed in a meander cut off from a river. They include forty-one complete hand-axes, six broken hand-axes and three hand-axe rough outs – there are ovate- and roughly triangular-shaped examples. The assemblage suggests skilled flint-knappers carefully selected local flint to make hand-axes they could use for a range of functions in a variety of circumstances.

Lynford Lakes, from the south-west. The excavation site is marked A and the car park P. (John Fielding)

The excavation of four mammoth tusks and a mammoth tooth at Lynford Quarry, 2002. (David Robertson)

Of more than 2,000 animal bones, over 1,300 could be identified to species, genus or family, of which 91 per cent are woolly mammoth. These are highly fragmented but represent at least eleven individuals, mostly large males. No definite cut marks were evident, but the lack of limb bones and the breaking of bones to recover marrow indicates human use of carcasses. Bones from at least ten other mammal species were identified (wolf, red fox, brown bear, spotted hyena, horse, woolly rhinoceros, reindeer, bison, ground squirrel and vole), along with pike, stickleback, perch, frog and crake.

Plant and invertebrate remains indicate the meander was located in an open landscape dominated by grasses, sedges and low herbaceous plants, with small stands of birch and scrub and areas of acid heath or bog. They suggest summer temperatures between 12 and 14°C, with winter temperatures between -8 and -15°C. These habitats and temperatures fit with the results of Optically Stimulated Luminescence (OSL) dating of the organic sediments, which determined when they were last exposed to light. This gave a date range of 65,000 to 57,000 years ago, during the last glaciation.

Although no human remains were discovered during the excavation, Neanderthals are the only human species known to have occupied north-western Europe around 60,000 years ago; modern humans arrived much later. The evidence collected suggests Neanderthal groups were moving through the landscape, fully equipped in preparation for hunting opportunities. The riverside location would have attracted individual and herds of large mammals, providing Neanderthals the chance to ambush animals that were using the meander, or scavenge from the carcasses of those that had fallen into it.

The excavation site is now within one of the Lynford Lakes (TF 824 948), to the north-east of the Lynford Arboretum car park. The car park is to the east of Lynford Hall and the A1065 at Mundford. (Car park: IP26 5HN)

FURTHER READING

Boismier, W.A., Gamble C. and Coward, F., 2012, *Neanderthals Among Mammoths: Excavations at Lynford Quarry, Norfolk* (English Heritage).

THE NEOLITHIC AND BRONZE AGE

INTRODUCTION

EARLY NEOLITHIC (4000 TO 3000 BC)

The Early Neolithic saw the farming of domesticated crops and livestock, and pottery was used for the first time in the British Isles. In the early years of archaeology their introduction was associated with invaders from continental Europe but from the 1960s onwards the spread of ideas rather than people was the favoured interpretation. However, recent studies of ancient DNA appear to suggest there was a widespread change in the British population around the start of the Neolithic period, with the Mesolithic people substantially replaced over several centuries by farmers whose ancestors came from the eastern Mediterranean. Neolithic Britons are likely to have had dark skin, brown hair and brown eyes.

The arrival of farming was accompanied by woodland clearance and the construction of the first monuments. Long barrows – rectangular mounds built to house the remains of the dead – are the county's most visible Neolithic monuments. At least four survive as earthworks (No. 3), with the outlines of the infilled ditches that surrounded others known from cropmarks visible from the air. Some excavated long barrows in south, west and north Britain contain stone chambers and the remains of many individuals. The lack of suitable stone in Norfolk means ours do not contain stone chambers but they may have had internal timber structures. Only the West Rudham long barrow has seen any excavation, when in 1937–38 the Norfolk Research Committee discovered the mound was built of turf and gravel and identified a small ditched enclosure that might have served as a 'forecourt'. Part of a raised platform within the enclosure had been heated to such an extent that the soil has turned red – this could have been the location of a cremation pyre.

Cropmarks of several circular or oval ditched enclosures interrupted by multiple crossing points have also been identified, including one associated with possible long barrow cropmarks at Roughton. The number of gaps in the ditches of these 'causewayed enclosures' suggest they were not defensive sites but perhaps community, religious and/or trading centres. The Neolithic enclosure on Broome Heath is a puzzle (No. 3). It is not a causewayed enclosure and does not appear to have been associated with burial; it may have been for a settlement, and its revetment and palisade indicate it had a defensive function.

LATE NEOLITHIC/EARLY BRONZE AGE (3000–1700 BC)

In the Late Neolithic and Early Bronze Age a new suite of monuments appeared: henges, timber circles and round barrows. The term 'henge' was first used in the 1930s to describe prehistoric places without a burial function. Graham Clark's publication of the Arminghall henge (No. 4) in 1936 revised the term to describe a circular area with stone or timber uprights, normally surrounded by a bank and ditch, with the ditch usually inside the bank. This definition has been used ever since, although from the 1950s henges have not necessarily needed to include internal structures.

Norfolk does not have any stone circles or standing stones, but at least four timber circles have been found. One was associated with a henge, another was freestanding (No. 5), and the other two were perhaps associated with round barrows. Nineteenth-century reports of a stone circle at Gorleston are probably based on fiction or relate to a folly. Like causewayed enclosures, henges and timber circles may have been used for community and religious gatherings and could have seen elaborate ceremonies, something that is suggested by their associations with the movement of the sun and moon.

Round barrows – circular or oval burial mounds – are Norfolk's most prevalent prehistoric monument. Over 200 survive as earthworks and a selection of the most accessible and impressive are described here (Nos 3 and 6–8). Many archaeologists classify round barrows based on their current appearance. The simplest and most common are 'bowl barrows' with mounds that look like upturned bowls. Some of these have surrounding ditches, from which material was excavated to make the mound. The best have outer banks around their ditches. Bermed barrows have a flat area or 'berm' between their mound and ditch. If this gap is wide and the mound small, they are called 'disc barrows'.

Most round barrows that appear ditchless today probably once had ditches that have infilled over the centuries and therefore are no longer visible. The construction of ditches means that we know of several thousand more round barrows identifiable from the air as 'ring-ditch' cropmarks. However, some barrows never had ditches; instead, their mounds were built of soil and turf scraped from the area around them.

Excavations have shown each round barrow had its own history – some appear to have been built over a single grave, whereas others had many people buried under and within them, perhaps over many centuries. In some cases complete bodies were carefully inhumed, on occasions with grave goods. Excavations at Mintlyn and Bowthorpe have revealed coffins, made from both planks and hollowed-out tree trunks. The head of one person at Bowthorpe may have been placed on a grass-filled pillow. The richest burial known in East Anglia was found at Little Cressingham in 1849 – here an important person was buried with a rectangular decorated gold plate, three small gold cylindrical boxes, a necklace of amber beads and two bronze daggers. In other cases, bodies were cremated and placed in the ground, some in pottery urns, some perhaps in bags.

Although some barrows were built in one go, others saw multiple phases of construction. At Witton an irregular hollow, possibly a grave, was covered by a small mound of clay and surrounded by a ditch. After a short period of time the top of the mound was flattened and a small pit dug in the centre. A cremation pyre was then constructed, from which cremated bone ended up in the pit. A larger mound was built over the top, made from material from a second encircling ditch and clay from the nearby valley. Several cremation burials were later inserted into the mound.

Only a few late Neolithic/Bronze Age settlements have been excavated and most of these are characterised by groups of pits. The post-holes of a circular 'roundhouse' were excavated at Redgate Hill, Hunstanton, in the 1970s. These would have supported walls of wattle and daub and a thatched or turf roof, while two post-holes to the south suggest the building had an entrance porch. Despite the lack of settlement evidence, the discovery of flint axe heads, scrapers, arrowheads and other worked flints attest to people living and farming across Norfolk during the Neolithic and Bronze Age. In most cases locally sourced flint was used to make tools, but the mines at Grime's Graves (No. 9) suggest organised exploitation of the highest-quality raw materials. Metal objects – copper, bronze and gold – first arrived around 2500 BC, at the same time as elaborately decorated 'Beaker' pottery. The majority of early copper and bronze objects are axe heads but weapons are also numerous (such as spearheads, swords and daggers) and many pieces of jewellery have been found (including bracelets and torcs [neck rings]). Many individual objects have been collected but hoards of numerous pieces are also well known; the largest contain over 100 items. Analysis of ancient DNA indicates the appearance of Beaker pottery in Britain was associated with people moving from continental Europe.

LATER BRONZE AGE (1700–700 BC)

During the Later Bronze Age many areas of Britain experienced intensification of farming, with the establishment of formal field systems and small but probably permanent settlements. Ditched fields have been recognised on the Cambridgeshire fen edge since the 1970s – in the recent years excavations and aerial photograph research have confirmed their presence in Norfolk, including at Ormesby. An impressive settlement with seven or eight roundhouses and post alignments was excavated near Horsford ahead of the construction of the Norwich Northern Distributor Road.

From around 1700 BC round barrows ceased to be built and it appears cremation burial in flat cemeteries was preferred. Mini-mounds at Salthouse Heath (No. 6) suggest some flat cemeteries could have had small earthen markers.

FURTHER READING

Ashwin, T., 1996, 'Neolithic and Bronze Age Norfolk', *Proceedings of the Prehistoric Society* 62, pp.41–62.

Ashwin, T., 2005, 'Late Neolithic and Early Bronze-Age Norfolk (c.3000-1700 BC)', in Ashwin, T. and Davison A. (eds), *An Historical Atlas of Norfolk* (Phillimore), pp. 19-20.

Ashwin, T., 2005, 'Later Bronze-Age Norfolk (c.1700-700 BC)', in Ashwin, T. and Davison A. (eds), *An Historical Atlas of Norfolk* (Phillimore), pp. 21-22.

Ashwin, T., 2005, 'Norfolk's First Farmers: Early Neolithic Norfolk (c.4000-3000 BC)', in Ashwin, T. and Davison A. (eds), *An Historical Atlas of Norfolk* (Phillimore,) pp. 17-18.

Bradley, R., Chowne, P., Cleal, R.M.J., Healy, F. and Kinnes, I., 1993, *Excavations on Redgate Hill, Hunstanton, Norfolk and at Tattershall Thorpe, Lincolnshire*, East Anglian Archaeology 57, pp.1–77.

Barringer, C. (ed.), 1984, *Aspects of East Anglian Prehistory: 20 Years after Rainbird Clarke* (Geo Books).

Davies, J.A., 2008, *The Land of Boudica: Prehistoric and Roman Norfolk* (Oxbow Books).

Gilmour, N., Horlock, S., Mortimer, R. and Tremlett, S., 2014, 'Middle Bronze Age Enclosures in the Norfolk Broads: a Case Study and Ormesby St Michael, England', *Proceedings of the Prehistoric Society* 80, pp.141–157.

Hogg, A.H.A., 1940, 'A Long Barrow at West Rudham, Norfolk', *Norfolk Archaeology* XXVII, pp.315–331.

Lawson, A.J., 1986, *Barrow Excavations in Norfolk, 1950–82*, East Anglian Archaeology 29.

Lawson, A.J., Martin, E.A. and Priddy, D. 1981, *The Barrows of East Anglia*, East Anglian Archaeology 12.

Wymer, J.J. 1996. *Barrow Excavations in Norfolk, 1984–88*, East Anglian Archaeology 77.

3. BROOME HEATH, DITCHINGHAM

The Broome Heath long barrow, C-shaped enclosure and two bowl barrows represent a rare surviving prehistoric landscape. At least three additional barrows were lost to quarrying in the nineteenth and twentieth centuries (the quarries survive as water- and tree-filled pits).

The long barrow has not been excavated but Neolithic pottery and worked flints have been found on its surface. A low bank is attached to its western end, extending for about 40m in a south-westerly direction.

The C-shaped enclosure is exceptionally unusual; there are no other surviving prehistoric earthworks like it in Norfolk. When constructed, its curving inner and outer banks enclosed three sides of an area measuring 150m by 100m; the fourth side on the east was left open. Only the inner bank is now visible, standing up to 0.6m high. In 1970–71 archaeological excavations revealed it had an external timber revetment and was topped by a timber palisade, suggesting it may have been defensive. The banks were associated with numerous pits – some of these were found inside the enclosure and were probably dug when it was in use but others pre-dated it, having been infilled prior to the banks being built over the top of them. Pottery, over 20,000 flint artefacts and radiocarbon dating demonstrated the pits and enclosure were Neolithic. The pottery, flints and pits suggest the site was a settlement.

Broome Heath, Ditchingham, from the north-west. The long barrow is marked L, the enclosure C, the round barrows E and W, and the car park P. (David Robertson)

The Broome Heath long barrow. (David Robertson)

The western bowl barrow has an external ditch and an outer bank beyond this. Mesolithic and Neolithic flint artefacts, and Neolithic pottery, found on the surface of the eastern bowl barrow are probably evidence of earlier activity disturbed during its construction. A skeleton found in 1858 may have come from one of the round barrows but the exact circumstances and location of its discovery are uncertain.

Broome Heath's car park is on Green Lane, on the south side of Loddon Road, in Ditchingham village (TM 341 911). The C-shaped enclosure, long barrow and eastern round barrow are shown on the Ordnance Survey Explorer Map OL40. Bushes and trees mean the enclosure's banks can be difficult to see. The western round barrow is on the heath's southern boundary, partly in the heath and partly in a private garden. (Car park: NR35 2RD)

FURTHER READING

Wainwright, G.J., 1972, 'The Excavation of a Neolithic Settlement on Broome Heath, Ditchingham, Norfolk', *Proceedings of the Prehistoric Society* 38, pp.1–97.

4. ARMINGHALL HENGE

Arminghall is Norfolk's only confirmed henge. A low bank is all that is visible on the ground today but from the air two dark green circular rings, the circuits of infilled ditches, are visible among paler grass in very dry weather. On occasions eight dark patches arranged in a horseshoe-shape can also be seen inside the central area. This was the case when the site was discovered from the air on 18 June 1929 by Wing Commander Insall, three years after he had identified concentric timber circles at Woodhenge in Wiltshire. It was then partially excavated by Graham Clark in 1935, acting for the Norfolk Research Committee.

Clark investigated two of the dark patches, which were large infilled post-holes with ramps on their southern sides. In both post-holes he identified the shapes of the lost post – these were up to 0.9m in diameter and sunk up to 2.25m below ground. Charcoal at the base and on the edge of the posts suggests they were charred before they went into the ground; radiocarbon dating of the charcoal suggests they were installed between 3500 and 2700 BC. The ramps sloped down into the post-holes, indicating the posts were slid down into their sockets, before being pulled upright. If we work on the theory that two-thirds or three-quarters of each post would have been above ground, they may have stood 4–6m tall. They could well have been carved or painted.

The horseshoe of posts was 14m in diameter, with an opening on the south-west side. Surrounding it was the inner ditch, which Clark found was over 8m wide, over 2m deep and had a causeway entrance on the south-west. At the base of the ditch was a layer of charcoal from which sixteen sherds of decorated Beaker pottery, 107 flint flakes and nine flint cores were collected. Upper layers contained Iron Age and Roman pottery and Roman coins.

The surviving bank stood between the inner and outer ditches. By 1935 it had been damaged by ploughing and was around 15m wide. Clark established the outer ditch enclosed an area measuring 80–90m across and was about 3.6m wide by 1.4m deep. He found a Roman hearth and pottery in its upper fills.

The location of the ramps on the south side of the post-holes suggest the timbers were brought from an area to the south. However, the entrance to the inner ditch is on the south-west, which, if it had already been dug, would have made bringing the posts from the south exceedingly difficult. Clark therefore thought the posts were installed first and the ditches were dug immediately afterwards. The Beaker pottery from the base of the inner ditch is later than the radiocarbon date for the posts, which indicates the ditch could have been dug quite some time after the posts were installed.

Clark believed 'the monument was a sacred one' and that the upright posts were 'of an open air temple'. The south-west alignment of the entrances also suggests this – several authors have suggested they were deliberately aligned on sunset at

Arminghall henge from above, with the dark rings of the inner and outer ditches marked A and B and the horseshoe of post-holes marked C. This remarkable picture was taken in 1996 during exceptional dry conditions; the post-holes are not normally visible. (Derek Edwards, Norfolk County Council)

midwinter, which suggests links to beliefs associated with the movement of the sun. Research using virtual reality has also suggested an association with the setting sun, in this case as it was seen rolling down the prominent spur of land to the south-west known as Chapel Hill. The choice of the henge's location close to the confluence of the Rivers Tas and Yare would also have been important, as would its association with the numerous burial mounds constructed in the surrounding area.

The henge is marked on Ordnance Survey Explorer Map 237 (TG 239 060). It is located in grassland on the southern outskirts of Norwich, between Lakenham and Trowse. It can be seen to the south of a public footpath (part of Boudica's Way) that links White Horse Lane to the east and Stoke Road to the west. (NR14 8SH)

FURTHER READING

Clark, J.G.D., 1936, 'The Timber Monument at Arminghall, and its Affinities', *Proceedings of the Prehistoric Society* 2, pp.1–51.

Walker, K. 2018, 'Questions unanswered and questions unasked: A reflection on Arminghall Henge 90 years after its discovery', *The Annual* 27, pp.55–62.

5. SEAHENGE AND ITS SISTER

In 2049 BC more than fifty people gathered at Holme-next-the-Sea. They felled more than thirty oak trees growing on dry land, then carried and dragged them through saltmarshes to two favoured sites (where Holme Beach is today). At one location they placed the stump of the largest tree upside down in a large pit, so its roots pointed up towards the sky. A trench was then dug to take fifty-six timbers, creating a surrounding palisade that stood about 2m tall. This created the timber circle we know today as Seahenge. About 100m to the east, a second 'sister' timber circle (Holme II) was built: here two logs were laid on the ground, surrounded by a fence of wicker and enclosed by an arc of posts and a palisade. The palisade encircled an area more than four times larger than that inside the palisade at Seahenge.

Seahenge was reported to archaeologists in 1998, then fully excavated by the Norfolk Archaeological Unit the next year. Careful study revealed perfectly preserved and distinctive tool marks from the fifty or so different axes used to fell, split and shape the timbers. Holme II was not excavated but instead was surveyed and monitored on the beach; almost all of it has been destroyed by the sea since the late 1990s. Analysis of tree rings from both circles showed the trees were felled in the spring or summer of 2049 BC. This means they are the only two monuments in British prehistory we are certain were built at the same time.

It is likely a body was placed on the Seahenge central stump's upturned roots, perhaps to offer them to the heavens and so birds could remove the flesh. The stump's trunk pointed downwards, potentially creating a portal for the person's spirit to enter the underworld of the dead. Impressions on the top of the two oak logs in the centre of Holme II suggest an object was laid across them; this could have been the coffin of

Seahenge on Holme Beach, December 1998. (David Robertson)

Palisade timbers from Seahenge, in the Seahenge gallery at Lynn Museum. (Norfolk Museums Service [Lynn Museum, King's Lynn])

the deceased. If this was the case a small burial mound may have been placed over the coffin and logs, revetted by the wicker fence. The time and effort it took to build both structures would have been considerable, suggesting a person of some importance, possibly a local leader or religious figure. During construction and use it is likely they hosted celebrations and commemorations – the entrance into Seahenge's palisade is aligned on the midwinter sunset, suggesting these ceremonies could have been associated with the movement of the sun.

Neither of the structures had a surrounding bank and ditch so, despite the popular name 'Seahenge', they were not henges. Instead they fit into the tradition of Neolithic and Bronze Age timber circles – they are two of around 100 currently known in Britain. They stand out from the others because of the preservation of timbers, something that only happens in waterlogged and low-oxygen conditions like those on Holme Beach. To date, only one other timber circle (Bleasdale in Lancashire) has been found with surviving timbers.

> *Seahenge's central stump and half of its palisade are on display in a purpose-built gallery in Lynn Museum, Market Street, King's Lynn. The remaining palisade timbers are held in safe storage by Norfolk Museums Service. The few timbers left of Holme II are most often concealed by the sea or sand and therefore are rarely visible. (Lynn Museum: PE30 1NL)*

FURTHER READING

Bond, C.J. and Robertson, D. (eds.), Forthcoming. *Seahenge 2018: A Conference to Celebrate the Bronze Age Timber Circle* (Poppyland).

Brennand M. and Taylor M., 2003, 'The Survey and Excavation of a Bronze Age Timber Circle at Holme-next-the-Sea, Norfolk 1998–9', *Proceedings of the Prehistoric Society* 69, pp.1–84.

Pryor, F., 2001, *Seahenge: A Quest for Life and Death in Bronze Age Britain* (Harper Collins).

Robertson, D., 2016, 'A Second Timber Circle, Trackways, and Coppicing at Holme-next-the-Sea Beach, Norfolk: use of Salt- and Freshwater Marshes in the Bronze Age', *Proceedings of the Prehistoric Society* 82, pp.227–258.

Watson, C., 2005, *Seahenge: An Archaeological Conundrum* (English Heritage).

6. SALTHOUSE HEATH ROUND BARROWS

Salthouse Heath and adjacent land at Gallow Hill contain the densest concentration of round barrows in the county and one of the most extensive barrow cemeteries in East Anglia. There are at least eighteen large burial mounds and numerous 'mini-mounds' on publicly accessible land, with others on private property.

Gallow Hill is on the eastern side of the heath and at least nine of the large burial mounds can be seen here. The largest is north of the east–west road that bisects the heath; it is 28m across, 2m high and surrounded by a bank and ditch. It may also be the earliest in the group. The eight or nine smaller mounds to the south of the road are arranged in two parallel lines, with degraded ditches and a bank running between them. The name of this area of heath suggests there may have been a gallows here in medieval times. As far as we know, none of the Gallow Hill barrows has been excavated.

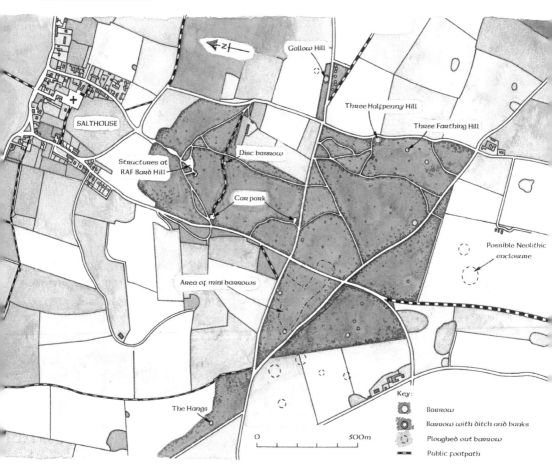

Map of Salthouse Heath, showing the locations of the round and mini-barrows. (Jason Gibbons)

The largest barrow at Gallow Hill, Salthouse Heath, from the west. (David Robertson)

On the eastern edge of the heath, to the south of the east–west road, are two bowl barrows named after coins that were produced between 1827 and 1862. 'Three Halfpenny Hill' stands next to the Salthouse–Kelling parish boundary, which (in a later period) may have been deliberately aligned on it. Its mound stands 2m tall and has a surrounding ditch and bank. Excavations in 1849 recovered a small urn decorated with chevrons. Further south is 'Three Farthing Hill', its name presumably reflecting how it is smaller than its neighbour. It was partly excavated in 1850 after being disturbed by a boy digging for rabbits; discoveries included a plain urn surrounded by a wall of flints and an urn decorated with scored lines containing the cremated remains of several different people. Aerial photographs taken in 1946 suggest a trench dug into the mound was created during Second World War military training.

North of the east–west road, next to a junction of paths, is a disc barrow. As one of only two disc barrows known to survive in Norfolk, it is incredibly important (the other is on Litcham Common). Here an outer low bank surrounds a shallow ditch, both of which enclose an area about 12m in diameter. A small mound stands towards the north-east of this central platform.

In the west of the heath, south of the east–west road and west of a north–south road, are two large barrows and most of the mini-barrows. In the 1930s A. Q. Watson discovered at least thirty small mounds, each of which was around 3m across and 30cm tall. He excavated three, Stuart Piggott investigated a fourth – all four contained cremated human remains and Late Bronze Age urns. It was thought the mini-mounds were destroyed in the 1940s during military training, but since the 1980s they have been rediscovered – during the 2000s Ray Loveday increased the number of possible examples to around seventy. In 2012 one of the possible mini-mounds was excavated in an attempt to further understand these features. Unfortunately, it was found to be a pile of soil that had accumulated naturally, possibly around the base of gorse bushes.

Salthouse Heath is located to south of Salthouse village. There are two car parks hidden behind bushes – one is accessed from the north–south road that links the heath with the village (Bard Hill), the other is off the east–west road that bisects the heath (Bridgefoot Lane). There are also a few roadside pull-ins close to the junction of the two roads. In summer the barrows can have tall vegetation growing on them, so it may be worth visiting in winter when this likely to be at its lowest. (NR25 7EA)

FURTHER READING

Chester, G.J. 1859, 'Account of the discovery of Ancient British Remains near Cromer' *Norfolk Archaeology* V, pp.263–267.

7. WEST RUDHAM ROUND BARROWS

There is a compact group of three bowl barrows on the easternmost section of West Rudham Common. They are located on level ground, with views across land that slopes down into a shallow dry valley to the north. The later boundary between West and East Rudham parishes lies immediately to the east.

All three have reasonably large and well-preserved mounds. The north-western mound in the biggest: it is about 1.5m tall. Located only 10m away, on the other side of a track, is the eastern mound. Both are surrounded by ditches, with low outer banks. Prehistoric worked flints have been found on both sites, but neither barrow has been excavated. The third barrow is 75m to the south-west of the other two. It does not have a ditch nor bank and is therefore harder see when visiting.

Other burial mounds are known from the surrounding area, including at least three (possibly more) on other sections of West Rudham Common.

The three barrows are shown as 'Tumuli' on Ordnance Survey Explorer Map 238 at TF 8335 2570. The easternmost part of West Rudham Common is open access land. It can be entered from a public right of way through a gate in its south-western corner. This path heads north-west from the road that links former RAF West Raynham (No. 97) with Little Massingham and Harpley. Providing the path is not obstructed, it is possible to park at its southern end, next to Gravelpit Wood (at TF 83799 24897). (NR21 7DQ)

Opposite above: *Three round barrows on West Rudham Common, from the north. The north-western barrow is marked A, the eastern mound B, the third barrow C and the public right of way F. (John Fielding)*

Opposite below: *The eastern barrow at West Rudham Common, from the south-east. (David Robertson)*

8. HARPLEY COMMON ROUND BARROWS

One of the best-preserved groups of round barrows in Norfolk stands on Harpley Common and adjacent land at Bunkers Hill and Anmer. Eight mounds are known to survive well, and archaeological investigations, faint earthworks and cropmarks suggest another ten may have been constructed nearby.

Four of the round barrows survive spread out over about 450m on open farmland to the east of the Peddars Way (No. 13). Three of these were excavated in 1843 by F.C. Lukis, who studied the construction of their mounds and recovered pottery and cremated bones. His observations and discoveries are recorded in notebooks curated by Guernsey Museums.

Across the country many burial mounds feature in folklore, although unfortunately very few in Norfolk are associated with local myths. One is the north-western barrow on Harpley Common, which legend suggests contains 'treasure' and rabbits will not dig into it. Lukis excavated a trench about 2.7m wide to investigate the mound's south side. He did not encounter treasure, but he did find two layers of burnt bone and wood, collected pottery sherds, and may have identified a prehistoric ground surface preserved below the mound. Pieces of Beaker pottery decorated with string impressions were recovered from the surface of the mound in 1993.

The south-western barrow is of an unusual form for Norfolk: its mound is sited on an earth platform that stands about 0.8m high above the surrounding land. It has not been excavated but in 1973 excavations by Andrew Lawson of a levelled barrow immediately to the east recovered three fragments of cremated bone, pottery and 159 flint artefacts.

The eastern group of round barrows at Harpley Common, from the south-east. (John Fielding)

The larger of the eastern round barrows at Harpley Common, from the south-east. (David Robertson)

Two bowl barrows close together form an eastern group. The asymmetrical shape of the western example is the result of disturbance caused by gravel quarrying on its southern side – Lukis noted the quarry had exposed bones and burnt material. The east barrow is smaller and was partially excavated by Lukis.

Like many barrows in Britain, these four have suffered damage during the cultivation of adjacent land. Since 2000 the owners of the barrows, with the support of the Norfolk Monument Management Project, Historic England and agri-environment schemes, have been able to establish grassland around the mounds to ensure their future survival.

The four barrows on Harpley Common are located south of Anmer Road, between Anmer and New Houghton (TF 763 280). They are labelled 'Tumulus' and 'Tumuli' on the Ordnance Survey Explorer 23 map. The western barrows are adjacent to the Peddars Way and can be viewed from it; there is a pull-in for parking where Anmer Road crosses the Peddars Way. The north-western and eastern barrows can be seen from the roadside. (PE31 6ZD)

FURTHER READING

Lawson, A., 1976, 'The Excavation of a Round Barrow at Harpley', *Norfolk*, East Anglian Archaeology 2, pp.45–63 .

Robertson D. and Paterson H., 2010, 'The Norfolk Monuments Management Project 1990–2010: Twenty Years Conserving the County's Rural Historic Environment', *Norfolk Archaeology* XLVI, pp.15–28.

9. GRIME'S GRAVES FLINT MINES

Grime's Graves is the only Neolithic/Bronze Age flint mine complex open to the public in the United Kingdom. Hundreds of mine shafts are still visible, with many other infilled shafts hidden below ground. Visitors can use a ladder to descend 9m though solid chalk to the base of one of the shafts to see the radiating galleries and the high-quality black flint 'floorstone' targeted by prehistoric miners.

From the late seventeenth century onwards antiquarians discussed the origins of the site. It was suggested the hollows could be the remains of an Iceni village, fortifications or a Viking camp. In 1867–68 Canon Greenwell from Durham Cathedral took part in the excavation of prehistoric flint mines at Cissbury in Sussex and he believed Grime's Graves was a similar site, which he was able to demonstrate during excavations he organised in 1868–70.

The visible flint mines occupy over 14ha and include at least 433 shafts, making them the largest prehistoric flint mining complex in England. On the surface the mines are circular, oval or linear depressions up to 7m deep, with diameters of the circular and oval examples between 6–20m. Mounds around and between the depressions are made of material excavated from the shafts and left behind. Geophysical surveys have identified evidence for further buried mines to the north and west of the visible examples.

The Neolithic–Bronze Age flint mines at Grime's Graves, from the south-west. (Mike Page)

Excavations have identified deep galleried shafts, 'intermediate pits' 6–7m deep with short galleries, and shallow open-cast workings. The depth of shafts and pits vary according to the depth of the floorstone, with the deepest extending 13m below ground level. Underground galleries radiating from individual mines are known to connect with those from other shafts. Linked galleries could have given miners escape routes in the event of shafts collapsing.

The shafts and galleries were excavated through solid chalk using just antler and bone picks; hundreds of antler picks have been found where they were left by their prehistoric users. We must imagine small groups of people working together, gradually digging further and further down, using ladders made from notched tree trunks to get in and out of the holes they created. When they reached a depth beyond the length of their ladders they built timber platforms across the width of the shafts, so they could use multiple ladders. The galleries are up to 1.5m high, 3.5m wide and 15m long – it is likely miners had to lie down to prise out flint nodules, increasing the length of the galleries as they worked. The nodules were broken into smaller pieces. Then, as shown by marks left by ropes in the chalk, these were hauled out in baskets. It is highly likely ritual activities took place in the shafts, both during their use and on and after their abandonment. A Cornish greenstone axe and skull of a phalarope (a wading bird) were found between two antler picks in Greenwell's Pit. In the 1970s two decorated pots were discovered on a chalk platform and a dog was found carefully buried in a gallery. Ox, pig, horse, sheep and goat bones could be the remains of celebratory feasts (or perhaps miner's usual meals).

Radiocarbon dating of bone and antler tools and charcoal demonstrate that flint mining took place at Grime's Graves between 2600 and 1500 BC. This suggests the site is slightly later than all other English flint mines that have been dated using scientific techniques. It also indicates mining was not intensive, with perhaps only one or two mines active each year over a thousand-year period.

Although the miners were attracted by the high-quality floorstone flint, it is likely the process of digging deep and the effort involved gave the tools made from it special meaning. On the surface most nodules were worked into rough shapes (including axe 'rough-outs') and then taken elsewhere for conversion into tools – only a few were worked on site to make objects like scrapers and piercers for immediate use. Of all the flint artefacts found in the wider Brecks, a minority are made from floorstone, suggesting most of the mined material left the area. Although some archaeologists have suggested it was taken across the south and midland England, it is difficult to scientifically link flint with its source areas, so we are not sure how far that mined at Grime's Graves travelled. However, the axe made of Cornish greenstone found in Greenwell's Pit indicates Grime's Graves flint could have been transported long distances, as the does the discovery of tools made of Lake District stone all over Britain.

Managed by English Heritage, Grime's Graves is located between the A1065 and A143, north-west of Thetford and north-east of Brandon (TL 816 899). It is open to the public seasonally, please check the English Heritage website for details. (IP26 5DE)

FURTHER READING

Barber, M., Field, D. and Topping, P., 1999, *The Neolithic Flint Mines of England* (English Heritage).

Topping, P., 2011, *Grime's Graves* (English Heritage).

THE IRON AGE

INTRODUCTION

The Iron Age covers the period from about 700 BC to the defeat of Queen Boudica by the Romans in AD 60–61. The arrival of ironworking technology using locally sourced ore transformed agriculture with the introduction of iron tips to wooden ploughs so that more marginal land could be brought into cultivation, particularly on heavier soils. This was a period when the population grew, more woodland was cleared and there was increasing competition for the best farmland. Some of the easily worked soils of Breckland were perhaps already over-exploited and were becoming heath, while the central clay lands became much more extensively developed by the end of the Iron Age. Settlement evidence has been excavated at several locations, including West Harling, Harford, and Lynford.

With this growing prosperity tribal groupings were emerging and their chieftains were competing for dominance. The arrival of the iron blade transformed tribal warfare. Cattle raiding was probably common, and communities centred on hill forts were commonplace in many parts of Britain. Indeed, hill forts in all their various forms and sizes can be found from the south coast of England to the north of Scotland (although the term 'hill fort' seems to be a little inappropriate when Norfolk has so few steep hills).

Evidence for dating hill forts in Norfolk is limited, so the best we can say is that they were constructed and used during the Iron Age. It is interesting that all the forts we know about, bar one, are in north-west Norfolk, at Warham (No. 10), South Creake (No. 11), Narborough and Holkham with an outlier at Thetford (No. 12). There is also an undated earthwork enclosure at Tasburgh that could be Iron Age or much later. With no extensive area excavations using modern techniques on any of these sites, the function of the Norfolk forts is still uncertain.

The extraordinary wealth of the tribal elites of the time is reflected in spectacular discoveries of gold and silver treasure mostly in west Norfolk dating from the first and second centuries BC. At least eleven hoards have been recovered on Ken Hill in Snettisham, containing complete and fragmentary torcs, ingot rings, coins, bracelets and scrap metal. Most of the treasure was made of gold, silver and electrum (an alloy of gold and silver). The way the items were very carefully buried in nests on Ken Hill suggests that they were offerings to the gods by a tribe or its leaders at a major tribal or religious centre. Other torcs have been found at North Creake, Bawsey, Sedgeford and Marham, all in the west of the county.

East Anglia has more recorded Late Iron Age gold and silver treasure than any other part of Britain. Metal detector finds of non-precious metalwork from all over Norfolk are just as significant as the treasure. Horse harness and chariot fittings suggests horse-mounted warfare was now very much central to the Iron Age way of life. Elaborately decorated bridle and harness fittings, linchpins to secure wheels to chariot axles, and an enthusiasm for putting horses onto the coins shows horse riding in all its forms had become central to their culture. The Iceni, the tribe that controlled Norfolk, north Suffolk and the eastern fens, had emerged as dominant in a prosperous, vibrant and warlike society. It is perhaps not surprising that Roman generals found it much easier to agree a peace treaty with the Iceni rather than take them on during the early years of the invasion. It could help to explain why the Iceni were nearly successful in ejecting the legions from Britain in AD 60–61.

Meanwhile, the topography of the county was changing. At about 250 BC sea levels were rising and a wide inland sea, known today by archaeologists as the Great Estuary, spread over the whole of the Acle Marshes. In the Fens at the same time the sea reached as far inland as Downham Market, but then gradually receded during the first century AD leaving the fertile marine silts available for the Roman administration to create a great imperial estate.

Ken Hill is on private land and has been extensively excavated by the British Museum. Objects from the site are on display in the British Museum and Norwich Castle Museum.

FURTHER READING

Davies, J., 1996, 'Where Eagles Dare: the Iron Age of Norfolk' *Proceedings of the Prehistoric Society* 62, pp.63–92.

Davies, J., 1999, *Land of the Iceni* (Centre of East Anglian Studies).

Davies, J., 2008, *The Land of Boudica: Prehistoric and Roman Norfolk*, pp.85–132 (Norfolk Museums and Archaeology Service).

Davies, J.A., 2011, *The Iron Age in Northern East Anglia*, British Archaeological Reports British Series 549 (Archaeopress).

Davies, J.A., Gregory, T., Lawson, A.J., Rickett, R. and Rogerson, A., 1992, *The Iron Age Forts of Norfolk*, East Anglian Archaeology 54.

Hutcheson, N.C.G., 2004, *Later Iron Age Norfolk*, British Archaeological Reports British Series 361 (Archaeopress).

Hutcheson, N. and Ashwin, T., 2005, 'Iron Age Norfolk' in Ashwin, T. and Davison, A. (eds), *An Historical Atlas of Norfolk*, pp.23–27 (Phillimore).

Hutcheson, N., 'The End of Prehistory: Gold, Silver, Boudica and the Romans' in Ashwin, T. and Davison, A. (eds), *An Historical Atlas of Norfolk*, pp.23–27 (Phillimore).

10. WARHAM ST MARY IRON AGE FORT

Warham Camp is surely the most impressive prehistoric monument in the county. It has a double bank and ditch enclosing an area of 1.5ha. There are three entrances, although none of these are thought to be original. Excavations have demonstrated that the defences continued into the valley, and estate maps show that the earth-works in the marsh were levelled when the old meandering course of the River Stiffkey was straightened. So, where was the entrance, and why was the whole fort built, not on a hill or on high ground, but on a valley side sloping down and actu-ally into the valley floor? A possible explanation is that there could have been a causeway across the valley bottom leading to the fort. With marshes on either side, this may well have created a perfectly defendable entrance.

There were excavations here, in 1914, 1929 and 1959, but none provided clear dating evidence from sealed locations and only eleven Iron Age sherds were recov-ered in total. The most interesting discovery from 1959 was a series of post holes and trenches for holding timbers along the crest of the inner bank probably representing a palisade and a fighting platform. The Norfolk Archaeological Trust used this signifi-cant evidence to show a palisade on top of the bank on the information panel near the site entrance. If the inner and outer banks both held continuous timber palisades then the amount of timber needed to provide an effective defence was extraordinary. One can only imagine the resources needed to build such a place.

The Iron Age fort known as Warham Camp, with its massive double bank and ditch, from the south-west. None of the three entrances are thought to be original. (Mike Page)

The east side of the inner ditch of Warham Camp. The original bottom of the ditch is probably 2m below the present ground surface. (Peter Wade-Martins)

The fort is owned by the Holkham Estate, which permits access from the end of a footpath running down a long, straight green lane off the Warham St Mary to Wighton Road (NR23 1NZ). Care needs to be taken to find a place to park the car beside the road without obstructing the lane or the road.

FURTHER READING

Gregory, T., 1986 'Warham Camp' in Gregory T. and Gurney D., *Excavations at Thornham, Warham, Wighton and Caistor St Edmund, Norfolk*, East Anglian Archaeology 30, pp.22–26.

St George Gray, H., 1993, 'Trial-excavations in the so-called 'Danish Camp' at Warham, near Wells, Norfolk', *The Antiquaries Journal* XIII, pp.399–413.

11. BLOODGATE HILL, SOUTH CREAKE, IRON AGE FORT

This fort, with a single bank and ditch enclosing an area of 3.5ha, lies on high ground to the west of the River Burn. The very circular shape has obvious parallels with the fort nearby at Warham (No. 10). We know from a parish map of 1619 that the interior was then still being cultivated as medieval strip fields, and the earthworks marked on the map as 'Burgh Dykes' were then still intact. But, an entry in the parish records for 1827–28 describes how the 'Burrow Dykes' 'were removed and set on land' as a part of a wholesale land improvement scheme. It was then ploughed regularly until the Norfolk Archaeological Trust bought the site in 2003.

The most informative aerial photograph of the fort was taken in 1975 when the field was under plough, and it shows the outline of the earthworks and the locations of three possible entrances. To protect the earthworks from yet further cultivation, the site was put down to permanent grass with the aid of a grant from the Heritage Lottery Fund. Before that the interior was field-walked in 2001 and surveyed by metal detectorists in 2004, but nothing was found from either survey to give a clear indication of when the fort was occupied. In 2003 a geophysical survey enhanced the information on the aerial photograph, and the two together were used to produce the artist's reconstruction of the fort depicted on the on-site information panels.

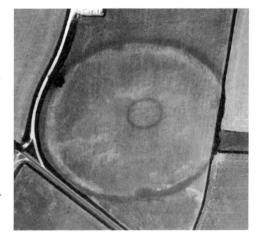

Excavations in 2003 showed that the main fort ditch was re-cut once, and a radiocarbon date from primary deposits suggests it was constructed between 400 and 170 BC. Near the middle was a much smaller ring-ditch believed to be contemporary with the fort because Iron Age pottery was recovered from all levels of the ditch fill and because the narrow entrance in the ring was aligned with the main fort entrance to the east. Internal features picked up in the geophysical survey fit well with this layout and create the suggestion that there was a ceremonial area inside the main gate leading up to the circular inner sanctum.

The outline of the ploughed down earthworks of the Iron Age fort on Bloodgate Hill, South Creake, from the east, showing the cropmarks of the single bank and ditch. Inside the fort there is a small circular ditch found on excavation also to be Iron Age. These cropmarks showed up well under a crop of cereals in 1975 before the field was put down to grass in 2003. (Derek Edwards, Norfolk County Council)

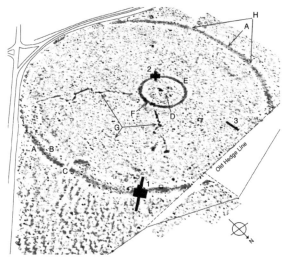

The geophysical survey

1-3 Excavation trenches
A   Outer ditch
B   Rampart, outer bank
C   Main entrance
D   Possible round house
E   Ring-ditch and inner bank
F   Ring-ditch entrance
G   Timber palisades or fences
H   Western entrances

The results of a resistivity survey in 2003 highlighted internal features and three possible entrances marked C and H. (Survey by C. Gaffney / GSB Prospection annotated by Sue Walker White)

Reconstruction of the fort based on the 1975 aerial photographs, the 2003 resistivity survey and subsequent excavations. (Reconstruction by Sue Walker White)

The Norfolk Archaeological Trust provides open public access. There is a car park off the South Creake to Syderstone road that is signposted and there are two information panels. (Car park: NR21 9LZ)

FURTHER READING

Penn, K., 2006, 'Excavation and survey at the Iron Age fort at Bloodgate Hill, South Creake, 2003', *Norfolk Archaeology* XLV, pp.1–27.

12. THETFORD IRON AGE FORT AND MEDIEVAL CASTLE

Thetford castle was first constructed in the Iron Age as an earthwork fort and was converted into a Norman motte and bailey castle more than a thousand years later. So, any understanding of the site involves working out which earthworks were built in the Iron Age and which were built, or rebuilt, by a Norman baron. We know that the Great Danish Army of possibly several thousand men wintered in Thetford in 869–870 and they may have set up camp in the old fort.

Only the northern half of both the fort and the castle are visible, while the southern half was levelled when the town expanded. There are two ramparts visible running along the north side of the castle bailey, the inner one being much more substantial than the outer one. Excavations in 1962 demonstrated that the outer bank and ditch are both Iron Age, and the inner bank was heightened and widened to build the castle. The outer ditch is mostly infilled but was originally massive, 3.3m deep and 4.5m wide at the bottom. Low down in the ditch fill there was an Iron Age jar; above that was Roman pottery and above that Middle Saxon sherds, so the date for the gradual infilling of this earthwork is clear. The inner and higher bank is thought to be entirely Norman and contemporary with the castle motte.

The very tall Norman motte of Thetford Castle with the castle bailey to the left surrounded by a double bank and ditch. The outer bank is partly Iron Age and partly medieval. (John Fielding)

Within the bailey, small-scale excavations have produced strong evidence for both Iron Age and medieval occupation. The motte stands to an impressive height of 25m above the castle bailey, making it one of the tallest castle mottes in Britain. It is dished at the top with a rim running around the edge, but we have yet to discover if it carried a timber or stone keep.

There is no clear evidence for the line of the southern ramparts. On a street plan it looks obvious that the curving lines of Ford Street and Old Market Street follow the outer perimeter, but excavations in 1985–86 in gardens to the east produced no sign of these ditches. One guess is that they lie undiscovered somewhere south of Ford Street near the River Thet and would then be comparable to Warham where the defences were partly dug into the flood plain (No. 10). Another possibility is that there was no southern side and the defences of both the fort and the later castle were provided by the river. Further excavations are surely needed to clarify this part of the site plan.

The fort earthworks are located within an urban park managed by Thetford Town Council that is open to the public. There is a car park on Castle Street. (IP24 2DN)

FURTHER READING

Davies, J. and Gregory, T., 1992, 'Excavations at Thetford Castle, 1962 and 1985–6', in Davies, J.A., Gregory, T., Lawson, A.J., Rickett, R. and Rogerson, A., 1992, *The Iron Age Forts of Norfolk*, East Anglian Archaeology 54, pp.1–30.

THE ROMAN PERIOD

INTRODUCTION

In AD 43 the emperor Claudius sent an army of 50,000 well-trained fighting men in four legions with auxiliaries to invade, conquer and incorporate Britain into the Roman Empire. The army was ruthless in its aims of subjugating the tribes, and those chieftains who did not submit were defeated. King Prasutagus of the Iceni quickly reached a treaty relationship with Rome so that he could be left in peace as the Roman army moved north. But that did not last, and Norfolk people, then as now, 'did different'. There was clearly a push-back against Roman interference, resulting during AD 60–61 in an open revolt led by Prasutagus's widow Queen Boudica. Her army drove south, sacked Colchester and burnt London, but she was defeated, and the territory of the Iceni fell firmly under Roman rule. It then remained within the empire until the troops eventually withdrew some 350 years later. That should have been long enough to ensure that Norfolk was completely subjugated and integrated into Roman culture, but Boudica's legacy lived on in many subtle ways.

Rome, nevertheless, did leave a strong imprint on the Norfolk landscape. Today the most obvious sign of this imprint is the road system, the most prominent road being the very straight Peddars Way, a military road probably dating to the late first century (No. 13). This ran, with just a slight bend, in a line from the north coast to the Suffolk border. Another is the Pye Road from Caistor St Edmund to Scole and on down to Colchester, followed today by the busy A140. The evidence for other roads is more subtle, but several of them formed a network over the county with one crossing the Fens on the Fen Causeway. There is a detailed map of Roman Norfolk showing all the known roads in *An Historical Atlas of Norfolk* (Ashwin and Davison, 2005, pp.28–29), but there are certainly more to discover.

Caistor St Edmund, or *Venta Icenorum,* was the new regional capital laid out with its grid of streets beside the River Tas (No. 14). It does not seem to have had an Iron Age predecessor, although there are Iron Age finds from the area. At about the end of the third century massive stone walls were built around the town at a time when the east coast was being disrupted by raiders penetrating inland from across the North Sea. Norfolk's second major town at Brampton on the River Ant was an industrial centre that specialised in pottery production. This was also protected, in this case, by a single line of earthwork defences. There were probably up to fifteen other smaller undefended towns or large villages in the county where market centres grew up on crossroads or at river crossings, like Billingford. None are visible on the surface today except as scatters of pottery and coins in ploughed fields and sometimes as cropmarks visible from the air.

Although Caistor had a grid-iron layout of streets, with a forum, a theatre and public baths, it had few of the other numerous monumental buildings of a Roman municipal centre, as at Colchester and Lincoln. The Roman army was perfectly capable of transporting suitable stone, but except for one small piece with an unintelligible inscription no stone inscriptions honouring the emperor, or indeed anybody else, has been found. Roman influence, even in the *civitas* capital, was kept low key.

Norfolk's economy remained based on agriculture, as it had been in the Iron Age when there was enough surplus wealth to produce such extraordinary quantities of gold and silver (pp.41–42). But this wealth was not exhibited in the Roman period by its architecture in the capital or in the rural estates, including higher-status villas clustered along the fen edge between Snettisham and Gayton Thorpe. Only one, at Gayton Thorpe, is known for certain to have had a mosaic floor. Most people who owned and farmed the larger estates appear to have shunned the more lavish lifestyle which Rome had to offer. Norfolk had some of the most fertile soils in England and this apparent lack of investment in elaborate buildings was certainly not due to regional poverty. But they did invest in possessions. As John Davies says in his perceptive study of Roman Norfolk in *The Land of Boudica* (2008):

> The process of Romanisation had been a relatively short-lived veneer upon this local culture, which was able to survive in many ways through the Roman occupation and manifested itself on occasions, especially at times of stress, through the deposition of material in the ground, which is now being found by archaeologists.

Any understanding of the Roman landscape needs also to take account of the massive coastal erosion and deposition that has taken place over the last 2,000 years, with up to 2km of land along the north-east coast being lost to the sea. The Great Estuary with open navigable seaways now reached inland as far as Acle, and the rivers feeding into this tidal sea were probably wider, deeper and more navigable than today. Hence our east coast was particularly attractive to the Anglo-Saxon raiding parties in the fourth century. That is why Caistor St Edmund and Brampton needed defences and why massive stone shore forts were built on either side of the entrance to the Great Estuary at Burgh Castle (No. 16) and Caister-on-Sea (No. 17). The amount of Roman building material in Reedham church strongly suggests that there was another on the estuary there as well. There was certainly one on the north coast at Brancaster (No. 15) and there may even have been a fifth near Cromer, now lost to the sea, midway between Brancaster and Caister-on-Sea. It is sometimes suggested that these forts functioned as fortified centres of trade, but the scale of the walls shows that they were primarily designed to resist enemy attack. These forts as a group were poorly integrated with the road system and it appears that they were intended primarily to be naval bases rather than centres for trade.

As the Fens dried out there was a great burst of new activity with roads, canals, salt extraction and livestock farming, possibly managed as one great imperial estate from a centre at Stonea in Cambridgeshire. It nevertheless remains a puzzle why the Fens dried out while the Acle marshes apparently remained a tidal inland sea.

Coin supply from the empire ceased about *c*.400 and commerce and trade gradually disintegrated. Troops were withdrawn from the shore forts *c*.410, and thereafter the coast was wide open to invasion and settlement. The defences could no longer hold back the tide of Germanic and Scandinavian settlers who arrived in large numbers hoping for a better life. The sub-Roman population was quickly overwhelmed and absorbed, but we know little about what happened to them because they disappear so comprehensively from the archaeological record. The old Latin and Celtic languages quickly gave way to Old English, and the Roman church was replaced by beliefs in the pagan gods of the settlers' homelands. There are traces of a substantial, but ploughed-down, earthwork fort within the Roman town at Great Walsingham that might have been the town's last stand, although we do not know that for sure. The massive earthwork banks piled over the stone town walls at Caistor St Edmund still need to be explained, and they might also just belong to a similar final phase of sub-Roman resistance. We have much to learn about the Roman–Anglo-Saxon overlap.

FURTHER READING

Davies, J.A., 2008, *The Land of Boudica: Prehistoric and Roman Norfolk*, pp.133–235 (Norfolk Museums and Archaeology Service).

Gurney, D., 2005, 'Roman Norfolk' in Ashwin T. and Davison, A. (eds), *An Historical Atlas on Norfolk*, pp.28–29 (Phillimore).

13. PEDDARS WAY ROMAN ROAD

On any map of Norfolk there is no historic feature that is more prominent than the Peddars Way Roman road. It runs straight all the way from the north-west coast at Holme-next-the-Sea down to Great Hockham, where it turns slightly to the south before passing over the Rivers Thet and Little Ouse. In Suffolk it is not so easy to follow to Ixworth and then it runs on to Long Melford and eventually to London. For most of its Norfolk route it can be followed along green lanes and minor roads, making it ideal for walkers.

One could expect to find a Roman military installation, or at least a port, where the road reaches the sea, but nothing has been found so far. Its exact terminus remains a mystery. As Bruce Robinson wrote in his 1978 guide to the road, 'It is a road with no beginning, no certainty and no end.' The best guess is that there was at least a ferry port on the coast for military traffic to cross the Wash to Lincolnshire, and evidence for that may have been lost to the sea.

There is a significant site on the route at Saham Toney, where the road passed through a first-century fort recorded on aerial photographs. At Brettenham at the crossing of the River Thet there are extensive traces of settlement with pottery, coins, brooches and other domestic metalwork indicating that the main period of occupation here was in the fourth century.

> Peddars Way is a long-distance walking route that joins up with the North Norfolk Coast Path. It can be enjoyed by walking through some of Norfolk's best landscapes, and we recommend parts of the northern section from Ringstead through Fring south to Massingham. (c.PE36 6LG to c.IP22 2SY)

FURTHER READING

Robinson, B., 1978, *The Peddars Way* (Weathercock Press).

Robinson, B. with Robinson M. and Lidstone-Scott, T., 2017, *Peddars Way and Norfolk Coast Path Official National Trail Guide* (Aurum Press).

Smith, P., 2019, *Walking the Peddars Way and Norfolk Coast Path* (Cicerone).

Opposite: *The very straight line of Peddars Way Roman road stretching from Castle Acre (below the camera) past Great Massingham and north to the coast. (Mike Page)*

The grid of Roman streets shows well during exceptionally dry weather, from the east. The dark line of a drain runs along the centre of the main street. Walls alongside some of the streets and traces of various buildings are also visible. (Mike Page)

Above left: *A closer view of the Caistor amphitheatre from the east. The dark central oval of the arena is surrounded by a lighter band indicating embankments for seating that are in turn surrounded by a darker rectangle. An entrance into the arena is visible at the left-hand end. (Mike Page)*

Above right: *Caistor St Edmund Roman town from the south showing the amphitheatre as a dark oval area in the foreground just beyond the sewage works and beyond that the town centre with its grid-iron layout of streets surrounded by the late Roman defences. Across the road to the right an area of suburban streets can also be seen visible as light areas in the greener grass. (Mike Page)*

14. CAISTOR ST EDMUND ROMAN REGIONAL CAPITAL AND THE DUNSTON FIELD ANGLO-SAXON TRADING CENTRE

Caistor, or *Venta Icenorum* as it was called, was the Roman equivalent to a modern-day county town and it was the centre of administration for an area that stretched over Norfolk and into Suffolk and Cambridgeshire. From Caistor, roads radiated north to the Roman industrial town at Brampton, west to the Fens and south along the Pye Road to Scole and beyond to Colchester. It is a rare example of a Roman regional capital that has remained a green field ever since, the only other examples being Silchester in Hampshire and Wroxeter in Shropshire.

This Roman town is probably the best-known archaeological monument in the county following recent well-publicised excavations. The town was initially extensive, covering approximately 28ha surrounded by triple-ditched earthwork defences. The only place where these can now be seen is just as you approach the modern bridge to Dunston Field where the ground drops more steeply near the river. But the more obvious late-Roman defences consist of massive stone walls that enclosed a much smaller rectangular area of 14ha, and within this the Roman streets are usually visible as lines of dead grass in dry weather. Although the town was close beside the River Tas, the limited evidence we have so far suggests that ships could not have reached upstream from the Great Estuary. Indeed, it is still a matter for much debate as to how navigable our rivers were in the Roman period.

Excavations suggest that the streets originated early in the second century, while the visible town walls were probably not added until the later third or early fourth centuries. These late-Roman stone walls are clear in several places, particularly on the north side, while elsewhere they are covered by the earthwork banks that are not yet understood. The walls, originally up to 7m high, have a flint and mortar core with a dressed flint facing interspersed with layers of tile. But the tiles are not so decoratively ordered as at Burgh Castle (No. 16). There was a single gateway through the centre of each side, and projecting forward from these walls were alternating semicircular and rectangular bastions still just visible in the grass on the south side. One semicircular example stands above ground on the west side near the river.

The Roman buildings are all buried below the turf, but excavations and an extensive geophysical survey have located the forum, the public baths, two temples and possibly a theatre. Outside the town in the field to the south an amphitheatre is just visible as a slight hollow, and aerial photos show that this had an oval shape with entrances probably at both ends all set within a larger rectangle.

The curious observer will notice that the parish church not only stands within the town walls but is aligned closely with one of the east-to-west streets. Roman

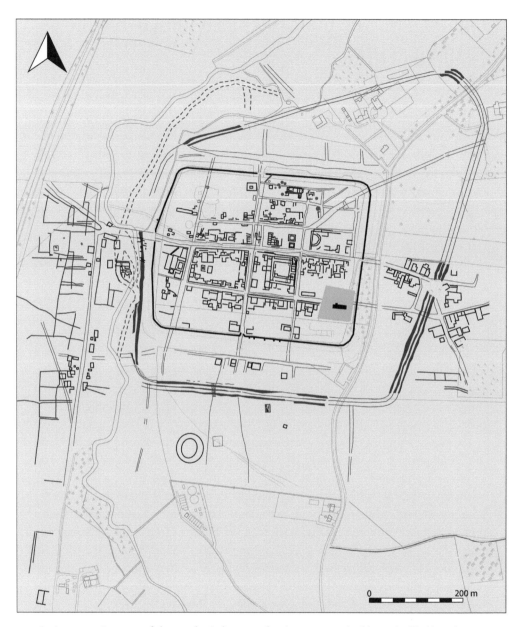

An interpretation map of the geophysical survey showing masonry buildings (in black) and streets surrounded by the rectangle of the late Roman defences These are all set within an earlier extensive second-century triple-ditch circuit (in red) with its distinctive kite-shape outline. The postulated course of the river in the Roman period is shown with blue dotted lines, while possible pottery kilns in the northern part of the town are shown as red dots. An oval indicates the amphitheatre to the south. (This contains OS data, © Crown copyright, and aerial investigation and mapping data © Historic England licensed to Norfolk County Council).

tiles built into the south-west corner of the nave superficially give the impression that this building has a Roman origin. But excavations have located human bones underneath the foundations with a radiocarbon date of AD 890 to 1030. These burials may, of course, be associated with an Anglo-Saxon wooden church close by that has yet to be located.

There is little sign of activity within the walled area after the early fifth century, although there are three cemeteries on the hills around. There is good evidence of Middle Saxon activity on all sides outside the walls, and in Dunston Field across the river to the west there is extensive evidence of Middle Saxon occupation, suggesting that there was a strong revival of Caistor as a trading centre here before there was a move in the ninth century to Norwich beside the more navigable River Wensum.

The Roman town and Dunston Field are both owned by the Norfolk Archaeological Trust and are fully open for public access. While there is no charge, there is a donations box in the car park. The site is signposted from Caistor village, and a series of information panels provide a self-guided walk around the defences starting at the car park. A new bridge takes you across the river to Dunston Field where the Archaeological Trust has developed an extensive area of wild flowers that are magical in the summer months. (Car park: NR14 8QN)

FURTHER READING

Bowden, W. 2013. 'Townscape and identity at Caistor-by-Norwich' in Eckardt, H. and Rippon, S. (eds) *Living and Working in the Roman World: Essays in Honour of Michael Fulford on his 65th Birthday*, pp.47–62 (Portsmouth, Rhode Island).

Bowden, W., 2013, 'The urban plan of *Venta Icenorum* and its relationship with the Boudican Revolt', *Britannia* 44, pp.145–169.

Bowden, W., 2020, *Venta Icenorum: A Brief History of Caistor Roman Town* (Norfolk Archaeological Trust).

Davies, J. A., 2001, *Venta Icenorum: Caistor St Edmund Roman Town* (Norfolk Archaeological Trust).

Wacher, J., 1995, *The Towns of Roman Britain*, pp.242–255 (BCA).

15. BRANCASTER 'SAXON SHORE' ROMAN FORT AND *VICUS*

This fort was one of up to five built around the Norfolk coast during the late Roman period in response to the constant threat of Anglo-Saxon raids from across the North Sea. They were parts of a string of defences stretching from Porchester on the south coast up to Brancaster. The other forts we are sure about are at Caister-on-Sea (No. 17) and Burgh Castle (No. 16), There is much debate about their purpose because none have produced any evidence that they had naval facilities, yet we assume that they were to protect coastal shipping and to intercept raiders arriving by boat. We do know that some had cavalry units to confront the raiding parties once they had landed. The earliest forts included Brancaster and Caister-on-Sea, both built in the early 200s. Burgh Castle was added a little later so that Caister-on-Sea and Burgh Castle could then together protect the entrance to the Great Estuary now covered by the Acle and Halvergate Marshes.

Brancaster was the most northerly of the shore forts, and, as at Caister-on-Sea, there are extensive marshes separating the fort from open water. There is an old record that the walls here were still 4m high in 1600, but they were demolished in

Brancaster Roman fort from the west taken in about 1984 when the site was still growing cereals. The cropmarks of four entrances in the middle of each side are clear, and so also is the large headquarters building, or principia, to the right of centre. In the distance the outlines of the civilian settlement, or vicus, outside the fort can also be seen. (Derek Edwards, courtesy of Norfolk County Council)

The Roman fort in 2020 looking north. These 'Saxon Shore' forts were originally built close to the sea. So, we can see here how much the coastal mud flats and marshes have accumulated over the last 2,000 years. (John Fielding)

the eighteenth century. The squared grey stones robbed from the walls can now be seen reused in local buildings and churches at Brancaster, Burnham Deepdale and Titchwell. After demolition the fort was reduced to ground level, so it now appears just as a 2.5ha square raised area with ditches still visible on three sides. The fourth side is followed by the present coast road. From excavations in 1935 we know that the fort had rounded corners, internal corner turrets and gates in the middle of each side. Otherwise our information about the fort and the very extensive areas of civilian settlement, or *vicus,* outside the fort has come largely from aerial photographs. The *vicus* to the west was partly excavated in the 1970s prior to it being covered by a housing development, but to the east it still lies largely undisturbed in the adjacent field.

The eastern *vicus* and the fort interior were both subject to an extensive magnetometer survey in 2012 organised by the TV *Time Team* programme. This enhanced the information we already had from the aerial photographs and showed the *vicus* to be a network of streets marked out with flanking ditches lined with carefully organised house plots measured to a uniform size. A plan of the *vicus* on both sides of the fort shows the main east-to-west street ran right through the fort emerging on the other side on the same alignment but not quite orientated with the fort. The only part of the fort aligned with this was the *Principia,* or headquarters building in the middle, suggesting that the *vicus* and headquarters building were contemporary with an earlier fort buried under the later one. The magnetometer survey also identified lines of barrack blocks in the south-east part of the fort.

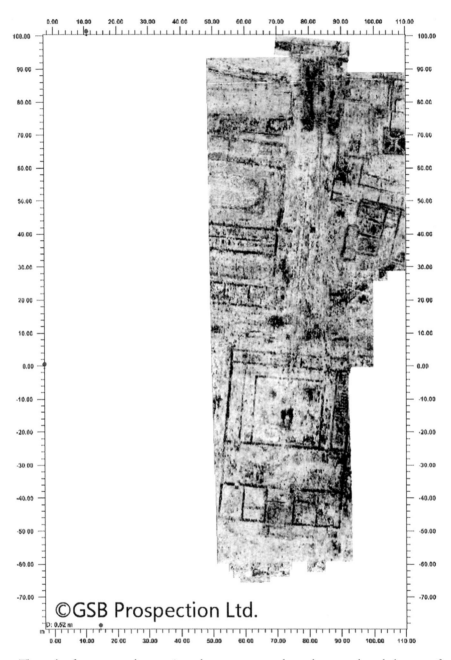

©GSB Prospection Ltd.

The results of a 2012 ground penetrating radar survey on a north–south transect through the centre of the fort showing the headquarters building and to the north of that a large granary and to the north of that an oval area within a rectangle. The oval area might have been an exercise arena for cavalry horses or possibly an amphitheatre. Nobody knows, but there are some possible similarities with the amphitheatre at Caistor St Edmund on page 54. (Survey by Dr John Gater/GSB Prospection)

As well as the magnetometer survey, *Time Team* organised a ground-penetrating radar (GPR) survey over a north-to-south transect about 50m wide across the fort, and this revealed in astonishing detail individual rooms within buildings and even the heating systems in some places. There is a larger building that looks like a granary – a standard feature in many forts – and an oval area that may have been an arena or exercise yard for cavalry horses. If the GPR survey could be extended to include the whole of the fort and the *vicus* to the east the result would be extraordinarily interesting. Brancaster certainly has many more secrets to reveal.

The site is owned by the National Trust and is open to the public, accessible only from the coastal footpath. (PE31 8XD)

FURTHER READING

Brennan, N., 2016, 'The Roman Fort at Branodunum: A Time Team Evaluation', *Norfolk Archaeology* XLVII, pp.374–394.

Fields, N., 2006, *Rome's Saxon Shore*, p.25 (Osprey).

Frere, S.S. and St Joseph, J.K., 1983, *Roman Britain from the Air*, pp.81–83 (Cambridge University Press).

Gurney, D., 2002, *Outposts of the Roman Empire: A Guide to Norfolk's Roman Forts at Burgh Castle, Caister-on-Sea and Brancaster*, pp.15–19 (Norfolk Archaeological Trust).

Hinchliffe, J. and Sparey Green, C., 1985, *Excavations at Brancaster 1974 and 1977*, East Anglian Archaeology 23.

Johnson, S., 1976, *The Roman Forts of the Saxon Shore*, pp.37–40 (Paul Elek).

Pearson, A., 2002, *The Roman Shore Forts*, pp.107–108 (Tempus).

St Joseph, J.K., 1936, 'The Roman Fort at Brancaster', *The Antiquaries Journal* XVI, pp.444–460.

Taylor, T. 2013, 'Mapping Roman Brancaster', *British Archaeology* 129, pp.20–25.

16. BURGH CASTLE ROMAN 'SAXON SHORE' FORT, ANGLO-SAXON MONASTERY AND MEDIEVAL CASTLE

This quite spectacular Roman fort sits on high ground overlooking the River Waveney, where it joins Breydon Water, and the Halvergate marshes beyond. In any tour of archaeological sites of East Anglia this one is not to be missed. The fort walls stand to their full height on three sides enclosing an area of 2.2ha; the fourth side fell into the marsh many centuries ago.

The gap in the middle of the east wall was the main landward entrance, and at regular intervals around the walls are semicircular projecting bastions designed to increase firepower when the fort was under attack. Holes in the bastion tops held heavy posts probably to support timber superstructures on the bastions that ran all along the wall tops.

The best-preserved section of the front face is along the south side where bands of tiles are separated by four or five courses of knapped flints. The observant visitor will notice that the bastions were not part of the original design but were added and bonded into the walls when they were half built. Evidence from aerial photographs and geophysical surveys show that there was also an extensive civilian settlement or *vicus* in the fields outside the fort.

Burgh Castle Roman fort from the east looking across the River Waveney and beyond to the River Yare and the Berney Arms windmill with the Halvergate marshes (No.98) in the distance. (Mike Page)

The south-east corner bastion showing the central hole seen in the tops of all the bastions, probably to support timber superstructures that extended all along the walls as a wall walk. (John Fielding)

In the Anglo-Saxon period the fort appears to have been occupied for a while as a monastery founded by St Fursey in AD 633, although it is possible that his monastery was in the fort at Caister-on-Sea (No. 17). Or, perhaps both forts were reused as monasteries during this period. Certainly, in excavations carried out at Burgh Castle between 1958 and 1961 a cemetery containing more than 160 Christian graves was found inside the fort at the southern end, and nearby there was also a timber building that may have been a church.

Soon after the Norman Conquest a large earth mound, surrounded by a deep ditch, was built in the south-west corner of the fort to form a Norman castle motte, no doubt with a timber keep on top. This explains the substantial gap in the south wall where the motte ditch cuts through the Roman masonry. The castle was short-lived and its motte was finally levelled in the eighteenth century. The only surface trace of the Norman castle now is the hollow following the line of the partly filled ditch.

The south-east bastion and south wall with the decorative bands of Roman tiles between the knapped flints in the wall facing. (Peter Wade-Martins)

The fort is owned by the Norfolk Archaeological Trust and the walls are in the care of English Heritage. There are information panels at the car park and at the fort and at a viewing platform overlooking the reed beds and the marshes. The car park is well sign-posted from the village. Whether the visitor is interested in archaeology or in bird watching, Burgh Castle is a very special place with wonderful views over the old Roman estuary. It is not difficult to imagine a Roman fleet drawn up on a beach where reed beds now grow. Extensive areas of bee orchids can be found in the fields around the fort. (Car park: NR31 9QD)

FURTHER READING

Campbell, A. (ed.), 2004, *Heritage Unlocked, Guide to Free Sites in the East of England*, pp.54–56 (English Heritage).

Fields, N., 2006, *Rome's Saxon Shore*, pp.28–29 (Osprey).

Gurney, D., 2002, *Outposts of the Roman Empire: A Guide to Norfolk's Roman Forts at Burgh Castle, Caister-on-Sea and Brancaster*, pp.15–19 (Norfolk Archaeological Trust).

Johnson, S., 1976, *The Roman Forts of the Saxon Shore*, pp.37–40 (Paul Elek).

Johnson, S., 1983, *Burgh Castle, Excavations by Charles Green 1985–61*, East Anglian Archaeology 20.

Pearson, A., 2002, *The Roman Shore Forts*, pp.107–108 (Tempus).

17. CAISTER-ON-SEA 'SAXON SHORE' ROMAN FORT

Compared with Burgh Castle and Brancaster, the setting of this shore fort is disappointing with no fine views across marshes; there are just extensive housing estates. One is left with a great sense of real regret that the post-war planning system treated this critically important Roman monument so badly. It is likely that there was also a civilian *vicus* to the west that lay open and largely unexcavated in farmland until it was covered by a housing estate as late as 1986. Planning laws at the time did not require developers to allow access for excavation, and only minimal recording was permitted. Just two years later, after the county council's structure plan was introduced in 1988, permission for development here could have been refused, or there could have been a condition attached to the planning consent requiring access and funding for excavation. It is easy to forget how quickly standards and environmental awareness have changed.

The excavated part of the Roman fort at Caister-on-Sea from the south. This includes the south fort wall, a part of the south gate (near the red car) and one long building with its hypocaust heating system near the left-hand end. (Mike Page)

This fort, probably called *Gariannum*, was built in the early 200s on the north side of the entrance to the Roman Great Estuary. Later, Burgh Castle was built (No. 16) so that the two could act in unison to control river-born access into the inland waterways. The fort was roughly square, covering 3.5ha, and modern housing now covers much of it. The rest is open to the public and in the ownership of English Heritage. Foundations of the south wall, a part of the south gate and some late Roman buildings excavated in 1951–55 have been consolidated and are on view. One guard chamber in the gate is visible, and it is assumed that this was part of a double gateway with towers over both guard chambers linked above by a parapet walkway. Within the fort one long building and parts of another are completely exposed, and they are the only Roman buildings in the county open to public view. One of the rooms still has its underfloor hypocaust hot air heating system.

The fort was abandoned with the collapse of the Roman Empire in the early fifth century, and it was all levelled by the eighteenth century. In the intervening years there was some particularly interesting activity that we do not fully understand. Caister-on-Sea may have been the place where St Fursey established his monastery in 633 and called it *Cnobheresburg*, or perhaps it was on the other side of the estuary at Burgh Castle. There were four cemeteries located in and around the fort, including one just outside the south gate partly excavated in the 1950s. The evidence for these cemeteries is confused, but they appear to range in date from Roman to Christian Middle Saxon. How much Caister-on-Sea may have developed as an Anglo-Scandinavian trading settlement at the mouth of the Great Estuary is an open question. With a dense concentration of thirteen Scandinavian place names ending in *-by* (such as Filby and Mautby) just to the north, it seems likely. This is a question that would certainly justify further research.

The site is owned by English Heritage and open during reasonable hours without charge. (Layby at NR30 5RP)

FURTHER READING

Brown, M.P., 2001, *The Life of St Fursey*, pp.17–19 (Fursey Pilgrims).

Campbell, A. (ed.), 2004, *Heritage Unlocked, Guide to Free Sites in the East of England*, pp.56–57 (English Heritage).

Darling, M.J. with Gurney, D., 1993, *Caister-on-Sea Excavations by Charles Green 1951–55*, East Anglian Archaeology 60.

Fields, N., 2006, *Rome's Saxon Shore*, pp.25–27 (Osprey).

Gurney, D., 2002, *Outposts of the Roman Empire: A Guide to Norfolk's Roman Forts at Burgh Castle, Caister-on-Sea and Brancaster*, pp.15–19 (Norfolk Archaeological Trust).

Johnson, S., 1976, *The Roman Forts of the Saxon Shore*, pp.37–40 (Paul Elek).

Pearson, A., 2002, *The Roman Shore Forts*, pp.107–108 (Tempus).

THE ANGLO-SAXON PERIOD

INTRODUCTION

The Anglo-Saxon, or Early Medieval, period, between the end of Roman rule and the Norman Conquest, is traditionally divided by archaeologists into three: Early (*c.*410–*c.*650), Middle (*c.*650–*c.*850) and Late Saxon (*c.*850–1066). None of the dates are meant to be precise except for the last one.

EARLY SAXON

This period runs from the time the Roman army left in about AD 410 until the Christian missionaries started to convert the region in the seventh century. With the coast undefended, waves of migrants soon arrived from north Germany in the hope of a better future. They had pagan beliefs and their religion was based on the worship of the gods of their homelands. Traces of their settlements are difficult to locate, while their cemeteries are easier to find. In the early years cremation was the more usual method of burial, but later there was a gradual switch to interment. The men were often laid in their graves with their weapons and shields while the women were buried with their jewellery.

We now know a lot more about these early migrants thanks to the excavations of a great cemetery of over 2,000 burials on Spong Hill in North Elmham. The burials were mainly cremations with just a few inhumations from the final phase of the cemetery. The cremated remains, some with grave goods, were put into urns, many decorated, and buried only just below topsoil. The whole cemetery was excavated when it became clear that the urns were being severely damaged by modern cultivation. These burials represented the earliest phase of Anglo-Saxon settlement in Norfolk, which began in the first quarter of the fifth century and finished with a short phase of inhumation in the middle of the sixth century. The overall sample from the site was large enough to show that the early settlers were 'Anglian' from north Germany, where similar cemeteries have been found in Schleswig-Holstein. The later immigrants were primarily 'Saxon' from the

Elbe–Weser area. So, overall, this new population that settled in East Anglia by the end of the fifth century was from mixed cultural backgrounds (Hills, 2015).

Although there are surface traces of cemeteries from this period visible as finds in the plough soil, evidence for the settlements is much harder to detect and none is visible above ground. However, reconstructions of excavated Early Saxon houses can be seen in Suffolk at the West Stow Country Park. Their buildings were all of wood, and while it is possible some of the derelict Roman stone buildings continued in use, no such evidence has yet been found. There are no upstanding field monuments, except some linear earthworks. That is why these earthworks may be so important and why one of them, the Fossditch (No. 18), is featured below.

It is strange that from the early fifth century there is an almost complete lack of archaeological evidence for the Romano-British people, who were quickly subsumed within the new Germanic way of life. There was a small Roman town not far from Spong Hill at Billingford where excavations have located just a single phase of Early Saxon timber buildings and a Roman cemetery, but there is no sign of the continued use of this cemetery into the fifth century. So this town seems to have just disappeared by the mid-fifth century.

As the Anglo-Saxon settlements became established, the conflicting tribal groups were brought together under a single East Anglian king by the mid sixth century, probably based at Rendlesham in the Deben Valley in Suffolk. Here recent metal detecting, geophysical surveys and some limited excavations have revealed strong evidence for a high-status settlement, which became a magnet for long-distance trade from the late sixth century until the early eighth century. This appears to be linked to the princely burials found at Sutton Hoo and Snape nearby. It was probably King Raedwald who was buried in the great ship burial at Sutton Hoo in 624 or 625.

MIDDLE SAXON

From the 630s onwards the conversion of the region to Christianity began in earnest with the arrival of St Felix at Walton Castle (now lost to the sea) near Felixstowe and another missionary, St Fursa (or Fursey), in 633 at either Burgh Castle (No. 16) or Caister-on-Sea (No. 17). There were probably many other missionaries sent into Norfolk, but we hear of none of them from the records.

The conversion can be followed through the evidence of excavated cemeteries with the replacement of cremation by inhumation in the early seventh century and then the very gradual abandonment of the practice of putting grave goods with the body. But it was not that simple, with some of the wealthier people, particularly women, being buried with quite astonishingly rich 'Final Phase' jewellery into the early eighth century.

As Christianity spread, the old pagan cemeteries were quickly abandoned in favour of fresh burial grounds that were being created around new churches. These churches were made of timber and are therefore hard to find, especially as most were replaced in stone and have continued in use up to the present day. There was then a widespread population movement to form new villages around these churches. It is certainly true that we seldom find evidence of Early Saxon settlements under villages or near churches today. Unlike early Saxon settlements, Middle Saxon villages are much easier to find because the hard-fired Middle Saxon pottery, called Ipswich Ware, lasts relatively well in the plough soil in fields and can be picked up around many now-isolated churches.

LATE SAXON

Following a period of peace in the kingdom there were great upheavals in the ninth century caused by Viking raids from Scandinavia. The first recorded encounter in East Anglia with these 'heathen men' was in 841 in King Athelstan's reign. The year 865 saw the arrival of 'a great heathen army' causing much distress. After rampaging in the north of England the army returned to East Anglia in 869 and set up winter quarters in Thetford. These raids and the settlers who followed them extinguished the Christian church in the region for a century, and it is from that time that the burnt-out remains of a substantial timber-framed building have been excavated from a well near to the likely site of the Late Saxon cathedral at North Elmham (No. 31).

The best evidence for Scandinavian settlement in East Anglia comes actually not from monuments but from metal detector finds over the last forty years. Tim Pestell's recent book *Viking East Anglia* (2019) is a masterpiece in how to interpret the past from these finds. The most visible evidence for this ninth- and tenth- century Danish settlement today is in the place names with the ending -*by,* such as Filby and Stokesby. There are more than twenty of these, and half of them are in a tight cluster on the old Isle of Flegg close to the coast north of Caister-on-Sea. Recent research by Trevor Ogden has shown that it is also in Flegg that the strongest concentration of the surname 'Tooke', derived from the Old Norse, can be found (Ogden 2021). Flegg appears to have been a real stronghold of Viking settlement.

In the longer term the impact of this new influx of Danish settlers encouraged an unprecedented level of trade and prosperity with the Continent. One wonders how much the Roman fort at Caister-on-Sea and its *vicus* (the adjacent Roman settlement) became an early centre for this Anglo-Scandinavian activity (No. 17).

Norwich and Thetford grew into major towns, with Norwich replacing the old trading centre in Dunston Field close to the Roman regional capital at Caistor St Edmund (No. 14). Thetford became a main pottery producer for the region by the 850s, and there was a mint in Norwich by the 920s, By the Norman Conquest, Norwich had become one of the largest and most prosperous towns in England. With 1,300 burgesses, suggesting a population of over 5,000, it was comparable in size to London. No wonder King William decided to build one of his great royal castles here soon after the Conquest (No. 28).

We have no visible monuments in the county that can be described with certainty as Late Saxon, other than a much-modified length of Thetford's earthwork defences and the early phases of the great sea bank in Marshland (No. 19). This extraordinary piece of engineering was built to protect the Fens from flooding, and it demonstrates a level of wealth and vitality in the eleventh and early twelfth centuries not seen in our region since the Iron Age. There is also, of course, the beautifully preserved stone cross from Whissonsett churchyard (No. 20) and a part of a Scandinavian-style cross shaft from the site of St Vedast's church in Norwich Castle Museum.

There is much debate about the date of our earliest stone churches and there probably always will be until some have been excavated. Some architectural historians now argue that in East Anglia there was no building in stone before the Norman Conquest. There is a convincing case for saying that following the Viking invasions in the ninth century East Anglia became increasingly under Scandinavian influence, where building in timber was the tradition – a tradition made famous by the early twelfth-century stave churches of Norway. Indeed, the only churches in our region that have been unambiguously dated as Anglo-Saxon have been wooden examples excavated in Norwich, Thetford and at Brandon in Suffolk. Even the cathedral at North Elmham (No. 31) was described as a wooden church at the time the Norman bishop moved to Thetford in 1072 and ultimately to Norwich.

FURTHER READING

Chester-Kadwell, M., 2009, *Early Anglo-Saxon Communities in the Landscape of Norfolk* (British Archaeological Reports British Series 481).

Hamerow, H., 2012, *Rural Settlements and Society in Anglo-Saxon England* (Oxford University Press).

Heywood, S., 2013, 'Stone building in Romanesque East Anglia' in Bates, D. and Liddiard, R.. *East Anglia and its North Sea World in the Middle Ages*, pp.256–269 (Boydell).

Higham, N.J. and Ryan, M.J., 2013, *The Anglo-Saxon World* (Yale University Press).

Hills, C. and Lucy, S., 2013, *Spong Hill Part IX: Chronology and Synthesis* (McDonald Institute for Archaeological Research, University of Cambridge).

Hills, C.M., 2015, 'Spong Hill and the origins of England', *British Archaeology* 143, pp.20–27.

Hoggett, R., 2010, *The Archaeology of the East Anglian Conversion* (Boydell).

Margeson, S., 1996, 'Viking Settlement in Norfolk: A study of new evidence' in Margeson, S., Ayers, B. and Heywood, S. (eds) *A Festival of Norfolk Archaeology*, pp.47-57 (Norfolk and Norwich Archaeological Society).

Margeson, S., 1997, *The Vikings in Norfolk* (Norfolk Museums Service).

Ogden, T., 2021, 'Old Norse-derived surnames and place-names in Norfolk', *Society for Name Studies in Britain and Ireland Newsletter* 22.

Penn, K., 2005, 'Early Saxon Settlement' in Ashwin, R. and Davison, A. (eds), *An Historical Atlas of Norfolk'*, pp.30–31 (Phillimore).

Pestell, T., 2019, *Viking East Anglia* (Norfolk Museums Service).

Pestell, T., 2005, 'Viking Settlement in Norfolk' in Ashwin, T. and Davison, A. (eds), *An Historical Atlas of Norfolk*, pp.36–37 (Phillimore).

Rogerson, A., 2005, 'Middle Saxon Norfolk' in Ashwin, T. and Davison, A. (eds), *An Historical Atlas of Norfolk*, pp.32–33 (Phillimore).

West, S., 1999, *Understanding West Stow* (Jarrold Publishing).

West, S., 2001, *West Stow Revisited* (West Stow Anglo-Saxon Village Trust).

18. THE FOSSDITCH

In west and south Norfolk there are six linear earthworks consisting of long defensive banks and ditches. However, proving their date and explaining their purpose when there is such a real shortage of hard facts is a struggle. In the west of the county there are three of these, with the two northern ones, the Bichamditch and the Fossditch, apparently forming parts of the same boundary. They run north to south roughly in a line, with their ditches to the east of their banks. With streams and river valleys filling the gap between them, the two appear to form a frontier of some significance about 28km long. To the south-east there is also the Devil's Ditch on Garboldisham Heath, which terminates in river valleys. But this one is puzzling because it may have been started in the Iron Age and was then later modified. All these earthworks are crying out for further excavation and research. They appear to represent a turbulent period in our history when there was hostility between local tribal groupings. This rather narrows their time down to either the Iron Age, which was clearly an unsettled period when hill forts were built, or to the fifth or early sixth centuries after Roman rule had collapsed and before the region was unified under the new kingdom of East Anglia.

The Fossditch where it is best preserved in the Thetford Forest, with the ditch visible to the left of the bank. (Peter Wade-Martins)

The Fossditch where it emerges from Thetford Forest as a bank and ditch at A running south as a straight line over Weeting Heath to B. (Mike Page)

We have chosen the Fossditch to describe here because it is the most easily accessible, with much of it running alongside a road through the Breckland forests, and because excavations have demonstrated that it is post-Roman. The earthwork runs for 9km from the River Wissey in the north down to the River Ouse in the south. Through the forest the top of the bank is in some places up to 2m above the base of the ditch. The ditch terminates at both ends in riverside marshland offering some security to the flanks. Essentially this is an east-facing military installation providing some protection for the prosperous areas along the fen edge to the west.

The date for the earthwork was established in 1949 by Rainbird Clarke, who was an active archaeologist in the county in the post-war years. He recognised that at the south end where the dyke follows the Hockwold-cum-Wilton and Weeting parish boundary it runs through an area of Roman settlement. He predicted that it should be possible by cutting a trench through the dyke here to show if it was built before or after the Romans. His excavation clearly demonstrated that the rampart had been built *over* an old topsoil that contained Roman pottery, so it could not be Iron Age. Some of this pottery was dated to the fourth century, including pieces that were probably late fourth century. The pottery and coins from the Roman settlement suggested that the settlement remained in use until 390 or even later.

So, this long earthwork was either very late Roman or Early Saxon. A late fifth- or early sixth-century date seemed most likely. Further excavations on all these dykes, making use of modern techniques of scientific dating, should eventually clarify the matter further.

The Fossditch is best followed on the ground using the Ordnance Survey Explorer map 229 from the crossroads at TL 767 940 to TL 760 904 through the Thetford Forest, where it is labelled 'Fossditch' on the map in Roman script. Further south the earthwork runs across Weeting Heath, a nature reserve of open grassland managed by the Norfolk Wildlife Trust where the nesting areas of stone curlew are protected, and access is not permitted. (IP26 5JN to IP26 4NP)

FURTHER READING

Clarke, R.R., 1955, 'The Fossditch – a linear earthwork in south-west Norfolk', *Norfolk Archaeology* 31, pp.178–196.

Wade-Martins, P., 1974, 'The Linear Earthworks of West Norfolk', *Norfolk Archaeology* 36, pp.23–38.

Wade-Martins, P., 2016, 'The Date of the West Norfolk Linear Earthworks – an unresolved debate', *Norfolk Archaeology* 47, pp.329–333.

19. THE LATE SAXON SEA BANK AROUND MARSHLAND KNOWN AS 'THE ROMAN BANK'

The 'Roman Bank' was a part of a great earth bank that ran the whole way around the Wash and up the tidal valleys of the major rivers. It was first called the 'Roman Bank' by antiquarians in the seventeenth century, and it is clearly marked as 'The Old Roman Sea Bank' on Faden's map of Norfolk published in 1797, but its date has until recently remained unproven. More recent historians assumed that it was probably medieval, but there was no clear evidence. Then, excavations by archaeologists working for the Fenland Management Project between 1991 and 1995 at Clenchwarton, West Walton and Terrington St Clement showed that the bank originated as a Late Saxon sea defence.

At Banklands in Clenchwarton in 1992 a partial section was cut through the bank demonstrating that at that point it was built directly on the edge of tidal mudflats where periodic flooding had prevented the accumulation of topsoil. Late Saxon Thetford Ware pottery was found *within* the body of the bank, so it could not have been built before the eleventh or early twelfth centuries, thus solving one of the riddles of Norfolk's archaeology. Evidence from the soil stratigraphy in the excavation confirmed that after the bank was constructed there was no more marine silt deposition on the inside of the bank, but in places silt deposition continued on the outside of the bank where the adjacent soil levels are sometimes higher.

The landward side of the 'Roman' sea bank at Clenchwarton from the west. (Peter Wade-Martins)

The bank was a great earthwork representing a single co-ordinated attempt to provide continuous flood protection between the River Ouse to the east and the Nene to the west. For its time it was a massive and impressive undertaking. Place names along its route, such as Walsoken, West Walton and Walpole, may refer to the sea wall, but while that sounds logical, place name experts don't necessarily agree.

For most of its length the bank is now about 18 to 20m wide and up to 2m high, although no doubt originally it would have been higher. It seldom runs straight and meanders a lot, presumably following the shoreline at that time. The bank protected the villages of Marshland and provided opportunities for developing more farmland. The extraordinary resources needed for such a major undertaking are difficult to imagine, and it is even more impressive when one realises that there were no more attempts to push back the sea here any further with new flood banks until the eighteenth century – a gap of 700 years!

It is important to say that while the origins of the sea bank appear to be Late Saxon, there were no doubt many later attempts to strengthen the bank, especially along the Ouse and the Nene.

Much of the Roman Bank has been heavily eroded over the centuries, but the Ordnance Survey Explorer map 236 shows a good section running westwards from Point Farm beside the River Ouse to the north of Clenchwarton, where it is labelled 'Sea Bank' and 'Clenchwarton Parish Walk'. It is not so clear to the north of Terrington St Clement, where it is confusingly called the 'New Roman Bank' and then the 'Old Roman Bank'. It is only obvious again to the south of Walpole Cross Keys, where it is called 'Eastlands Bank', then Walpole Bank and then the King John Bank heading south-west to Wisbech. In places this route can be followed by car. From Point Farm near the Ouse a rebuilt and modified version runs south around Clenchwarton, curving to the east of Tilney All Saints alongside the old course of the River Ouse and then on to Wiggenhall St Germans. (Banklands at PE34 4DB)

FURTHER READING

Crowson, A., Lane, T., Penn, K. and Trimble, D., 2005, *Anglo-Saxon Settlement on the Siltlands of Eastern England*, pp.190–205 (Lincolnshire Archaeology and Heritage Reports Series 7).

Darby, H.C., 1968, *The Draining of the Fens*, second edition (Cambridge University Press).

Darby, H.C., 1983, *The Changing Fenland* (The Press Syndicate of the University of Cambridge).

Faden, W., 1797, *Map of Norfolk* (republished by The Larks Press in 1989 with an Introduction by Chris Barringer).

Godwin, H., 1978, *Fenland: Its Ancient Past and Uncertain Future* (Cambridge University Press).

Hall, D. and Coles, J., 1994, *Fenland Survey: An Essay in Landscape and Persistence*, p.127 (English Heritage).

Silvester, R.J., 1988, 'Clenchwarton', *The Fenland Project Number 3: Marshland and the Nar Valley, Norfolk*, East Anglian Archaeology 45, pp.17–22.

20. THE WHISSONSETT LATE SAXON CROSS

There are only a few pieces of Anglo-Saxon decorative sculpture known in Norfolk, no doubt because there was no suitable local stone to carve, and the pieces we do have were made from imported material. One of them, an almost complete early eleventh-century wheel-headed cross, is sitting in a niche in Whissonsett church, having been dug up in the churchyard in 1900. Because of the way the cross was placed in the niche in the 1920s or '30s only one face can now be seen, but luckily photographs of both faces and the edges were published in *Norfolk Archaeology* in 1904. The cross was probably a grave marker standing originally about a metre high rather than a tall preaching cross. It was made of Barnack limestone and was carved with 'Stafford Knot' interlace on both faces. There is no inscription; the base is missing, and there is a small central boss in the head.

There are no other examples, or even fragments, of cross shafts decorated in this style on our side of the Wash despite extensive searches in churches and churchyard walls in the area. The carving is in fine condition, suggesting that this rare piece spent most of the last thousand years covered with soil in the churchyard.

The cross is on display in a niche at the end of the south aisle of the church. For more information look no further than the excellent booklet by Trevor Heaton on sale in the church which is open during reasonable hours. (NR20 5AE)

FURTHER READING

Collingwood, W.G., 1904, 'The Whissonsett Cross', *Norfolk Archaeology* XV, pp.316–323.

Everson, P. and Stocker, D., 1999, *The Corpus of Anglo-Saxon Sculpture: Vol. V: Lincolnshire* (Oxford University Press).

Heaton, T., undated, *The Story of the Whissonsett Cross.*

The Whissonsett cross set within a niche in the south aisle of the church. (Peter Wade-Martins)

Above: *The ruined church at Bawsey on a slight hill surrounded by cultivated fields where surface finds indicate the site of a Middle Saxon trading centre. (John Fielding)*

Below: *The interior of the Norman ruined church at Bawsey. (Peter Wade-Martins)*

21. NORMAN RUINED CHURCH AT BAWSEY SURROUNDED BY EVIDENCE OF A HIGH-STATUS MIDDLE SAXON TRADING CENTRE

Isolated churches are a characteristic feature of the Norfolk countryside, and a surprising number have been abandoned. There are 101 ruined ones in the county, and a further 153 have disappeared completely. In many cases this is because the villages they served have decayed or have been deserted in favour of more attractive locations. The spectacular remains of Bawsey church stand on high ground in complete isolation visible from the King's Lynn bypass. The village has long gone, but in the fields around surface finds show that this was once a very prosperous trading centre, particularly in the Middle and Late Saxon periods.

The church, dedicated to St James, is partly Norman built about 1120, with an axial (central) tower, as at Great Dunham (No. 33), standing partly to full height but looking perilously unsafe. Of the fourteenth-century chancel only the south-east corner survives, although the outline of the original eastern apse was discovered in excavations in the 1930s. The arch between tower and nave is the most impressive feature with zigzag decoration and double roll-moulding above. A number of these stones fell off in the 1970s and '80s, and before they were replaced some were found to have signs of Anglo-Saxon interlace carving on their hidden faces. In the nave no windows remain, but the position of the south door is clear, and a gap in the north wall suggests there was also a door on this side. The church is recorded as being in bad repair in 1679, although baptisms and burials are recorded up to the 1770s.

Information from earlier periods comes from aerial photographs, geophysical surveys, surface finds from the surrounding fields and from a *Time Team* three-day excavation filmed live for Channel 4 television in 1998. There are important Iron Age finds near the church, but the main period of special interest is Middle Saxon of seventh- to ninth-century date. Coins, dress fittings and pottery continued to be used and lost on the site right into the medieval period. One human burial found in the excavation had a radiocarbon date centring on AD 760–880 and the repurposed carved stone provide a strong suggestion that there was a church on the site before the present ruin.

The exceptional number of surface finds, particularly the eighth and ninth century coins, strongly suggest that site was 'a focus of economic exchange' within the kingdom of East Anglia, known by archaeologists as 'productive sites'. In other words, a key market centre, like Dunston Field to the west of the Roman town at Caistor (No. 14). The sea was much closer than it is now, and we can visualise this hilltop as a place for international trade and for exchanging both local and imported goods. Bawsey was probably replaced by King's Lynn in the eleventh and twelfth centuries as a market centre as Dunston Field was by Norwich in the ninth century.

A public footpath runs close by the church, which is in a dangerous condition on private land. (PE32 1EU)

FURTHER READING

Batcock, N., 1991, *The Ruined and Disused Churches of Norfolk*, East Anglian Archaeology 51, pp.114–116.

Pestell, T., 2014, 'Bawsey – a 'productive' site in west Norfolk' in Ashley, S. and Marsden, A. (eds), *Landscapes and Artefacts: Studies in East Anglian Archaeology Presented to Andrew Rogerson*, pp.139–165 (Archaeopress).

Rogerson, A., 2005. 'Middle Saxon Norfolk' in Ashwin, T. and Davison, A. (eds), *An Historical Atlas of Norfolk*, pp.32–33 (Phillimore).

FROM CASTLES TO GREAT HOUSES

INTRODUCTION

The Norman Conquest in 1066 had a great impact on the social structure and landscape of England. As far as we know, there were no castles in Norfolk before the Conquest, but when the barons took control of the territories they had conquered, mainly from about 1070 onwards, their castles sprang up in both strategic and not-so-strategic locations. They were built primarily to demonstrate power and dominance over the lands they had conquered. Around twenty-five castles were built in Norfolk, perhaps fifteen in the eleventh and twelfth centuries, and about a further ten in the thirteenth to fifteenth centuries. At least three, at New Buckenham (No. 23), Castle Acre (No. 26) and Castle Rising (No. 24), had planted medieval planned towns directly associated with them.

RINGWORKS

A ringwork was essentially a circular, or near circular, embanked enclosure, and within it stood the keep built either of wood or stone. At the lower end of this hierarchy was the little structure at Moot Hill, Wymondham (No. 22), and at the upper end must surely be Castle Rising castle (c.1138) where an elaborately decorated stone keep stands within a massive embankment (No. 24).

MOTTE AND BAILEY CASTLES

The motte was a mound with a keep (a fortified wooden or stone tower) on top beside an embanked enclosure, or bailey, which provided a defended area for subsidiary buildings and protected access to the keep. The smallest is the tiny Denton Castle, a gem that lay undiscovered in woodland until the nineteenth century (No. 25). Thetford Castle has the tallest motte we have in Norfolk, and it is interesting that this castle was constructed by refurbishing an Iron Age fort built over 1,000 years earlier (No. 12). At Burgh Castle the motte was built in one corner of the Roman fort, and the fort itself became a rather large bailey (No. 16). We also have one fascinating hybrid castle at Mileham where there is motte and bailey, with a stone keep on the motte, all surrounded by a ringwork (No. 27). And the greatest motte and bailey of all is the royal castle at Norwich, where the original timber castle was strong enough by 1075 to withstand a siege (No. 28).

The only castles to be excavated on any scale so far are Castle Acre (No. 26), where a complex sequence of keeps was uncovered, Castle Rising (No. 24) and Norwich (No. 28). At Norwich the castle's two baileys were excavated in 1979 in advance of the construction of the Anglia Television office development, and from 1987 to 1991 in advance of the extensive Castle Mall shopping centre with its underground car park.

At the tail end of castle building, in the fifteenth century, manorial lords were erecting grand but quite undefendable castle-like manor houses, as at Baconsthorpe (No. 29) and Oxburgh (No. 30). They demonstrated the owner's wealth and prestige, but would have quickly disintegrated under cannon fire. After that there were no illusions about defence, and for this period we illustrate (in a later section) a series of great houses that represent changing fashion and design over time (Nos. 85–89).

The creation of parks was an adjunct to great house building starting with deer parks for hunting in the Middle Ages, as at Castle Rising, leading to designed landscapes for visual pleasure from the seventeenth century, as at Houghton (No. 86).

FURTHER READING

Cushion, B. and Davison, A., 2003, *Earthworks of Norfolk,* East Anglian Archaeology 104, 186.

Dallas, P., Last, R. and Williamson, T., 2013, *Norfolk Gardens and Designed Landscapes* (Norfolk Gardens Trust).

Liddiard, R., 2000, *Landscape of Lordship: Norman Castles and the Countryside in Medieval Norfolk, 1066–1200,* British Archaeological Reports British Series 309.

Liddiard, R., 2005, *Castles in Context: Power, Symbolism and Landscape, 1066 to 1500,* pp.134–139 (WINDgather Press).

Rowley, T., 1997, *Norman England* (English Heritage).

22. MOOT HILL RINGWORK, WYMONDHAM

This oval earthwork, which lies in dense woodland hemmed in between a railway line and the Wymondham town playing field, is a small early and rare type of ringwork castle, although documents give no clue to its history. The ringwork is about 100m across at its widest point, and the outer ditch is 15m to 18m across, wet in places, with an entrance causeway to the north-west. Quoting from Brian Cushion and Alan Davison in *Earthworks of Norfolk* (2003): 'This earthwork is a mystery. It was probably an early ringwork fortification, soon abandoned and apparently forgotten.' It sits in a very boggy location on heavy clay – a bad choice – which probably explains why it was soon abandoned but also why it has survived.

It is nevertheless well worth a visit because it was apparently not used for long and it is a largely unspoilt example of an early medieval ringwork dating from the time of the Conquest or possibly from the Anarchy of King Stephen's reign (1135–54).

The Moot Hill ringwork is most difficult to photograph buried deep in the dense Gristle Wood sandwiched between a housing estate, an industrial estate, a railway line and Wymondham town's Kett's Park playing fields! (John Fielding)

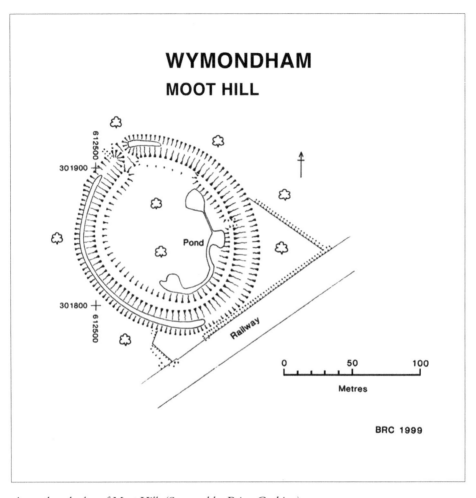

An earthwork plan of Moot Hill. (Surveyed by Brian Cushion)

The ponds inside are a puzzle, although they may have provided clay to strengthen the defences. An aerial photograph does not illustrate this site well, and it is best appreciated from an earthwork plan.

There is open access to the monument from Kett's Park playing field, using informal paths through thorn thickets into the woodland. (NR18 0YE)

FURTHER READING

Cushion, B. and Davison, A., 2003, *Earthworks of Norfolk*, East Anglian Archaeology 104, p.186.

23. NEW BUCKENHAM RINGWORK CASTLE AND PLANNED TOWN

THE CASTLE

The castle is an enormous ringwork with two outer baileys. It was built by William d'Albini II, a powerful and wealthy Norman baron, in about 1146 during the reign of King Stephen as a replacement for his castle in Old Buckenham. He was also responsible for building Castle Rising castle on an even grander scale with an elaborate square keep (No. 24).

The ringwork has a circular bank surrounded by a wide and deep water-filled ditch containing an area 75m across. Buried in the eastern bank is the original gatehouse, and close by, and also partly buried, is the circular keep – the largest round keep in England. The gatehouse was replaced in the thirteenth century by another on the south-west side where there is a nineteenth-century bridge over the moat, no doubt masking traces of an earlier structure.

A near vertical view of New Buckenham with the great ringwork of the castle containing the circular keep to the left, the grid iron pattern of streets of the planned Norman town and a market green near the centre. Outside the town to the right is New Buckenham Common. (John Fielding)

The outer wall of the keep is 3.7m thick, mainly built of flint rubble, and the circular interior is divided by a cross wall. On the exterior, close to the top, there is a deep groove, suggesting that some ornamental stonework has been torn out. The entrance doorway has lost all detail and is probably not original, but the head of the inner doorway through the cross wall is formed with thin slabs of stone and is genuine. It is likely that the ground floor was for storage, and the flat top of the cross wall supported the beams for the floor of the main living space above. There is no sign now of the outer stairway for the first floor, where the original entrance was probably ornate. Both walls retain traces of an original smooth plaster face.

In the meadow to the east, and contemporary with the original eastern gatehouse, is a horseshoe-shaped bailey surviving only as a low bank separating the castle from the town. Visible on aerial photographs, there is a cropmark in ploughed fields to the south-west of a second bailey, or barbican, to protect the later entrance. There are also long straight banks and ditches, representing the boundaries of the extensive deer park that lay mainly to the north. This is depicted as an area of wood pasture labelled 'Parke' on a map of 1597. Beside the lane up to the castle entrance is the small twelfth-century St Mary's chapel, now converted into a house. This appears to have served both castle and town before the parish church was built within the town in the mid-thirteenth century.

THE PLANNED TOWN

Beyond the eastern bailey is the planned town also founded by William d'Albini II in about 1170. He created a small parish for his new borough taking land from Old

The circular castle keep of New Buckenham castle within its ringwork from the south-west. (Mike Page)

Buckenham, Banham and Carleton Rode. The town was well located to be a market centre on the road between Norwich and Bury St Edmunds and was laid out in a square with a grid of streets surrounding a large market green. Outside the town, d'Albini also created an extensive common for the benefit of the town's livestock traders. With no cultivated land of its own, this was a place for craftsmen and traders rather than farmers. A regular market was held, and by about the middle of the twelfth century the town was thriving sufficiently for it to be given a charter to confirm its status as a borough. The church was not part of the original design and was inserted into the grid in about 1254.

The town has fine timber-framed buildings, many covered with later brick skins. These buildings have been studied in detail by the Norfolk Historic Buildings Group, which took samples for tree ring dating. The oldest sample was in the Old Vicarage in Chapel Street dating from the winter of 1451–52, and the next oldest was in 'Oak and Yellow Cottage' on the south side of the market green dating from the spring of 1473. In one corner of the green stands the open-sided Market House of 1754 built partly with reused earlier materials. Look out for the whipping post with arm clamps. In Chapel Hill there is a wonderful jumble of restored early seventeenth-century cottages.

Surrounding the town was a moat, known as the 'borough ditch' in 1493, and the 'greate ditch' in 1598. If there was a defensive bank on the inside of the ditch, as at Castle Acre (No. 26), no visible trace remains. It is interesting to follow the line of the defences, as far as one can, starting where the moat is best preserved along the north side and at the north-east corner, then down the east side between the town and the common. On the south side it is totally buried along Marsh Lane. Here the ditch has been recorded as 3m deep and 9m wide in archaeological excavations. It was filled in during the fifteenth and sixteenth centuries. To the west there was the castle bailey. On the north side the ditch is visible again at St Martin's Gardens, which take you back to your starting point. It is reasonable to assume that there were town gates, perhaps like the Bailey Gate at Castle Acre (No. 26), but none have been found.

In the church there is an excellent guidebook to the church and there are leaflets to help you explore the town. The very extensive unenclosed common, which is open for public access, is managed by the Norfolk Wildlife Trust as an important wildlife reserve, where green-winged orchids can be seen in flower in May and June. The castle is in private ownership, but it is usually possible to obtain a key for a fee from the village stores in King Street. (NR16 2AG)

FURTHER READING

Beresford, M. 1967, *New Towns of the Middle Ages*, p.467 (Lutterworth Press).

Cattermole, P. and Rutledge, P., 2007, *New Buckenham Church: A History and Guide*. On sale in the church.

Cushion, B. and Davison, A., 2003, *Earthworks of Norfolk*, East Anglian Archaeology 104, pp.175–177.

Renn, D., 1961, 'The Keep at New Buckenham', *Norfolk Archaeology* 32, pp.232–235.

Rutledge, P., 2007, 'New Buckenham in 1542', *Norfolk Archaeology* XLV, pp.222–231.

Rutledge, P., 2019, *New Buckenham* (Poppyland).

Longcroft, A. (ed.), 2005, *The Historic Buildings of New Buckenham*, Norfolk Historic Buildings Group 2.

24. CASTLE RISING RINGWORK CASTLE AND PLANNED TOWN

The most imposing Norman Castle in Norfolk after Norwich (No. 28) is Castle Rising, with its intact stone keep, faced with Barnack stone, and its enormous ringwork. It was built by William d'Albini II in *c.*1138, when he married the widow of King Henry I. He also built New Buckenham, and his two Norfolk castles formed an impressive manifestation of his power and standing in the county. To the north of the castle the village also has strong elements of a planned town, with a rectilinear street pattern and a central market green, but without town defences. The probability that d'Albini created a planned town here as well at New Buckenham is reinforced by a map of the parish of 1588 showing the streets set at right angles to each other. To the east of the market green stands the fine late Norman church of St Lawrence with a central tower and a west front described by Pevsner and Wilson (1999) as 'a swagger piece of Norman decoration'. There was a mint here during the reign of King Stephen, and a 1298 document refers to a burgage plot, suggesting that the place was regarded as a borough. The town, which has for long since been a small village, famously sent *two* members to Parliament until the Great Reform Act of 1832.

Castle Rising castle with its square stone keep and gatehouse standing within its impressive earthworks. In the foreground is the earthwork barbican protecting the gatehouse and bridge, and to the rear is another barbican. (John Fielding)

Above: *The castle keep from the south-east with its elaborately decorated forebuilding housing the stairway up to the first floor.* (Peter Wade-Martins)

Right: *The impressive stairway in the forebuilding.* (Peter Wade-Martins)

The castle consists of an ovoid-shaped ringwork with a very substantial bank surmounted by a curtain wall, a deep ditch and a twelfth-century gatehouse, complete with the slots for a portcullis. Protecting this entrance to the east is another massive earthwork barbican with an equally high bank and ditch. A causeway to the north where these two ditches meet gave access to the town. There is a smaller rectangular outer ward to the west, but its purpose is unclear, although it may well represent the remnants of an earlier larger ringwork. Partly buried in the north embankment are the ruins of an eleventh-century church. There is strong evidence that the eleventh-century village was also here but was moved off the hill to make way for the castle and re-established to the north as a part of the new planned layout with the new church.

The square stone keep is one of the greatest and finest in England, with walls over 2m thick, similar to the even grander keep at Norwich Castle. It is decorated with clasping corner buttresses and shallow buttresses on the north and south sides. The east wall, which faces the gatehouse, is the most richly decorated and was clearly designed to impress. It has a forebuilding with a wide magisterial stairway with arched doorways at the bottom, halfway up and at the top leading to a grand upper doorway (converted into a fireplace in the sixteenth century). This gave access to the first floor, which was divided in two with a spine wall separating the Great Hall from the Great Chamber (or sleeping area) and chapel. To the west was the kitchen and latrines. Newel stairs in the north-east and south-west corners take you up to the battlements and down to the ground-floor storage basement, and there are arrow slits at basement level. An upper floor was added to the forebuilding in the sixteenth century.

Excavations from 1970 to 1976 and in 1987 suggested that the earthworks were heightened and the ditch deepened in probably about 1200, and that the keep was abandoned by the fifteenth century. The map of 1588 shows that there was an extensive park for deer hunting to the south and west of the castle.

The castle is owned and managed by the Duke of Norfolk in association with English Heritage. Don't hurry this visit and enjoy the grandeur of the place. Check the castle website for opening times. The estate has produced its own guidebook. (Car park: PE31 6EJ)

FURTHER READING

Cushion, B. and Davison, A., 2003, *Earthworks of Norfolk*, East Anglian Archaeology 104, pp.166–167.
Castle Rising castle site guidebook – no author, publisher or date quoted.
Morley, B. and Gurney, D., 1997, *Castle Rising Castle, Norfolk*, East Anglian Archaeology 81.

25. DENTON CASTLE

The castle stands isolated 2km from the present village of Denton in a flat boulder clay landscape, and it is difficult to imagine why an unnamed Norman baron chose this spot to build himself a castle since its location appears to have had no strategic advantage. The earthworks lay undiscovered in Darrow Wood until 1850 when the wood was felled, and the site was recognised as a castle in 1884.

The castle has a tiny but complete motte measuring only 40m in diameter with a ditch 10m wide. It is unusual in that the low motte has a raised rim up to 2m above its centre, only just above the level of the surrounding meadow. It is tempting to interpret the arrangement here as an earth bank piled against a pre-existing timber keep. The horseshoe-shaped bailey, which is only 65m by 35m, has a bank 1m high with an entrance through the bank and ditch to the north-east. As at Moot Hill, Wymondham (No. 22), we have used an earthwork plan to illustrate the site layout because the features are so buried in woodland.

A view from the north-east of the earthworks of this tiny motte and bailey castle just visible in the trees in Darrow Wood, Denton. (John Fielding)

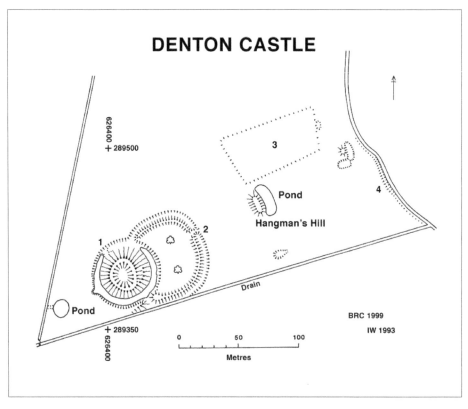

An earthwork plan of Denton Castle. (Surveyed by Brian Cushion)

This miniature earthwork castle is in the ownership of the National Trust with easy access across the meadow from a footpath. It can be found in their property list under Darrow Wood rather than Denton Castle. Each time the writers have been to the site, access onto the motte has been deep in nettles, so it is best to visit in winter. (IP20 0AY)

FURTHER READING

Cushion, B. and Davison, A., 2003, *Earthworks of Norfolk*, East Anglian Archaeology 104, pp.168–169.

Manning, C.R., 1884, 'Earthworks at the 'Castle Hill', Darrow Wood, Denton, Norfolk', *Norfolk Archaeology* 9, pp.335–342.

26. CASTLE ACRE CASTLE AND PLANNED TOWN

The village of Castle Acre is dominated by the massive earthworks of the motte and bailey castle sitting on the south-facing slopes of the Nar valley. To the west of the castle is the grid-iron pattern of streets of the Norman planned town. Immediately outside the town to the west is the parish church and beyond that is the Cluniac priory in its extensive walled precinct (No. 45). This whole complex is one great Norman creation imposed on a subjugated earlier landscape to be the focal point for the de Warenne family's Norfolk estates.

THE CASTLE

The castle has a circular motte and a rectangular bailey with a small triangular barbican to the north-east protecting the north-east entrance. This whole massive construction was cut into the side of the chalk valley, and it must have been gleaming white when first built. Around the top of the motte (inner ward) is a curtain wall and set within it is the stone keep. The keep was excavated between 1972 and 1977, revealing a complex structural sequence starting around 1100 with a double two-storey house set in a simple ringwork. Then, the outer walls of the house were thickened and increased in height while the lower levels of the building were partly buried and converted into a basement. Finally, the dividing wall was thickened to become an exterior wall and the southern half of the house was demolished, creating a tall narrow keep by about 1150. There was also a gatehouse on the motte controlling access from the bailey.

The bailey has a wall running along its perimeter bank and within it lie earthworks of unexcavated buildings. There were two stone gates, one controlling access from the town to the west and one from the barbican to the east. The west gate, which faced the town, was the most elaborate with flanking towers, a guard room and slots for a portcullis. At the lower end of the bailey there is a rather puzzling doorway said to be for access to a quay at the river's edge, although it is doubtful that the river was ever navigable this far upstream.

THE PLANNED TOWN

Just to the west of the castle lies the impressive planned town of Castle Acre with its own substantial defences, which were joined on to the castle to the north and south and enclosed a rectangular area of 5ha. The bank and ditch, known as Dyke Hills, can best be seen from a footpath that runs from the churchyard through the defences into the town. Bailey Street was the main street running north to south, with gates at either end. All trace of the southern gate has gone but the northern one, the so-called Bailey Gate, survives remarkably well; dating from around 1200, it has two round towers faced with whole flints and simple ashlar dressings forming two arches with upper hinge pins for the doors and slots for the portcullis still in place. English Heritage has now installed a replica portcullis.

Above: *Castle Acre castle and planned town from the north-east. A curtain wall around the top of the motte (inner ward) surrounds the excavated keep. Earthworks of unexcavated buildings are clear within the bailey. Beyond the castle is the Norman planned town still surrounded to the west and south by a massive bank and ditch. Beyond that stands the parish church. (John Fielding)*

Left: *The north gate of the town known as the Bailey Gate. (Peter Wade-Martins)*

Except for the Bailey Gate the defences on the north side have all been removed and replaced with houses that front on to Stocks Green, which is located over the infilled north town ditch. The original market green lay in the town centre, and the name is preserved in the street name Pales Green, which forms a loop to the west off Bailey Street. Probably the whole of this loop formed the original outline of this central open market space. Pales Green is now built over, while the areas of burgage plots to the west and south are allotments or gardens. The archaeology of these plots ought to be very well preserved below garden soil level. The fact that the church was first constructed in the twelfth century *outside* the town in the space left between the town and the Cluniac priory suggests that, unlike New Buckenham, by this date the town was already full.

The castle became derelict by the late fourteenth century, and the town seems to have declined at about that time since it was allowed a 40 per cent reduction to the 1449 Lay Subsidy return, although markets continued to be held here until the seventeenth century. Moving the marketplace from Pales Green to Stocks Green could only have occurred after the north ditch was filled in. A walk down Bailey Street will reveal pieces of dressed ashlar stone from the castle and priory set into some of the houses, mainly on the east side of the street.

The setting of the town and castle is of particular interest since this whole layout was built across the Peddars Way Roman road (No. 13), thus diverting traffic to the west through the planned town. On leaving the town heading south the traveller was required to make a further detour to the west passing around the priory precinct walls before fording the river and resuming the Roman alignment 4.8km to the south. This was all a power statement of the 1140s. But there is one element of a grand design that is strangely missing. There is no known original stone bridge – just a ford – over the River Nar near the priory.

There is open access to the castle from the town and from the car park to the north-east. Both castle and Bailey Gate are in the care of English Heritage. (Car park: PE32 2AN)

FURTHER READING

Campbell, C. (ed.), 2004, *Heritage Unlocked: Guide to Free Sites in the East of England*, pp.58–60 (English Heritage).

Coad, J.G. and Streeten, A.D.F., 1982, 'Excavations at Castle Acre Castle, Norfolk 1972–77; country house and castle of the Norman earls of Surrey', *Archaeological Journal* 139, pp.138–301.

Cushion, B. and Davison, A., 2003, *Earthworks of Norfolk,* East Anglian Archaeology 104, p.165.

Impey, E., 2008, *Castle Acre Priory and Castle* (English Heritage).

27. MILEHAM CASTLE

At the time of Domesday Book in 1086 Mileham was a place of unusual significance. The king owned a holding here consisting of ten carucates of land (about 490ha). With outlying estates in Litcham, Dunham and elsewhere, the influence of Mileham extended to some twenty places in Norfolk. It is reasonable to assume that the castle was built by Count Alan of Brittany, the son-in-law of William the Conqueror. The castle is unusual because it has a motte and a bailey entirely surrounded by a circular ringwork that formed an outer bailey – the only time in Norfolk the two techniques of castle building were combined. A causeway on the west side of the inner bailey links the two. It is not clear which came first or if they were parts of a single design. Within the motte there is a 15m square stone keep. On the north side of the inner bailey two lumps of flint masonry may be supports for a bridge to the outer bailey. A break in the bank on the north side of the ringwork forms an entrance on to the village street. There is no record of the castle after 1154, so its life was short.

The motte and bailey of Mileham castle surrounded by a ringwork. The stone keep set into the motte is just visible in the bushes. The outer rectangular moated enclosure to the left is on the other side of the street just beyond the Burwood Hall farm buildings. The medieval village ran between the castle and the church in the distance. (Mike Page)

On the opposite side of the street surrounding Burwood Hall Farm is an unusual rectangular-moated enclosure clearly linked to the castle, and the ditch on its west side is in line with a ditch running across the outer bailey. It is not difficult to imagine that there were stone gateways on the street at both entrances to this outer earthwork to complete the defences. But it is not so easy to understand what these outer defences were for. The area is too big to represent an outwork to the castle, but there is a parallel in the larger rectangular earthwork around the planned town at nearby Castle Acre (No. 26). Perhaps at Mileham we have a smaller Norman attempt to create a defended market centre. This one seems to have failed, although it was situated on the main east-to-west route between Norwich and King's Lynn, well-placed for extracting lucrative tolls from cross-county traffic.

Running south from the castle is a long curving hedgerow that at the far end abuts an even older earthwork, the Launditch, forming the outline of an extensive deer park. A document of 1302 describes a capital messuage in Mileham of 242 acres of arable, four acres of pasture and woodland in a park with two windmills and a water mill. There were similar extensive deer parks also attached to castles at New Buckenham (No. 23) and Castle Rising (No. 24).

There is permissive access to the castle through a kissing gate off the village street. Once on the monument, keep to the right to reach the motte and stone keep. (PE32 2RA)

FURTHER READING

Cushion, B. and Davison, A., 2003, *Earthworks of Norfolk,* East Anglian Archaeology 104, pp.173–175.

Above: *Norwich Castle motte with its stone keep and adjacent prison buildings converted into the county museum after the prison closed in 1887. The castle bailey in the foreground was dug away after it was archaeologically excavated to install the underground Castle Mall car park and shopping centre completed in 1993. (Mike Page)*

Below: *Norwich Castle keep, refaced in 1834–39, and the bridge up to the motte to the right. (John Fielding)*

28. NORWICH CASTLE, PRISON AND MUSEUM

In the heart of Norwich is the great royal castle standing high overlooking the city. Unlike the other Norfolk castles, this was a royal fortress and was owned and built by the king. A castle here was probably under construction soon after the Norman Conquest, and the Domesday Book records that this involved clearing ninety-eight houses. We know from excavations that two timber churches were also removed. The stone keep stands on a very prominent mound, part natural and part man-made, with a large bailey to the south (now replaced by the Castle Mall underground shopping centre with a landscaped green above) and a smaller bailey to the north-east (where the old Agricultural Hall is located), the whole covering an area of 5.6ha. The timber castle was sufficiently complete by 1075 to withstand a siege when the Constable rebelled against the king, although the garrison eventually surrendered.

The castle was the third in a series of great fortified royal palaces constructed by William the Conqueror after the Tower of London and Colchester Castle. Architectural historians believe that the present stone keep was built to replace the timber keep by William's sons, King William Rufus and his successor King Henry I, in the years following 1100. It is a remarkable building, constructed mainly of flint but with shiploads of dressed limestone from Caen in Normandy. Norwich had become a boom town by the end of the eleventh century, equal only to London, and there was heavy Norman investment here in both the castle and the cathedral (No. 34). It is quite clear from masons' marks on the dressed stone in the two buildings that they were being built at the same time as a pair.

Although the keep was refaced by the Victorians in 1834–39, we do have elevation drawings from the late eighteenth century that show all the external detailing that the Victorians attempted to replicate in their refacing. To build a massive and very heavy stone keep on a new, and not fully consolidated, mound was a great risk, and indeed there was a major split in the centre of the north side that had to be strengthened by an extra buttress. On the other sides there are five buttresses but on this side there are six. The ground floor, which was used for storage, was largely plain on the exterior, while the main first floor was heavily decorated with rows of blind arcades and windows.

The keep was originally entered on the east side through the Bigod Tower forebuilding with a stairway, just as at Castle Rising (No. 24). Even though the Bigod Tower has gone, the doorway that gave access from the tower into the Great Hall survives without much Victorian alteration. This highly decorated doorway, with some traces of paintwork remaining, is the least damaged and most impressive part of the building. To reach this, visitors should ascend the modern stairway to the doorway, noting especially the Pegasus winged horse near the top of the doorway arch. The only time where such a figure is seen in the Bayeux Tapestry is over the head of Duke William as he is riding into battle with his knights at Hastings.

Inside the keep, much Norman stonework survives although all the interior dividing walls have gone. The decorated doorway is level with the main living space, which was divided into the Great Hall and the Great Chamber (or sleeping space). In the north-east corner a spiral staircase leads both up to the battlements and down to the basement. The latrines were located at the far end of the Great Hall on the west side, as at Castle Rising (No. 24), and the apse of the chapel in the south-east corner also survives.

In 1230 Henry III designated the castle as the county gaol, both for local and for state prisoners, but it was recorded as derelict by 1371. As the conditions in the keep deteriorated, new prison buildings were erected inside the keep walls, and in 1793 a separate prison block was added to the east of the keep, but later demolished. The prison was surrounded by the very forbidding medieval-looking granite walls in 1823, and in 1824–28 new prison buildings were erected inside consisting of three main wings radiating from a central open space. Public hangings took place on gallows erected on the castle bridge, with the last taking place in 1867. After the site was closed as a prison in 1887 it was converted by the Norwich architect Edward Boardman into a museum. The three main prison wings became display galleries, and the keep with a new glass roof was adapted to be both a part of the museum and also a great open space for civic ceremonies. The formal opening of the museum was performed by Duke and Duchess of York (later King George V and Queen Mary) in 1894. The central open space from which the galleries radiate was roofed over to form The Rotunda in 1969.

The main castle bailey became the Norwich Cattle Market in 1738 until it was moved out of the city in the early 1960s. Extensive archaeological excavations all over this bailey took place between 1989 and 1991, followed by the construction of the Castle Mall underground shopping centre with spaces for a thousand cars.

Opening times for the Castle Museum are advertised by the Norfolk Museums Service. (NR1 3FS)

FURTHER READING

Ayers, B., 1994, *Norwich* (Batsford/English Heritage).

Heslop, T.A., 1994, *Norwich Castle Keep* (Centre of East Anglian Studies).

Shepherd Popescu, E., 2009, *Norwich Castle: Excavations and Historical Survey, 1987–98,* East Anglian Archaeology 132.

29. BACONSTHORPE CASTLE

The site of Baconsthorpe Castle has been the subject of much detailed research, including archaeological excavations, a study of the surviving fabric and a review of the documents. The importance of the castle today is its place in castle development between the construction of heavily defended castles, such as Castle Acre (No. 26) and ornamental moated manor houses like Oxburgh (No. 30). Retaining the castle-like appearance helped to emphasise the owner's status, so gunloops for hand guns were built into the curtain walls, although the walls would certainly not have withstood the cannon that were by then available.

The original moated and fortified manor house was begun in about 1450 by Sir John Heydon and completed by his son Sir Henry in 1504. The Heydons were one of Norfolk's leading families and they also built Heydon Hall, otherwise known as Saxlingham Place, in Saxlingham in 1550.

Sir John first built the massive three-storey gatehouse without gunloops but with a drawbridge, which was itself a contradiction. He followed this with a curtain wall

Baconsthorpe Castle from the north-west surrounded by its moat and a large ornamental pond. In front stands the partly ruined outer gatehouse. (Mike Page)

that runs west from the gatehouse and then north as far as a square tower. This wall had gunloops and there was a gun port in the square tower. It was also the outer wall of a substantial courtyard house, since demolished, built by Sir John's son Sir Henry in the south-west corner of the moated platform. Perhaps forty years later the rest of the curtain wall and service buildings were added.

In *c.*1560 Sir Christopher Heydon added a new outer gatehouse with a pair of picturesque octagonal towers in front of the castle to create an outer court between the two gatehouses. The ornamental mere was added early in the seventeenth century, but by the mid-seventeenth century the Heydon family was in debt. Most of the buildings in the inner court were sold and the materials removed by the cartload from 1650. The outer gatehouse was retained, and *c.*1810 it was given a new doorway with a castellated top. The end came in 1920 when the west side of the outer gatehouse and one of the octagonal towers collapsed, and the place was abandoned.

Baconsthorpe was started possibly twenty-five years before Oxburgh Hall, and the contrast between the use of flint here compared with the flamboyant use of ornamental brick as the primary building material at Oxburgh is remarkable.

> *The castle is managed by English Heritage and is open at all reasonable times. (Car park: NR25 6LF)*

FURTHER READING

Campbell, A., 2004, *Heritage Unlocked: Guide to Free Sites in the East of England*, pp.44–47 (English Heritage).

Cushion, B. and Davison, A., 2003, *Earthworks of Norfolk*, East Anglian Archaeology 104, pp.163–165.

Dallas, C. and Sherlock, D., 2002, *Baconsthorpe Castle, Excavations and Finds, 1951–1972*, East Anglian Archaeology 102.

30. OXBURGH HALL

Oxburgh has been described as the finest late medieval house in Norfolk with good reason. It looks like a fairy tale moated manor house, with its perfectly formed fifteenth-century brick gatehouse overlooking a wide water-filled brick-lined moat surrounded by parkland. It was built by Henry Bedingfeld sometime between 1476, when he inherited Oxburgh, and 1487 when he was able to entertain Henry VII in his new house. The gatehouse with its polygonal turrets rises in seven stages culminating in double-stepped battlements. The two turrets have different window openings since one serves as a spiral staircase. The east turret has gunloops on the ground floor, although some are now blocked. The great wooden doors are original, and the gatehouse contains perhaps the only genuine priest's hole in Norfolk. The wooden drawbridge was replaced in the eighteenth century with a three-arched bridge spanning the moat.

The three wings completing the square were built soon after, but the Great Hall on the fourth side was (sadly) pulled down in 1775 and replaced in 1862 by a corridor joining the two side wings again.

The moated Oxburgh Hall from the north-west with ornamental gardens to the left and chapel in the foreground. (Mike Page)

The Bedingfelds were a prominent Catholic family who declared for the king in the Civil War. Sir Henry Bedingfeld's three sons fought for the king throughout the war, and their house was occupied by Parliament. The east range was damaged and it then lay in ruins until it was rebuilt by 1725. A south-west tower was replaced as a pavilion sometime after 1780. Close inspection of the exterior brickwork shows that there have been many alterations over the years, and there are further rather symbolic gunloops on the north and east sides. The sixth baronet employed the architect J.C. Buckler to carry out extensive repairs and alterations in the 1830s, which included replacing most of the windows, adding highly ornate chimneys and constructing the south-east corner tower. Buckler also designed the attractive walls and towers of the kitchen garden, now an orchard, and the chapel, which was opened in 1836. The Bedingfeld family still live in a part of the house, although it has been owned by the National Trust since 1952.

No visit to Oxburgh is complete without a look inside the partly ruined parish church. The tower fell in 1948 destroying the nave and south aisle, but the east end of the south aisle containing the fine early sixteenth-century terracotta Bedingfeld monuments miraculously survived.

Oxburgh Hall is run by the National Trust and is open at advertised times. There are walks through extensive areas of woodland at Home Covert south-west of the hall, including some fine old oak trees at the far end. (PE33 9QD)

FURTHER READING

Forest, A., 2014, *Oxburgh Hall* (National Trust).

CHURCHES AND CHAPELS

INTRODUCTION

Norfolk has more medieval churches than any other county in England. At least 921 were built between the eleventh and sixteenth centuries, which is an astonishing figure. The Domesday Book recorded 330 in 1086, but we know from Anglo-Saxon charters that there were others that were not listed. 'Competitive church building' by manorial lords to enhance their social status is the best explanation for the great number of churches built in the tenth and eleventh centuries (Williamson, 1993, p.158).

The numbers reached their peak in the late thirteenth century. There then followed a gradual decline, with the sixteenth and nineteenth centuries seeing the greatest number of church closures. About 610 churches are still in use, and ruined and abandoned medieval churches are a characteristic feature of the Norfolk landscape.

In the eleventh and twelfth centuries stone churches in East Anglia were mainly, but not always, built with round west towers, and some were later replaced with square towers. It used to be said that the reason for building round towers was because there was no suitable stone to construct square ones, but it is perfectly possible to build corners and window openings in flint. Some of these round towers, such as at East and West Lexham (No. 32) are early, but are any pre-Conquest? Are we right to say when discussing the Late Saxon period that all churches up to the Conquest were wooden (p.70)? One possible line of research would be to excavate around the outside of some churches with Anglo-Saxon characteristics to see if there are burials beneath them cut by the foundations that could be radiocarbon dated. This might be a way of dating some early buildings without disturbing church interiors.

For the later Middle Ages we have included two stunning churches entirely built in the fifteenth century at Salle (No. 39) and St Peter Mancroft in Norwich (No. 40). These represent the full flowering of late medieval architecture funded largely from the wool trade.

As church building went into decline, the rise of nonconformity from the mid-seventeenth century was particularly strong in Norfolk, with early dissent stimulated by an independently minded yeoman class and the county's proximity to a centre of dissent in the Low Countries. This led eventually to the building of dissenting chapels and meeting houses in almost every village, some with their own burial grounds. Many have since been sold and converted into houses, but we illustrate two, the Congregational chapel at Oulton of 1728 (No. 43), which is one of the earliest meeting houses in Norfolk, and the fine Unitarian Octagon chapel in Norwich of 1756 (No. 44). As a part of the revival of the Church of England in the nineteenth century churches were extensively renovated, while some were almost entirely rebuilt by Victorian 'restorers'.

FURTHER READING

Butcher, D., 2019, *Norfolk and Suffolk Churches: The Domesday Record* (Poppyland).

Cautley, H.M., 1949, *Norfolk Churches* (Norman Adlard).

Ede, J., Virgoe, N. and Williamson, T., 1994, *Halls of Zion* (Centre of East Anglian Studies).

Heywood, S., 2013, 'Stone building in Romanesque East Anglia' in Bates, D. and Liddiard, R., *East Anglia and its North Sea World in the Middle Ages* (Boydell).

Ladbrooke, R., 1843, *Views of the churches of Norfolk* in five volumes (Charles Muskett).

Mortlock, D.P. and Roberts, C.V., 2017, *A Guide to Norfolk Churches* (Lutterworth Press).

Taylor, H.M. and Taylor J., 1965 and 1978, *Anglo-Saxon Architecture* in three volumes (Cambridge University Press).

31. SITE OF THE ANGLO-SAXON CATHEDRAL AND EARLY NORMAN BISHOP'S CHAPEL, NORTH ELMHAM

The early Norman chapel, faced with ferruginous conglomerate (naturally occurring iron-bound gravel blocks), stands either very close to, or probably on, the site of the Anglo-Saxon wooden cathedral for the diocese of East Anglia. No clear evidence for the cathedral building has yet been found, but a very extensive Late Saxon Christian burial ground has been excavated in the park on the opposite side of the main road extending as far south as the parish church. These excavations have also revealed traces of Middle and Late Saxon timber buildings contemporary with the cathedral.

The bishops moved away in around 1071, and the cathedral, described at the time as being built of wood, was replaced with a stone Norman chapel. At some stage, and we are not sure when, the chapel was converted into domestic use and it was later fortified by Bishop Despenser as his rural retreat in 1387. He was the 'fighting bishop' of Norwich who put down the Peasants' Revolt in 1381. He was no doubt very unpopular and in need of a place to sleep safely at night! The converted chapel was fortified with massive earthworks, which must have disturbed thousands of Christian burials when Despenser piled the earth against the old Norman chapel

The Norman chapel at North Elmham with the interior subdivisions dating from the time it was converted into a fortified manor house in the fourteenth century. (John Fielding)

The Norman stair turret to the left was matched in the fourteenth century by another turret to the right to frame a first-floor fortified entrance into the manor house. (Peter Wade-Martins)

walls. So, the visible remains consist of the chapel converted into a fortified fourteenth-century manor house. The visitor needs to distinguish between these two main periods, and the key to the difference is that the conglomerate blocks are only used in the original chapel walls.

The chapel had a western square tower with thick walls and a stairway leading to a first-floor room. A blocked doorway can just be discerned in the west wall. The base of the tower arch is visible between the tower and the long, thin, aisle-less nave leading to an eastern apse with transepts to either side. In the external angles between the nave and the transepts are very distinctive quarter-round pilasters only found in Norman buildings. There were north and south doorways at the west end of the nave, and in the angles between nave and transepts there were small square towers.

The fourteenth-century conversion involved creating a first-floor living space and an internal stairway down to the Norman ground floor, which then became the basement – no doubt for the bishop's wine cellar. The Norman apse was removed in the digging of the inner moat, and a second half-round turret was added on the south side to flank the south door and to match the Norman stairway turret. The visitor will notice that this doorway is in line with the main street coming up the hill from the river crossing to the south, thus creating a sense of grandeur to impress the visitor.

The site is owned by the Norwich Diocese, in the care of English Heritage and managed by North Elmham Parish Council, which keeps it open at all reasonable times. (Car park: NR20 5JU)

FURTHER READING

Heywood, S. 1982, 'The ruined church at North Elmham', *Journal of the British Archaeological Association* 135, pp.1–10.

Heywood, S., 2014, 'The Elmhams re-visited', *Landscapes and Artefacts: Studies in East Anglian Archaeology Presented to Andrew Rogerson*, pp.181–188 (Archaeopress).

Rigold, S.E., 1962–63. 'The Anglian Cathedral at North Elmham, Norfolk', *Medieval Archaeology* 6–7, pp.67–108.

32. THE SAXO-NORMAN CHURCHES AT EAST AND WEST LEXHAM

EAST LEXHAM CHURCH

If any stone building in Norfolk looks pre-Conquest, then it is surely St Andrew's church at East Lexham. It stands within an unusual near-circular churchyard, and the primitive-looking round tower was built with flint rubble on the outside and chalk blocks, or clunch, on the inside. The way the tower tapers and bulges slightly suggests that it was constructed by masons with little experience of building in flint. The tower arch (behind a usually locked door) is cruck-shaped with sides which rise in a curve to meet at the top. This is rare, although there are a few other examples in Norfolk, as at nearby Newton-by-Castle Acre. The way the courses of large flints in the tower run around into the west wall of the nave shows that the two were built together. All four corners of the church are of dressed stone forming rather crude 'long-and-short' work, which is usually described as Anglo-Saxon, although it can be seen in some early Norman churches, as at Great Dunham nearby (No. 33). The unusual plan was a simple rectangle with no distinction outside between nave and chancel. However, on Ladbrooke's sketch of the church published in 1843 there is a trace of a possible butt-joint between the two. The flint courses in the nave are more regular than the uneven flint work in the tower and appear to have been built by more experienced craftsmen. Architectural historians will for ever debate the date and significance of this tower. All options make this a most intriguing building, which is well worth careful study.

There are three quite different bell openings in the tower. The east window is cut out of a solid piece of limestone in the form of a Maltese cross and set within a single-splayed opening. The one to the north-west is formed out of a thin piece of carved limestone with a central baluster, again set within a single-splayed opening. Can we be sure that these two carved stones are not later inserts? The opening to the south-west is formed of flint rubble within a round-headed opening and has a rendered cylinder of rubble supporting a flattened cushion capital. Visible only inside the tower on the east side there is a small blocked triangular-headed upper doorway once opening into the roof space. And above the bell opening level all around the tower is a series of twelve very unusual blocked cylindrical holes that are hardly visible on the outside. There are two pairs of somewhat similar ones near the top of the tower at Great Dunham.

The two doorways in the nave are probably late twelfth century. While most of the south side of the nave was rendered in 1975–76 and is difficult to study, the north side is built with coursed flints at the lower levels, but the coursing is disrupted higher up. The church also saw nineteenth-century restoration that has undoubtedly obscured further interesting early detail.

Above: *The round tower and nave of East Lexham church within its circular churchyard. The top of the tower was rebuilt during recent repairs. Is this one of the oldest buildings still in use to be found in Norfolk? (John Fielding)*

Above left: *East Lexham church tower with one of its three unusual windows. (Peter Wade-Martins)*

Above right: *The rather crude 'long and short' work in the north-west corner, a characteristic feature of all four corners, suggesting that the East Lexham church was just a simple rectangle without a separate chancel. The corner stones indicate that the original church was no more than about 3m high to the eaves. (Peter Wade-Martins)*

WEST LEXHAM CHURCH

East Lexham should be followed by a visit to neighbouring West Lexham church because the two need to be studied together. This also has a round tower built with a mixture of flints and clunch and with fascinating early features, but these features are hard to see. In 2018, when cement rendering was, at last, removed from the tower, three blocked, double-splayed, round-headed windows and one blocked circular opening were discovered in the upper part of the tower. Two of the round-headed windows are clear on the outside. Lower down there are two primitive-looking, triangular-headed windows on the north and south sides, but you need to look carefully to see them.

The two Lexham churches and the one at Hales (No. 35) are all good examples of isolated churches where the villages moved away from the churches in the eleventh and twelfth centuries, usually to village greens, and the churches were gradually left standing by themselves. No original village can be found near any of these churches, although in the case of West Lexham there is a late-sixteenth-century map of the parish showing a village to the east, but there is no trace of one today. The story of gradual rural decline and settlement movement away from churches was repeated so often all over Norfolk.

Both Lexham churches are usually open, although access into the East Lexham tower is locked. (PE32 2QL and PE32 2QN)

FURTHER READING

An unpublished report by Stephen Heywood entitled *The Church of St Andrew, East Lexham* (March 2014) is held in the Norfolk Historic Environment Record (NHER).

A report by Sarah Bates and Simon Underdown of the 2018 archaeological recording carried out at West Lexham church at the time of restoration is also available in the NHER.

33. THE EARLY NORMAN CHURCH AT GREAT DUNHAM

This church, which was constructed within twenty years of the Norman Conquest, is a fine example of the Saxon–Norman overlap when local craftsmen were inserting features sometimes regarded as Anglo-Saxon into churches being built in the new Norman tradition. At Great Dunham the use of well-formed 'long and short' work at the corners of the nave and the high central tower, the triangular-headed west doorway, the double-splayed lower windows in the tower and the mouldings around the chancel arch say 'Anglo-Saxon'. At the same time, the band of billet moulding around the west doorway, the decoration on the imposts of the tower arch and dog-toothing on the blind arcading in the nave say 'Norman'. High up in the tower on all four sides are two-light bell openings with central shafts and mysterious small circular holes above them to west and east.

The early Norman church at Great Dunham. The triangular-headed west door, the 'long and short' work on all the original corners and the unusual circular holes to west and east in the tower above the two-light openings make this a particularly interesting building. (Peter Wade-Martins)

The church was built at considerable cost involving the importation of some 20 tons of Barnack limestone when most Norfolk churches at the time were being built using local flint. It is part of a group of five early churches in the area: Newton-by-Castle Acre, which also has a square central tower; East and West Lexham churches, with round towers (No. 32); and Houghton-on-the-Hill, with remarkable early wall paintings. All are well worth a visit. The obvious reuse of Roman bricks in some door and window openings creates additional interest.

The nave inside with blind arcading on the side walls and the two arches supporting the central tower. (Peter Wade-Martins)

In its original form Great Dunham had a small west door and a long narrow nave ornamented inside with blind arcading. A large arched opening into the tower, and beyond that a smaller more ornate arch, takes the eye into what would have been a long narrow apse. Sadly, the east end of the apse was replaced with a square-ended chancel sometime before Robert Ladbrooke sketched the church for his five volumes of sketches of Norfolk churches published in 1843. In the east wall of the chancel there is a commemorative plaque to the Rev. Ambrose Pinlow, who was incumbent between 1721 and 1752. Assuming that the plaque is in its original position, it seems likely that the east end of the apse was replaced by him in the middle of the eighteenth century. There is a blocked doorway formed in Roman brick in a surviving part of the original south apse wall.

The tower separating nave from chancel could well have had deep ritual significance. Above the tower arch, midway between the east and west ends of the church, is a single projecting corbel that supported the foot of a crucifix or a crucifixion scene, implying that what lay further to the east was 'the realm of heaven, the sacred and unknowable place that is the goal of Christian life on earth' (Heslop, 2014).

The church is usually open. (PE32 2LQ)

FURTHER READING

Heslop, T.A., 2014, 'Great Dunham church and its eleventh-century context', *Landscapes and Artefacts: Studies in East Anglian Archaeology presented to Andrew Rogerson*, pp.189–197 (Archaeopress).

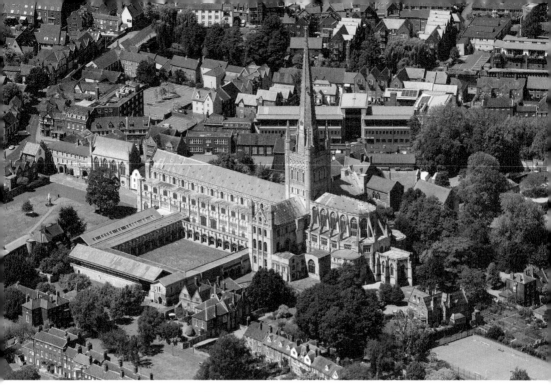

A fine view of Norwich Cathedral, cloisters and priory buildings. (John Fielding)

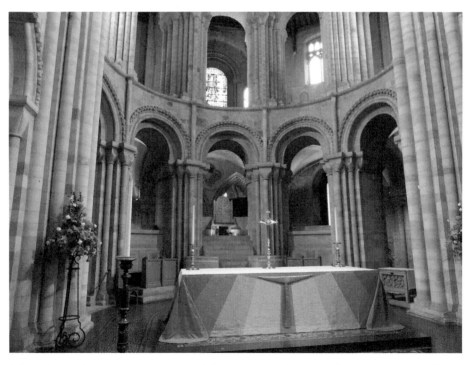

The modern bishop's throne at the east end that covers stone fragments of an earlier seat, possibly the original Anglo-Saxon throne brought from North Elmham. (Peter Wade-Martins)

34. NORWICH ROMANESQUE CATHEDRAL AND PRECINCT

The cathedral and castle were built at the same time, demonstrating the dominance the Norman barons and bishops quickly established over the subjugated Anglo-Saxon population both of Norwich and the wider region. As the guidebook says, 'The Cathedral was intended to overwhelm the English with the power and divine favour enjoyed by their Norman conquerors …' (Doll, 2017, p. 11). Significant areas of the town were cleared, and in the case of the cathedral this was not just for the church. The area had to be big enough for a bishop's palace to the north and the Benedictine priory to the south, all set within the largest cathedral close in England with two gateways opening on to Tombland, which had been the main Anglo-Saxon market centre for Norwich. It is one of the best-preserved Romanesque cathedrals in Europe, and it is both the scale of the work and the detailing that demonstrates the extraordinary energy of the Norman elite in the late eleventh and twelfth centuries.

The plan of the Norman cathedral survives almost in its entirety. Construction by Bishop Herbert Losinga began in 1096, and the eastern end of the church with its surrounding ambulatory, radiating chapels, transepts with corner turrets and the first four bays of the nave was completed by his death in 1119. The rest, including the west front with its now much-reduced corner turrets and the crossing tower, was completed by his successor, Bishop Eborard, by about 1140. The crossing tower, highly decorated with bold roundels, lozenges and blind interlacing arcades, again with corner turrets, is unique. Wisely, the Norman builders gave the church twenty years to settle before the tower was added, while at Bury St Edmunds, Lincoln and Ely they did not wait and their towers collapsed.

Visitors to this great building can only be impressed by its height, its extraordinary length and the quantity of dressed stone imported from Caen in Normandy and from Barnack. The stone was used to clad the flint walls and there is much decorative blind arcading both inside and out.

The door in the end of the north transept was the bishop's entrance from his palace. On the exterior (sadly, in an area not normally open to visitors) over the north transept doorway are heads of grotesque beasts under an arched niche containing a life-sized, rather archaic, representation of a bishop holding a crozier. The niche now contains a replica, and the original, still with much of its gold paint, has been moved indoors to the south side of the ambulatory. On the inside over the doorway there is a pair of triangular arches decorated with billet moulding and yet further heads of fierce beasts that seem to relate back to an earlier Anglo-Saxon style. It is such a pity that we now cannot understand the significance Bishop Losinga attached to this archaic symbolism.

Up at the east end of the church is the bishop's throne, and under the wooden seat, made in 1974, are two fragments of a far older throne that may have stood in the original wooden cathedral at North Elmham (No. 31). Norwich is the only cathedral north of the Alps that retains this Roman arrangement with the bishop seated at the east end. In the ambulatory directly under the throne is a relic chamber (or recess) with a flue up to the underside of the throne for the 'essence' of the relics to rise under the bishop to give him divine aid and assistance. By the eleventh century such a practice had been abandoned elsewhere in Europe, so its use here is a further sign of Bishop Losinga's liking for past traditions.

The ambulatory and the small circular chapels radiating from it are the best areas to find surviving paint on the stonework. It is not clear if this paintwork is original or was added after a serious fire in 1272. It looks original.

The 1272 fire was started in a riot, and both the cathedral and the priory were severely damaged. The king then required the townsfolk to pay an enormous sum for the repairs. Following a great gale in 1362, the previous spire fell onto the roof, and so the Norman clerestory windows east of the crossing were replaced with a much taller clerestory creating a wonderful feeling of light and space at this end of the church. The remarkable fan-vaulted roof, with its famous brightly painted stone roof bosses depicting Bible stories, replaced the wooden roof between 1480 and 1490. There are well over a thousand roof bosses in all, including those in the cloisters.

The nave windows were inserted and then the steep flying buttresses were added to stabilise the high eastern end in the fifteenth century. The 96m-high brick spire, clad in Weldon stone, was added to the crossing tower between 1472 and 1501, making this the second highest cathedral spire in England after Salisbury. The great west window and the west doorway (which still holds its original doors) were inserted in 1538.

The priory was closed by Henry VIII, but the prior and the remaining monks were then appointed as cathedral officials.

A stone figure of a bishop thought to represent St Felix originally located in the external niche above the door into the north transept. (Peter Wade-Martins)

The cathedral and the close have a feeling of great peace and tranquillity, but that was not always so. There was another major damaging fire in 1463, and during the fighting at the time of Kett's Rebellion in 1549 (No. 64) the wounded and dying from both sides were carried into the cathedral. In the Civil War in May 1643 a mob led by two city aldermen forced their way into the cathedral and smashed the stained glass, tore out monuments and fittings, and 'the cathedral was filled with musketeers drinking and tobacconing as freely as if it had been turned into an alehouse' (Meeres, 1998, p.70).

A comparison between the great nave piers of the cathedral, which are about 2.5m across, and the slender elegant mid-fifteenth century clustered piers of the high nave of St Peter Mancroft (No. 40), shows how much church architecture would evolve over the following 350 years.

Opening hours can be checked on the cathedral's website. The gift shop sells the guidebook, which does lack detail, and the enthusiast would benefit from having Pevsner and Wilson (1997) as well. A large mirror set on wheels in the nave will help you enjoy the remarkable roof bosses. This cathedral is a place not to be missed, especially by those who enjoy Romanesque architecture. (NR3 1HF)

FURTHER READING

Doll, P., 2017, *The Story of Norwich Cathedral* (Norwich Cathedral).

Heywood, S., 1996. 'The Romanesque Building', Atherton, I. and others (eds), *Norwich Cathedral: Church City and Diocese 1096–1996*, pp.73–115 (Hambleden Press).

Meeres, F., 1998, *A History of Norwich* (Phillimore).

Rose, M. and Hedgecoe, J., 1997, *Stories in Stone: The Medieval Roof Carvings of Norwich Cathedral* (Thames & Hudson).

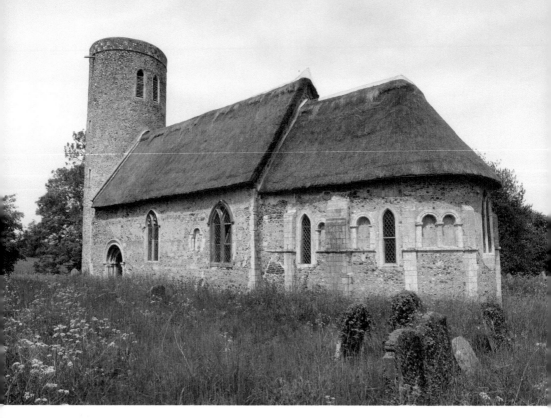

Above: *Hales church with its ornate Norman chancel and steep thatched roof. (Peter Wade-Martins)*

Left: *The highly elaborate Norman north door at Hales. (Peter Wade-Martins)*

35. THE NORMAN CHURCH AT HALES

This little isolated church, surrounded by a riot of wild flowers in the graveyard during the summer months, is a gem. The early Norman flint round tower is particularly interesting because it has inside two small perfectly preserved circular window openings, high up on the ground floor, now blocked on the outside. They were formed around conical basketwork that, remarkably, remains intact. Evidence that the tower is a part of the Saxo-Norman tradition is a blocked triangular-headed window at first-floor level that once opened towards the nave. In the angles between tower and nave are quarter round pilasters strongly suggesting that they are of one build and post-Conquest.

While the tower may be Saxo-Norman, the rest of the church is pure Norman in plan with nave and apse surviving unchanged from the mid-twelfth century. The nave is mostly built of flint with a strong scattering of ferruginous conglomerate obvious at North Elmham (No. 31). Pieces of Roman tile can be seen, especially low down in the north wall. The face of the apse has a blind arcade embellished with square imposts and decorated sills that continue around ashlar buttresses to form an attractive band. While it is a pity that this Norman composition is interrupted by thirteenth-century lancet windows, the original exterior composition is still a pleasure to behold. In the nave there were two small windows on each side matching the arcade, although only one on the south side now remains. Inside, the chancel arch is double-chamfered and simple.

The ornate north doorway is a masterpiece of Norman craftsmanship, probably created by the same stone mason who worked on the south doorway at Heckingham church nearby. Six orders of highly imaginative decoration surround the arch and spill over onto the wall above the capitals of the supporting columns. The south doorway is similar but simpler. How such a remote church serving a small community was able to commission such flamboyant stonework is remarkable.

Inside, a series of fourteenth-century paintings has recently been discovered. A near-complete St Christopher covers much of the west end of the south wall, while St James is illustrated behind the pulpit. Smaller fragments survive throughout the church reminding us how medieval churches were so different from the light lime-washed post-Reformation walls with which we are now so familiar.

Hales church is in the care of the Churches Conservation Trust and is usually unlocked, but it is a real shame that the Conservation Trust has no guidebook to such an interesting building. (NR14 6NL)

36. ST WILLIAM'S CHAPEL, MOUSEHOLD HEATH

A group of mounds and banks on Mousehold Heath hide one of the most unpleasant and controversial parts of Norfolk's history. They also have a wider role to play in the story of antisemitism in medieval Norwich and England.

William, a 12-year-old apprentice skinner, disappeared just before Easter 1144. When his body was found on the heath a few days later it was suggested he had suffered injuries reminiscent of the Crucifixion of Jesus. Word spread quickly and, despite a complete lack of evidence, members of the local Jewish community were accused of William's murder.

Although the accusations were completely unfounded, the story of William is an important one. It is the first known allegation of Jews murdering a child, an accusation that became known as 'blood libel'. Similar claims were made in other English cities and in other countries over centuries, contributing to the persecution of Jews. There are many accounts of persecution ahead of the Jewish community's expulsion from England by Edward I in 1290, including from London, Norwich, King's Lynn and York. In 2004 archaeologists discovered seventeen twelfth- or thirteenth-century skeletons in a well on the site of Chapelfield Shopping Centre. Seven were subject to DNA analysis, which suggested five could have been members of the same Jewish family.

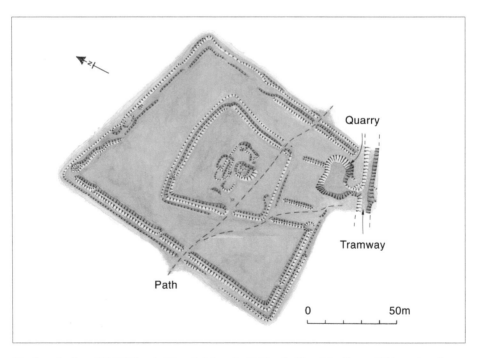

Earthwork plan of St William's Chapel, Mousehold Heath, Norwich. (Jason Gibbons, based on a survey by Brian Cushion)

At first William's body was buried close to where it was found, perhaps on the site where a chapel was established in his name in 1158 or 1168. However, within weeks the opportunity was taken to make William a religious martyr and his remains were moved to Norwich Cathedral (No. 34). They were buried in a number of different tombs, all of which attracted pilgrims and where miracles of healing took place.

The mounds and hollows in the centre of the site on Mousehold Heath are all that survive of two chapel buildings that stood here – the one dedicated to St William and a second to St Catherine. Flint rubble has been found among them. Sixteenth-century maps appear to show a stone church with a tower, but these are artistic rather than realistic representations of the site.

The remains of the buildings are surrounded by two earthwork enclosures, both defined by banks and ditches. The larger enclosure is substantial, measuring over 100m across with banks standing up to 1m tall. In the south of the site three banks link the outer and inner enclosures; it is possible that they were associated with a third chapel dedicated to St Thomas Becket or that they were used to direct pilgrims to the entrance of St William's chapel. The last recorded financial donation made at the site was in 1532–33, a few years before the chapel was closed.

The larger enclosure is shown on Ordnance Survey Explorer map 237 (TG 247 105) in the north of Mousehold Heath, just south of Mousehold Road and immediately south-east of Wingfield playing field. It can be reached from Gurney Road car park by taking one of the paths that head north-west. (Car park: NR1 4HG)

FURTHER READING

Nuthall, T., 2016, 'St William's Chapel, Mousehold Heath, Norwich – The site of three Chapels', *Norfolk Archaeology* XLVII, pp.334 346.

St Julian's church, Norwich, from the south. The rebuilt 'cell' is in the right-hand gabled extension. (John Fielding)

The interior of the cell at St Julian's church, Norwich. (John Fielding)

37. ST JULIAN'S ANCHORITE CELL, NORWICH

Along with Norfolk women such as Queen Boudica and Edith Cavell (No. 91), Julian of Norwich is part of national history. Unlike these two, however, her fame is not linked to war. Julian was a mystic who took her name from St Julian's church, just off King Street in Norwich, where she lived much of her life as a recluse, or anchorite. She was the first woman to write in English a book, which is recognised as one of the finest pieces of mystical writing.

Very little is known about her as a person except what she reveals in her book *Revelations of Divine Love,* written in about 1393. She was probably born about 1342 and we know nothing of her early life, or whether she was single, married or a widow when she received her 'revelations', or indeed, whether she ever became a nun. (Not all anchorites entered holy orders.) When she was critically ill at the age of 30, and while staring at a crucifix she received sixteen 'showings' or revelations. The first version of her book was written soon after her recovery, but a larger version of eighty-six short chapters was the result of twenty years of pondering. Written in the Middle English of the period, her literary style is spontaneous and unaffected. In her most famous saying from the twenty-seventh chapter of her book she identifies sin as inevitable and recognisable in the pain it causes but, 'All will be well and all will be well and all manner of things will be well.' Striking in our age of more gender equality is the way she emphasises the 'motherhood' of God, as creator and sustainer of life.

There is no record of how soon after her visions she became a recluse; in a will of 1394 she is described as a 'Recluse atte Norwyche' who lived in her anchorage at the church of St Julian and St Edmund in Conesford. Margery Kempe, a fellow mystic from King's Lynn, described her visit to Julian in Norwich in her *Book of Margery Kempe,* often seen as the first English autobiography and probably dictated in the 1430s (she could not write). She indicates that she spent several days with Julian comparing their religious experiences and Margery found her a sympathetic, shrewd and learned person. However, there is no indication of how long before 1430 the visit took place. Further wills of 1404 and 1415 mention gifts to Julian, so we can assume that she was still alive then.

Julian was part of a flourishing school of mysticism in the diocese of Norwich, and the solitary life shut away from normal society to live a life of contemplation and prayer was revered. The fourteenth and fifteenth centuries produced a whole crop of mystical writings resulting from revelations received from God and mostly written by women. At least seventy-three anchorites are mentioned living on forty-two different sites in the Norwich diocese between the mid-thirteenth century and the Reformation. Anchorages at St Peter Hungate, St John Sepulchre and St John Timberhill are recorded, among others. An applicant wishing to become an anchorite would be interviewed by the bishop and, if deemed suitable and could show that he or she had enough income to sustain the life, there would be a service of enclosure at which the applicant would be 'enclosed' in her cell, never to leave it alive.

These cells were not necessarily one-roomed; more usually they consisted of a suite of rooms, either attached to a church or set in its grounds, possibly with its own garden. Many anchorites had servants and we know of two, Sarah and Alice, who served Julian at different times. The anchorite might receive visitors and Marjory Kempe appears to have stayed with Julian. We know very little of what Julian's 'cell' looked like except that it was at St Julian's church. Blomefield, in his history of Norfolk published in 1806, describes an anchorage that had stood in the 'east part of the churchyard' in which a recluse dwelt until the Reformation when it was demolished. Confusingly, Richard Taylor's 'Map of Norwich previous to the dissolution of the monasteries' of 1821 shows a freestanding anchorage on the west side of the churchyard. What seems certain is that it was not where it has been reconstructed, attached to the south side of St Julian's church.

St Julian's church, with its round tower, was bombed during the Second World War and was rebuilt in 1953, mainly to act as a shrine church for Julian. Much of the north wall survived the bombing and three circular early Norman windows were found in the fabric of the wall. The shrine is a starkly simple room on the south side of the church in place of the long-lost anchorite cell. It is entered through an elaborate Norman doorway rescued from the bombed-out remains of nearby St Michael at Thorn. Against a bare wall under a plain wooden ceiling a large crucifix hangs behind an unadorned stone altar. It is a moving and tranquil place in which to meditate on the writings of this Norwich contemplative.

St Julian's church is in St Julian's alley off Kings Street opposite the fine fifteenth-century Dragon Hall, now the home of the National Writing Centre. The church is usually open but check the website for events and further information (Julianofnorwich.org). NR1 1QD

FURTHER READING

Gilchrist, R. and Oliva, M., 1993, *Religious Women in Medieval East Anglia* (Centre of East Anglian Studies).

Jantzen, G., 2011, *Julian of Norwich* (SPCK).

Meeres, F., 1998, *A History of Norwich*, pp.32–33 (Phillimore).

Opjohn, S. and Groves, N., 2018, *St Julian's Church, Norwich* (Friends of Julian of Norwich).

Sayer, F.D. (ed.), 1973, *Julian and Her Norwich* (Julian of Norwich Celebration Committee).

38. WORSTEAD CHURCH AND THE WORSTED WOOLLEN INDUSTRY

Much of the prosperity of Norfolk beginning in the thirteenth century was generated by the woollen industry. Worsted cloth, which takes its name from the village of Worstead in north-east Norfolk, is known throughout the world for its fine quality. The reign of Edward I (1272–1307) saw royal encouragement for worsted production and European trade. Rights were granted to 'alien' merchants, who paid taxes for the privilege. Described in the fourteenth century, when the industry reached its peak, as 'almost like silk', it found a ready national and export market. It made use of the medium and long staple wool produced in the county.

A second period of prosperity came in the second half of the sixteenth century when the arrival of religious refugees from Flanders brought new techniques for weaving, producing a cloth known as 'Norwich stuffs'. A map showing the distribution of weavers recorded in probate records from 1370 to 1857 shows a concentration in the north-east around North Walsham and Worstead. In this populous area of fertile soils there was the workforce available for this labour-intensive work and it was only in the sparsely populated west of the county that very few weavers were found. Gradually the centre of manufacture moved away from villages into Norwich.

Worstead church and marketplace. Much of the southern part of the original marketplace has been built over with later infilling. (John Fielding)

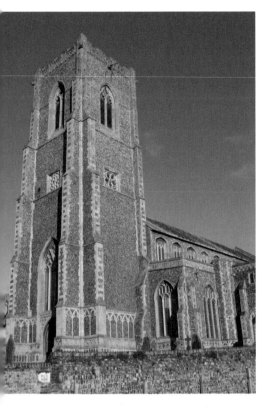

The richly decorated west tower of Worstead church with flushwork friezes of knapped flint within stone arcading. This demonstrates the astonishing wealth of this small textile manufacturing village by the late 1300s. (Peter Wade-Martins)

This fourteenth-century wealth is displayed in the flamboyant exterior of the huge church at Worstead, 'one of Norfolk's grandest' (Pevsner and Wilson, 1997, p.73). The earlier church was demolished and rebuilding began in the 1370s, starting at the east end and taking twenty years to complete. The tower, aisles and even the buttresses are wonderfully decorated with friezes of arcading, quatrefoils, trefoils, fleurons, chequer boards and roundalls infilled with knapped flints, known as 'flushwork'. The splendid two-storey south porch is a particularly fine example of the technique. The tower, 36m high, is richly decorated with intricate sound holes and a fine west doorway. Flushwork encircles the battlements, and grotesque gargoyles form waterspouts around the roof of the whole church.

Internally the first impression is of light and space in which, as the church guide says, 'men appear as grasshoppers'. The nave was heightened when the clerestory windows and the fine hammerbeam roof were inserted in about 1480. The rood screens across both the chancel and side chapels are early sixteenth century and survive to full height with coving and delicate tracery within ogee arches. The work is of high quality but there is some nineteenth-century repainting. Restoration of the 1970s revealed the bright colours and gilding of the original. The screen under the tower arch was built in 1831. Much of the nave is filled with box pews finished at the west end with fluted corner columns. The spectacularly tall wooden ladder dated 1846 is presumably no longer in use!

The church itself stands on one side of Church Plain, around which there is more evidence of the wealth the woollen industry brought to this small village. Houses date from the sixteenth century and later. Some have rooms with very high ceilings (up to 3m) possibly to house looms. A few also have cellars, one at least of which is medieval with a brick-arched opening into the roadway, in which cloth could be baled and stored.

The church is open during daylight houses and some of the houses and cellars are sometimes open for special events. (NR28 9RW)

FURTHER READING

Amor, A.R., 2018, 'The early History of Norfolk's Worsted Cloth' *Norfolk Archaeology* 48, pp.25–49.

Evans, N., 2005. 'Worsted and linen weavers' in Ashwin, T, and Davison, A. (eds), *An Historical Atlas of Norfolk*, pp.158–159 (Phillimore).

Priestley, U., 1990, *The Fabric of Stuffs: The Norwich Textile Industry from 1565* (Centre of East Anglian Studies).

Sutton, A.F., 1989, 'The early linen and worsted industry of Norfolk', *Norfolk Archaeology* 40, pp.201–225.

39. SALLE FIFTEENTH-CENTURY CHURCH

Mortlock and Roberts, in their 2017 guide to Norfolk churches, say '… this is a mighty church which draws one back again and again by virtue of its exceptional interest and great beauty'. This is surely the most magnificent rural church in Norfolk, standing within a group of other exceptional churches at Cawston, Heydon and Field Dalling, all built within forty years of each other. There is so much to see, both inside and out, and it is difficult to focus here on specific detail. Don't hurry your visit.

The church, with its tower 38m high, reflects the great wealth of the county derived from the wool trade. It stands almost alone in its landscape with little trace of a village nearby. Surely churches built on this scale were more to demonstrate the wealth and social standing of the donors than to serve the needs of the local community?

In the frieze of shields above the west door, the third from the right carries the royal arms of England for Henry V as Prince of Wales, and the fifth from the right has the royal arms of England after 1405, thus giving the tower a date of 1405–13. There is a dedication inscription by William Wode, the rector, stating that he built the chancel from the foundations and completed it in 1440. These and other indicators firmly place the construction of the whole building to a limited period in the first half of the fifteenth century.

Salle church with its remarkably tall tower. (John Fielding)

The west doorway of Salle church with angels wearing feather costumes waving censers in the spandrels above the west door. (Peter Wade-Martins)

Look out for the angels in costumes of feathers (or armour?) swinging censers in the spandrels over the west door. Similar costumes on angels can also be seen on the hammerbeam roof of nearby Cawston church, in a stained-glass window at Cockthorpe church, and on saints slaying dragons on the Ranworth screen (No. 42). On the west side of the highly ornate top of the tower are two 'P's, reflecting the dedication of the church to St Peter and St Paul. Note the richly decorated battlements over the two-storey porches, the transepts, aisles and nave and the elaborate tracery in the square sound holes in the tower.

Salle is an impressive and complete example that has retained many of its original furnishings. It is the sheer scale of the church with its soaring arcades on such slender clustered pillars, the wide chancel and the transepts that give a feeling of light and space. The slender columns rise towards the arch-braced roof. The bowl of the font depicts the seven sacraments and the crucifixion. On top of the bowl sits a very impressive unpainted wooden cover that can be raised on a rope through an original pulley on a painted crane fixed to the balcony above. The wineglass pulpit, with panels painted alternately red and green with stencilled devices, has been raised to be part of a three-decker Jacobean arrangement. There are several stained-glass figures dating to the 1470s, and on the floor are brasses of the 1450s, including one to John Brigge of 1454 showing him depicted as a very thin figure in a shroud. Upstairs in the north chapel are fine stone roof bosses repainted in the 1950s.

In the chancel the carvings on the misericords and the faces on the arm rests, polished by the sleeves of generations of choir boys, and the sound holes under the choir stalls should not be missed. The screen is less complete; some panels in the lower section have apostles, and on the doors are the 'Four Latin Doctors'. The communion rail is seventeenth century. Finally, look out for the parish chest heavily bound with iron straps secured with three locks requiring the presence of three parish officials before it could be opened.

The church is open at all reasonable hours, and there is plenty of parking space on the grass in front. Sadly, there is no guidebook. On advertised days the church tower can be climbed, and from the top the landscape of this part of Norfolk is laid out before you, including the spire of Norwich Cathedral just visible to the south-east. (NR10 4SD)

FURTHER READING

Parsons, W.L.E., 1937, *Salle: The Story of a Norfolk Parish, its Church, Manors & People* (Jarrold & Sons).

40. ST PETER MANCROFT FIFTEENTH-CENTURY CHURCH, NORWICH

This magnificent church, built between 1430 and 1455, with its richly decorated west tower with superb flint panels at lower levels, stands high over the Norman market-place. The open arches under the tower and the passageway under the sacristy create an unusual circular processional way around the building. Elegant buttresses support the aisles, and above the aisles are enormous clerestory windows, seventeen on each side, which give a wonderful feeling of space and light. This feeling is enhanced by the enormous east window and the tall arches of the eight-bay arcade. There is no chancel arch and the rood screen has long been removed, although its position can be picked out by the stairways in the side walls. The angel roof, with hammerbeams and fan tracery, resting on the wall posts between the clerestory windows, is one of the finest in Norfolk. The windows were filled with stained glass, but this was all blown out in a gunpowder explosion during the Civil War in 1648. The remnants were collected and installed in 1652 in the great east window but were then reassembled in 1881 with seven nineteenth-century panels in the centre and along the bottom. The rest of the window was made into forty-two colourful New Testament scenes to form probably the best surviving collection of Norwich School glass of the fifteenth and sixteenth centuries. All the side windows are now blissfully clear of coloured glass.

St Peter Mancroft church, Norwich, with its richly decorated tower and west window. (John Fielding)

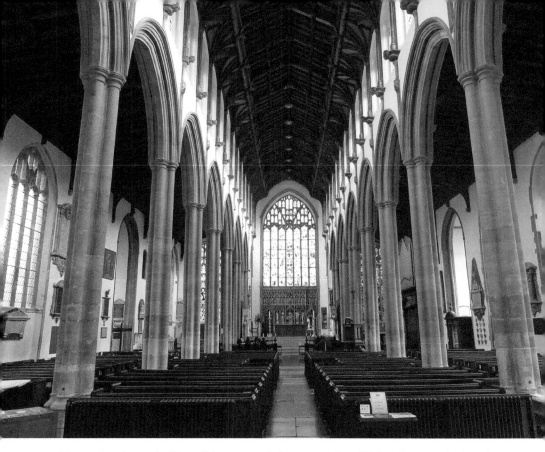

The soaring clustered pillars of the nave and the east window filled with Norwich glass. (Peter Wade-Martins)

The seven sacraments font of 1463 has been defaced, but the wooden cover remains. In the sanctuary high up on the south wall is a memorial to the famous local physician, scholar, scientist and antiquarian Sir Thomas Browne (died 1682), whose seated statue is in the Haymarket close by. On the opposite wall is one to his wife Dorothy (died 1685). Below the east window is a large reredos of 1885, originally of plain wood but gilded in 1930. The church is well known for its bells, and the first true peel was rung here as early as 1715. The church Treasury, opened in 1982, is on display in the north transept.

Just stand and enjoy and admire the skill of the fifteenth-century engineers who built this place.

The church is usually open and there are often friendly stewards on duty to answer your questions. Take binoculars to study the great east window. (NR2 1QE)

41. CLEY CHURCH AND THE GLAVEN PORTS

Norfolk's main ports were at King's Lynn and Great Yarmouth, but there were also smaller harbours all along the north coast such as at Thornham, Salthouse, Burnham Overy Staithe, Wells, Morston, Blakeney, Wiveton and Cley. Wiveton and Cley were on the estuary of the River Glaven which was tidal inland as far as the watermill at Glandford. From about 1200, when Blakeney Point had grown sufficiently far to the west, they were ideal havens well protected from sea storms.

The whole Glaven estuary was open water at high tide, and the deep water river channel divided into two, one passing close to Cley to the east and the other near Wiveton to the west. The port of Cley lay along the east bank centred on an inlet, now Newgate Green near the church. Cley and Wiveton were linked by a causeway over the estuary where a fifteenth-century stone bridge over the western channel remains in use today. It is easy to picture the old estuary as it was in the sixteenth century thanks to a remarkably informative map dated 1586 that showed the two Glaven ports and also Blakeney to the west. The original map does not survive, but there is a compilation by Godfrey Sayers based on two copies made in the 1840s.

The area of the old Glaven estuary from the south-west with Cley church on high ground on the far side and Wiveton church in the foreground. Joining the two old ports is a causeway with its fifteenth-century bridge over the main western channel of the River Glaven. (John Fielding)

In the Middle Ages the trade was mainly in locally caught fish that was landed, gutted and salted in barrels for export to London and inland. But, from the fifteenth century deep sea fishermen were also profitably importing fish from Iceland and the north Atlantic. The journey to Iceland took two or three weeks, and the ships set off with empty barrels and salt and returned laden with salted cod and ling for the English market.

Records show that by the mid-sixteenth century there were more than twenty ships of over 30 tons based in the two ports, and there was also traffic passing along the coast. In the seventeenth century some ships based in the estuary were up to 140 tons. Corn was being exported up and down the coast and to Holland, and coal was coming in from the north. There were shipyards at Wiveton for building and repairing vessels, and the women of Wiveton specialised in provisioning the vessels, particularly in ship's biscuits, for the long Iceland journey when seamen could be away for several months.

Both ports flourished until 1637, when the local landowning family callously built an embankment across the estuary despite the distress this caused local fishermen and merchants. This embankment is today approximately followed by the A149 Coast Road. It was part of a wider movement to embank coastal marshes to increase the areas available for grazing. Wiveton then went into rapid decline. But much of Cley had by then already expanded further north to near the present windmill along quays where deeper water was still available. Coastal trade continued at Cley and at nearby Blakeney, but as more salt marshes along this stretch

The area of the medieval port of Cley clustered around the triangular Newgate Green overlooked by the church. (John Fielding)

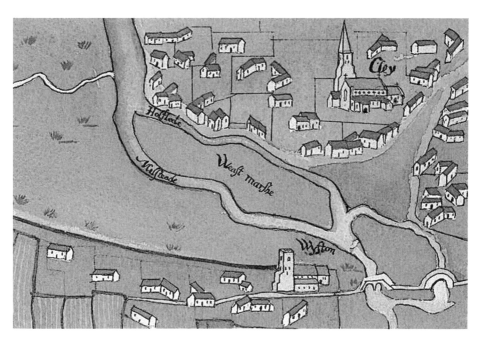

A part of the 1586 map of the Glaven ports showing Cley and Wiveton and the causeway and bridge linking the two. (Reproduced with the kind permission of Godfrey Sayers)

Ship graffiti on one of the south piers of Cley church. (Peter Wade-Martins)

of coast were embanked, so the tidal scour in the channels was reduced, and they both slowly silted up. The end of Cley as a port came rather suddenly in the late nineteenth century with the arrival of the railways.

No ships call at Cley today, but the signs of the town's medieval prosperity are obvious in the church with its fifteenth-century great west window overlooking the site of the old harbour at Newgate Green. The church is a marvellously exuberant piece of architecture that was intended to impress when seen from the south. The highly ornate, but ruined, south transept just adds to the impact of the place. The mainly fourteenth-century church with its splendid clerestory windows and lavish west door replaced an earlier church of which only the tower remains. It was embellished in the fifteenth century by the richly decorated south porch, the aisle windows and the great west window looking out over the estuary. Notice one of the roof bosses in the south porch showing a fox making off with a chicken chased by a furious old woman! By the sixteenth century the port had passed its peak when the north and south transepts were bricked up and abandoned.

Inside the church the soaring west window fills the building with light. Look at the wonderfully amusing figures between the arcade arches on the south side. From east to west there is an imp with a glass eye, a St George fighting an angry dragon, a lion happily eating a large bone, an angel with symbols and a musician with pipe and tabor. But especially look out for the informal graffiti of ships cut into three of the piers. If you use a torch you should pick out the scratch lines of the rigging, masts and sails.

In the churchyard is one of the best collections of eighteenth-century headstones to be seen in Norfolk. This suggests that a stonemason set up a workshop in Cley importing suitable stone and creating a wonderful range of decorative motifs – anchors, skulls, crossed bones, hourglasses and even coffins. Such a straightforward depiction of death contrasts with the draped urns common on nineteenth-century funerary monuments. At Wiveton there is a group of seven or eight similar stones that appear to be from the same workshop, including a fine one for a millwright depicting a millstone and the tools of his trade.

The church is open at reasonable hours, and there is a pub on Newgate Green. (NR25 7TU)

FURTHER READING

Hooton, J., 1996, *The Glaven Ports* (Blakeney History Group).

Hooton, J., 2021, *This was Formerly A Port Called Blakeney and Cley* (Poppyland Publishing)

Missen, M., 2013, *A History and Guide to the Parish Church of St Margaret of Antioch, Cley-next-the-Sea, Norfolk* (Cley Parochial Church Council).

42. FIFTEENTH-CENTURY ROOD SCREEN AT ST HELEN'S CHURCH, RANWORTH

The visual showpiece of many Norfolk medieval churches was the brightly coloured, beautifully painted and intricately carved rood screen. Fifteenth-century rood screens form the most important group of late-medieval English church painting and that at Ranworth is justifiably one of the most celebrated in East Anglia. Its structure and design are elaborate, and its painting, with a richness and delicacy of detail, was the work of a highly accomplished local school of painters.

The screen divided the sacred space of the chancel from the secular space of the nave frequented by the parishioners. The many complete or fragmentary screens across the county are an indication of both parish pride and the patronage of the leading families who commissioned these elaborate works of art and craftsmanship.

The late fifteenth-century highly decorated rood screen stretching across the chancel and the side chapels with rood loft above. (Peter Wade-Martins)

South chapel and side screen supporting an elaborate candle post and a panel showing St Michael slaying the seven-headed beast of the apocalypse. (Peter Wade-Martins)

Ranworth is one of the finest and most complete in Norfolk. It probably dates from the 1480s after Robert Iryng left money for 'painting over the altar'. It not only fills the chancel arch, but it stretches the full width of the church and retains its rood loft along its whole length. This was reached by a stair-case to the north of the chancel arch and is supported by coving intricately painted with flowers. It supported the 'Great Rood', which consisted of the crucifixion with St John the Evangelist to one side and Mary, the mother of Christ, to the other. During the ritual, one or more choir boys would climb to the loft to sing or recite in Latin to the congregation.

As very few could read or under-stand Latin, saints with their symbols depicted on the screen illustrated the basis of their Christian faith. Two pro-jecting wings (or parcloses) with tall carved candle posts separated the two side chapels, for which the screen provides the altarpiece. This arrangement is unique in Norfolk. On these partitions are some of the most dramatic figures on the screen. That to the north shows St George slay-ing the dragon and to the south is an equally impressive depiction of St Michael slaying the seven-headed beast of the apocalypse.

Like many other screens, the central part depicts the twelve apostles carrying their symbols, by which the illiterate in the congregation could recognise them. St James (fourth from the north) carries his pilgrim's staff, St Peter (sixth from north) carries his keys and St Paul (seventh from the north) carries the sword with which he was killed. They are all wearing luxurious clothing but their feet are bare, emphasising their humility. The backgrounds are alternately red and green with stencilled flower patterns. While the figures have survived, many of their faces were scratched out at the time of the Reformation. The panels were then whitewashed to ensure the saints themselves were not objects of veneration. In fact, the white-wash helped to preserve the paintings and protected them from further vandalism. They were uncovered in the nineteenth century and restored to their former glory by a team of conservationists in the 1960s.

The panels forming the altarpieces to the two side chapels are each painted with four figures. These are all female saints except for an unfinished figure of St John the Baptist, third from the north in the north chapel. In the lady chapel to the south all the saints are linked by tradition to the Holy Family, with the Virgin Mary second from the north. Within the panels above all eight figures there are demi-angels, all different and watching over the saints below.

The screen is not the only amazing treasure within this church. At the west end in a showcase and protected from light under a thick blanket is a richly decorated service book created by the monks of Langley Abbey for Ranworth church and bequeathed to the church in 1478. Scenes from Bible stories are illustrated in the illuminated capital letters at the beginnings of psalms and services for major festivals. The lavishness of the illustrations is an indication of the wealth of the donor.

The church is open during daylight hours. The saints and their symbols depicted on the screens are all identified on explanatory boards in the church. (NR13 6AH)

FURTHER READING

The excellent guidebook to the church by Patricia Mackridge is currently out of print.

Hayman, R. 2018, *Rood Screens* (Shire).

43. OULTON INDEPENDENT CHAPEL

A significant strand of Norfolk's history has been its religious non-conformity. The county's proximity to northern Europe meant that it was a frequent haven for religious refugees, particularly from Flanders (modern-day Belgium) who settled in Norwich and were known as 'the strangers'. The Dutch Reformed Church became a model for those with more radical Protestant beliefs and during the Commonwealth following the Civil War of the 1640s there was more tolerance of the various strands of nonconformity. Many Norfolk congregations whose chapels were rebuilt later can trace their foundations back to this period. The Restoration of the monarchy in 1660 heralded a return to a period of religious persecution that was brought to an end by the 1672 Declaration of Indulgence that allowed Dissenters to be officially recognised so long as their premises were licensed. The dissenting tradition continued through to the nineteenth century, when nearly every village could boast at least one Methodist chapel.

Oulton chapel, built 1724–26, has a domestic-looking exterior, unusual in chapel architecture. (Peter Wade-Martins)

Oulton Chapel interior showing the gallery still with its original box pews and nineteenth-century pews and reading desk on the ground floor. (Peter Wade-Martins)

The importance of religious nonconformity in Norfolk's history is clearly shown in the architecture of its chapels and meetinghouses. The architecturally finest of these are to be found in Norwich, such as the Octagon Chapel (No. 44) and the nearby Old Meeting House. Few other counties can boast so many examples of simple but beautiful neo-classical Georgian architecture in rural and often remote positions. While many remain externally intact, most have been altered internally, although at Oulton a complete early interior survives.

The earliest chapel in the Oulton area was at neighbouring Guestwick, founded in 1652, no doubt under the patronage of Oliver Cromwell's son-in-law Colonel Fleetwood of nearby Irmingland. It is now converted to domestic use and the original interior removed. The first meeting of Independents in Oulton, one mile west of Irmingland, was reported in 1669 under Abraham Coveney, the Fleetwoods' chaplain. In 1724 the Oulton congregation formed a separate chapel with Coveney as minister, but beyond that there were no gentry connections with the chapel. Typical of a dissenting congregation, the four men who signed the sale papers for the land were from the artisan class, one described as a weaver and another a carpenter.

The original dated wall ties, replaced in the restoration of 1990, read 1726 and indicate the date the present chapel was built. Services were held here into the 1970s, when the building became redundant. It was later bought by the Norfolk Historic Buildings Trust, which has since been responsible for its upkeep and restoration.

Unlike many other chapels in the county, Oulton has a simple domestic exterior. It is double depth with a pair of Dutch gables at each end and a later vestry to the rear. The original six-light leaded windows were replaced with large sash windows on the front and replaced with plate glass elsewhere allowing light to flood in, probably in the 1840s when the vestry was rebuilt.

The chapel's unique interest lies in its interior. The main valley beam of the roof is supported by two freestanding posts with moulded capitals. Originally there were galleries at the east and west gable ends of the building placed on sturdy Tuscan columns. A northern gallery along the length of the front of the building was added in the 1840s. The chapel was probably provided with box pews throughout at this date and they survive in their original unpainted state in the galleries. Those in the main body of the church were replaced with pews in the late Victorian era and the reading desk rebuilt, but some of the panelling from the old pews was reused along the walls. In spite of these later modifications the building retains the atmosphere of a simple rural meeting house in beautiful surroundings.

> The chapel is opened by the Friends of Oulton Chapel on the second Sunday of the month, 2–4 p.m. between April and October. At other times a key is available from the Manse next door. (NR11 6NU)

FURTHER READING

Ede, J., Virgoe, N. and Williamson, T., 1994, *Halls of Zion* (Centre of East Anglian Studies).

Stell, C., 2002, *Nonconformist Chapels and Meetinghouses in Eastern England*, pp.262–265 (English Heritage).

44. THE OCTAGON CHAPEL, COLEGATE, NORWICH

The high quality of the architecture of the Unitarian Octagon Chapel in Colegate and also the nearby Old Meeting House are an indication of the importance of dissent in Norwich. An independent chapel on the Colegate site was registered in 1689, and an illustration of 1723 shows a large rectangular building, but this was replaced by the far more original octagonal design by Thomas Ivory (1709–79) in 1754–56. Most of Ivory's work was confined to Norwich, where he was responsible for some excellent Georgian architecture. Elsewhere, at Blickling he was responsible for rebuilding the west front in a Jacobean revival style (No. 85). He began life as a carpenter, builder and timber merchant and by his death he was running a sizeable building company. The Octagon Chapel is his most notable piece of architecture, built of brick on an octagonal plan with a large classical porch and a pyramidal roof supported by eight Corinthian columns with wooden galleries between them. John Wesley described it as 'the most elegant Meeting House in Norfolk' and recommended its shape as a pattern for chapels across England.

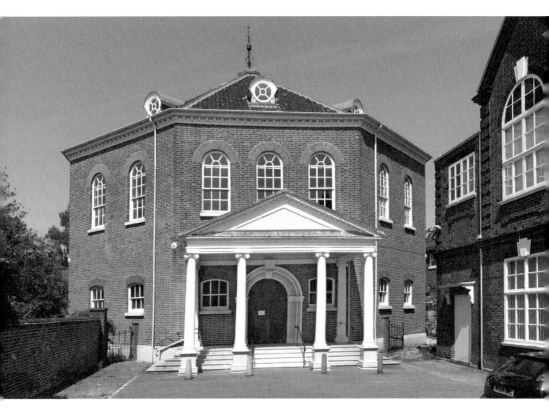

Octagon Chapel, Colegate, Norwich, built in 1754-56, with the front dominated by a fine classical porch. (John Fielding)

The Octagon was attended by many of Norwich's most prominent intellectual free-thinkers such as the Martineau family. Harriet Martineau (1802–76) is often described as the first female sociologist, while James was a renowned religious philosopher. The Norwich MP William Smith also worshipped here and was a strong supporter of the anti-slavery movement. A Sunday school, dedicated to Harriet Martineau, was built next door in 1907.

Ivory was also responsible, along with Sir John Burroughs, for enlarging and altering Chapel Field House, parts of which dated back to the Middle Ages, into a fine five-bay brick classical assembly rooms as a commercial venture. A more speculative enterprise undertaken by Ivory was the three-storey terrace of substantial houses in Surrey Street, reminiscent of the sort of building taking place in London at the time.

The chapel is open for organised groups and on specific occasions such as Heritage Open Days. (NR3 1BN)

FURTHER READING

Meeres, F., 1998, *A History of Norwich*, pp.122–123 (Phillimore).

Stell, C., 2002, *Nonconformist Chapels and Meetinghouses in Eastern England*, p.260 (English Heritage).

MONASTERIES

INTRODUCTION

Along with castles and cathedrals, monasteries are some of the most impressive medieval monuments in East Anglia. The earliest ones had a strong missionary role, which was to spread the gospel and convert the region to Christianity. The oldest we know about in the county were founded in the seventh century within the Roman forts at Burgh Castle (No. 16) and probably Caister-on-Sea (No. 17). There may well have been others, although none survived the Vikings. The next was St Benet's Abbey founded in about 1020 as a Benedictine house on the island of Cow Holme near Ludham in the Broads (No. 47). Most monastic communities were groups of monks or nuns living in isolation from the outside world, devoting their time to worship and to prayer for the intercession of the souls of the dead to help their journey from purgatory to heaven. Many followed a strict Rule laid down by the sixth-century Italian monk, St Benedict, which stipulated that these communities should be in remote places away from the distractions of the world and should follow a formal routine of regular services throughout the day.

After the Norman Conquest, the first monasteries to be founded in Norfolk were Castle Acre in 1090 (No. 45), or soon after, and Binham in 1091 (No. 46), followed by Norwich Cathedral Priory in 1096 (No. 34). In all, there were eighty-six monastic houses in the county in the Middle Ages. The church was usually the largest building and was the first to be built, starting at the east end. Then, the square of the cloister walk was usually laid out to the south with the chapter house (or meeting room) and the monk's accommodation along the east side. The refectory (or dining room) and kitchen lay to the south, while storerooms and lodgings for the prior or the abbot and guest rooms for visitors lay to the west. Many of these monasteries had working farms attached to them run by servants so that the monks could devote their time and energy to constant prayer, attending services and illuminating wonderful manuscripts like the one on display in Ranworth church (No. 42). The priory farm and subsidiary buildings usually stood within the walled precinct of the monastery, and the most complete example of a precinct wall is at Castle Acre. It is interesting how many gatehouses do survive even though most monastic buildings inside the precinct have long since gone, as at St Benet's, Walsingham (No. 48), Pentney, West Acre and (in a less complete condition) at Binham.

There were many different orders, the most popular in Norfolk being the Benedictines, the Augustinians and the Cluniacs. There were also friaries, of which the Franciscans and the Carmelites are best known. It was a complex picture of devotion and pilgrimage, not easy to describe in a short introduction.

Of the thirty-seven Norfolk monastic houses valued at the dissolution in 1535, the two richest by far were Walsingham and Norwich Cathedral, at over £700 each, followed by St Benet's at £583 and Castle Acre at £306. Of the rest, twenty-two were worth less than £200. Much of the income came from pilgrim donations, and the number of pilgrims was greatly influenced by the devotional importance of the relics each monastery held.

The most complete sets of buildings visible today are at Castle Acre, Binham and Norwich Cathedral. While the priory at Little Walsingham was the most important pilgrimage centre in England after Canterbury, little of it now remains. However, the survival at Walsingham of the late medieval timber-framed inns, hostelries and dormitories to cater for the faithful outside the priory gate is remarkable.

FURTHER READING

Le Strange, R., 1973, *Monasteries of Norfolk* (Yates Publishing).

Meeres, F., 2001, *'Not of this World': Norfolk Monastic Houses* (Frank Meeres).

Pestell, T., 2005. 'Monasteries' in Ashwin T. and Davison, A. (eds), *An Historical Atlas of Norfolk*, pp.66–67, third edition (Phillimore).

Rickett, R. and Rose, E., 1993 and 1994, 'Monastic Houses' in Wade-Martins, P. (ed.), *An Historical Atlas of Norfolk*, pp.64–65, first and second editions (Norfolk Museums Service).

Wilton, J.W., 1980, *Monastic Life in Norfolk and Suffolk* (Acorn Editions).

45. CASTLE ACRE PRIORY

The buildings at this Cluniac priory are some of the most intact in England, and they stand in splendour within the tranquil setting of the upper reaches of the Nar Valley. If you only have time to see a few of Norfolk's great monuments, then this should surely be high on your list.

As you approach the ruins you see the west front of the priory church described in the English Heritage guidebook as 'one of the most famous and beautiful of all twelfth-century facades … It was intended to be awe-inspiring, a humbling but uplifting statement of the priory and its purpose, the glory of God, and the wealth and piety of its founders' (Impey, 2008). The lower four stages of the wonderful blind arcades and doorways date from about 1140, and the upper levels with their pointed arches were added over the next twenty or thirty years. Into this, a large central window was inserted in the early fifteenth century.

The construction of these monastic churches usually progressed from east to west. Work started at Castle Acre in about 1090, or soon after, and the choir, which was the focus of the liturgy, was finished first. The piers of the choir were faced with Barnack stone mixed with local golden-brown Norfolk Carstone creating banded, chequered or spiral patterns to the piers. Construction then progressed to reach the monumental west front by about 1140.

Castle Acre Priory from the south-west set within its large walled precinct and with the gatehouse to the north. The parish church stands between the priory precinct and the planned town to the east. The recently repaired precinct wall that surrounds the meadow is visible to the rear. (John Fielding)

The west front of the priory church and the prior's lodgings to the right. (Peter Wade-Martins)

Notice as you step down from the nave into the cloister walk the book cupboards on the left, located in the same place as in Norwich Cathedral Priory (No. 34). These held the sacred texts that were taken each day into the services. Then, on the left, is the chapter house with seating for sixteen monks on each side. Beyond that are the stairs up to the monks' dormitory and below that the day room for monks to spend their time keeping warm in winter while reading the scriptures and copying religious books. A bridge from the dormitory led into the long toilet block or 'reredorter', with twelve open-fronted recesses each with seats with holes emptying into the stream below. This is one of the most intact medieval toilet blocks in England.

The square kitchen filled the angle between the refectory and the west range containing the prior's lodgings. This range is the most complex part of the site with its many periods of alteration and expansion, which culminated in the late fifteenth century with the fine flint chequerboard porch.

All these buildings, and more, were set within an extensive high-walled precinct with access controlled by a monk on duty in the gatehouse to the north. This gatehouse was built shortly before the priory was closed in the early sixteenth century, decorated with brick-lined openings and flint chequer board at the top. The long flint precinct wall, with its original capping, still preserved in places, was lost in ivy until it was cleared and consolidated on the initiative of the Norfolk Archaeological Trust in 2013–14. An examination of the join between gatehouse and the flint work of the precinct wall during this restoration work clearly showed that the gatehouse was later than the wall. The previous gatehouse has not yet been found.

Castle Acre is a popular visitor attraction with the castle, planned town, church and priory all easily accessible. English Heritage opening hours apply to the priory. Access to the castle is free and unrestricted. Do buy the excellent English Heritage guidebook to the castle and priory by Edward Impey, and don't miss the locally made ice cream in the priory ticket office. (Car park: PE32 2AA)

FURTHER READING

Cushion, B. and Davison, A., 2003, *Earthworks of Norfolk*, East Anglian Archaeology 104, pp.136–137.

Impey, E., 2008, *Castle Acre Priory and Castle* (English Heritage).

46. BINHAM PRIORY

The priory was founded in 1091 as an independent house of the Benedictine abbey at St Albans. The church stands up high at the north end of the village, and the nave is still in use as the parish church. The cloisters, the south aisle, the central crossing tower and the east end of the church all formed the monastic area, which was closed by Henry VIII in 1539. These buildings were then partly demolished, and many stones from the priory can be seen now built into houses in the village. The ruins were purchased by the Norfolk Archaeological Trust in 1933, excavated by the old Office of Works from 1934 to 1938 and are now in the care of English Heritage.

The nave demonstrates well the architectural progression from east to west, from Norman, starting about 1130, with round arches, richly decorated with zigzag and billet mouldings, at the east end; to Early English with pointed arches at the west end with the west front and its great window. This window, built with bar tracery before 1244, could well be the earliest surviving example of this style in England. Below that is the west door and the finely carved blind arcading to either side decorated with dog-toothing and crocket capitals. Although the window was bricked up rather crudely after it fell apart in 1809 the west front still remains an iconic symbol of Early English architecture. The building of the whole church took well over 100 years.

On the east side of the cloisters stood the chapter house, the monks' parlour and warming room with fireplace, and upstairs the dormitory. On the south side was the refectory with kitchen behind, and to the west were storerooms and accommodation for the prior and his guests. Various outlying buildings are less easy to interpret.

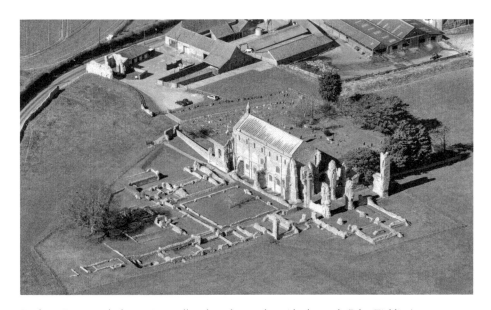

Binham Priory with the precinct wall and gatehouse alongside the road. (John Fielding)

The west front of the priory church, probably built before 1244, is an iconic example of Early English architecture. (Peter Wade-Martins)

The gatehouse, the adjacent precinct wall and the meadow were purchased by the Archaeological Trust in 2002 and then conserved. The conservation of the precinct wall had to be carried out with very great care because it is the only habitat in north Norfolk for a small and rare plant called wall bedstraw (*Galium parisiense*). In the adjacent meadow are clear earthworks of monastic outbuildings that have not been excavated.

> *The church is open at reasonable times and there is open access to the cloisters. (Car park: NR21 0DQ)*

FURTHER READING

Beckett, G., Bull, A. and Stephenson R., 1999, *A Flora of Norfolk*, p.192 (Gillian Becket).

Cushion, B. and Davison, A., 2003, *Earthworks of Norfolk*, East Anglian Archaeology 104, pp.148–151.

Hundleby, A. and Wade-Martins, P., 2004, *The Priory Church of St Mary & The Holy Cross and the Monastic Precinct* (Binham Parochial Church Council guidebook).

47. ST BENET'S ABBEY, HORNING

There is no better place in Norfolk to experience the wide-open skies of East Anglia than at St Benet's Abbey in the Broads. This Benedictine abbey is on the island of Cow Holme beside the River Bure, surrounded by extensive grazing marshes and reed beds. The ruins of the abbey church sit on the highest point with earthworks of the abbey all around. Encircling them is the water-filled drain that formed the medieval precinct boundary. On the west side of the precinct stands the ruined fourteenth-century gatehouse. Attached to it is an eighteenth-century wind-powered drainage pump that raised the water out of the drain and into the River Bure. The remains of the gatehouse and the wind pump have created a well-known landmark which has been painted by generations of local artists, some of whose work is on display in Norwich Castle Museum. Sadly, the sails blew off the wind pump in a gale in 1863 and were not replaced.

The site is owned by the Norfolk Archaeological Trust, and car access is permitted down a long concrete farm track. The abbey precinct covers 14.5ha beside the river, which is alive with holiday craft in the summer season. It was founded before the Norman Conquest in about 1020 as a Benedictine monastery, although there was a strong tradition that it had previously been occupied by hermits. The

The D-shaped precinct of St Benet's Abbey beside the River Bure from the west. The precinct is surrounded by a wide ditch, and the gatehouse and eighteenth-century windmill are to the right near the ornamental fishponds. The ruins of the abbey church stand on high ground near the centre of the island. (Mike Page)

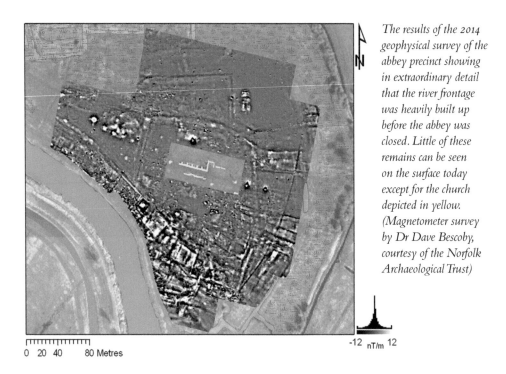

The results of the 2014 geophysical survey of the abbey precinct showing in extraordinary detail that the river frontage was heavily built up before the abbey was closed. Little of these remains can be seen on the surface today except for the church depicted in yellow. (Magnetometer survey by Dr Dave Bescoby, courtesy of the Norfolk Archaeological Trust)

0   20 40   80 Metres

-12 nT/m 12

monastery was closed under Henry VIII, but not officially dissolved since it passed into the ownership of the Bishop of Norwich. Today the current Bishop, who is also uniquely Abbot of St Benet's, sails down the River Bure by wherry each year wearing a golden cope and mitre for an annual open-air service at the abbey on the first Sunday in August. This is a very powerful image.

The most complete part of the monastery is the gatehouse. The top half was taken off in the eighteenth century to allow the sails of the wind pump to turn, but inside the mill the arch of the medieval gateway is well preserved, and in the spandrels above the arch are mythical figures of a hunter on the left and a lion-like beast on the right.

Beside the wide water-filled ditch that runs around the precinct are the foundations of a defensive wall dating from 1327 when the abbey was given permission to fortify the site. As the visitor walks up from the gatehouse towards the ruined church on the left there is a fine set of ornamental fishponds. A geophysical survey carried out in 2014 showed that there are stone foundations under the grass all along the riverbank, especially opposite the church, but none have yet been excavated. It was the isolation of the place that saved this site from antiquarian excavations in the nineteenth and twentieth centuries, and it is likely that deep in these waterlogged deposits there are undisturbed organic remains, possibly with the original Late Saxon monastery at the bottom.

Vehicle access is down a long farm concrete roadway across the marshes to the car park. But, better still, approach the site if you can by river. Remember that there are usually cattle grazing in the field, so do keep dogs under control. (Car park: NR29 5NU)

FURTHER READING

Cushion, B. and Davison, A., 2003, *Earthworks of Norfolk*, East Anglian Archaeology 104, pp.148–151.

Hutcheson, N., 2019, *St Benet's Abbey: A Brief History and Guide.* (Second edition Norfolk Archaeological Trust guidebook).

Pestell, T., 2007, *St Benet's Abbey: A Guide and History.* (First edition Norfolk Archaeological Trust).

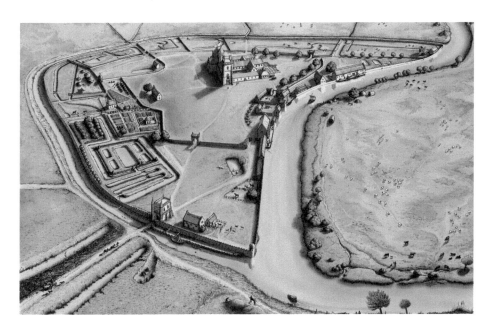

Above: *A reconstruction of how the abbey may have looked before its closure in 1545. This was drawn before details of the buried remains were located in the 2014 geophysical survey shown on the page opposite. The reconstruction nevertheless accurately indicates that the priory buildings were clustered along the waterfront. (Reconstruction by Sue Walker White)*

Right: *An 1856 photograph of the fourteenth-century gatehouse. The top half was removed in the eighteenth century so that the sails of drainage mill could turn. The scoop wheel to lift the water out of the precinct ditch and into the River Bure is just visible to the right.*

48. WALSINGHAM: A MEDIEVAL PILGRIMAGE TOWN

The Augustinian priory at Little Walsingham in north Norfolk, the home of the shrine of 'Our Lady of Walsingham', was one of the great pilgrimage centres of medieval Europe, second only in England to Canterbury. Founded in about 1153, it was visited regularly by Henry III and his son Edward I in the thirteenth century and it continued to have royal visitors, including Henry VIII, up until the dissolution in 1539. Only the fifteenth-century east wall of the priory church now survives as a folly in the gardens of Abbey House along with a vaulted undercroft in one corner of Abbey House. However, the gatehouse remains intact in the High Street. In 1347 the Greyfriars founded a house for their friars on the southern edge of town, and with the growing popularity of 'Our Lady' there was enough activity for both monasteries to flourish.

It has been estimated from the priory accounts for 1535 that, based on a likely donation of a penny for each pilgrim, there were on average 171 pilgrims a day, or 62,415 a year, arriving in this small somewhat isolated market town. There were, of course, great seasonal fluctuations, with pilgrims arriving mainly between May and October when the roads were passable. These pilgrims needed accommodation. The best reason to visit Walsingham now is to see the extraordinary wealth of late medieval timber-framed buildings that provided accommodation for the pilgrims in the High Street, Friday Market and Common Place.

Above left: *Walsingham from the south. The east end of the abbey church stands as a garden folly in the grounds of Abbey House to the right. The surviving pilgrimage hostels are mostly ranged along the High Street and Common Place to the north. (John Fielding)*

Above right: *The priory gatehouse on the east side of High Street. (Peter Wade-Martins)*

Above left: *No 31 High Street which had a continuous first-floor dormitory for pilgrims. (Peter Wade-Martins)*

Above right: *Three fifteenth-century shop windows on the jettied west end of 1 Common Place. (Photo by Peter Wade-Martins)*

After the dissolution of the priory, the town descended from great wealth to relative poverty. This explains why so many late medieval inns, hostelries, and dormitories for the faithful have survived, modified in different ways, but seldom replaced. Walsingham contains more buildings constructed before 1700 than any other town of similar size in the county.

In 2010 a team from the Norfolk Historic Buildings Group started a detailed buildings' survey lasting four years. The earliest buildings were fully timber-framed with ground-floor wall posts and studs and with jettied, timber-framed upper floors. During the fifteenth century the building tradition changed so that the ground floors were built of flint rubble while the upper floors remained jettied. By the seventeenth century, brick took over as the fashionable building material, and in many cases brick skins were simply added to reface earlier structures.

The priory and friary together owned most of the town and carried out the building works as speculative development. The ground-floor rooms were large, some with fireplaces and some without, and those without may have had portable braziers and back kitchens to cater for the hundreds of pilgrims. The upstairs rooms were also large, forming dormitories, 35m long in one case, open to the roof. Narrow unglazed windows with internal shutters were normal on both floors.

Good examples of the pilgrim hostels with first-floor dormitories can be viewed from the outside at 21/23 High Street, 31 High Street and 12 Common Place. The latter had an undivided 20m long upper chamber. By far the largest was in 47/49/51/53 High Street, which had a continuous dormitory of 35m long extending across all four modern properties. This was in a prestigious location immediately opposite the principal gateway into the priory, but it is difficult to appreciate the extent of the timber framing now from the outside because 47 and 49 are hidden behind a nineteenth-century brick front.

There must have been many shops as well. Although evidence for them is hard to find, there are three shop windows, two still with their arches, visible at the west end of 1 Common Place. The only other complete examples of medieval shop windows in Norfolk are four in the mid-fifteenth-century Green Dragon in Wymondham (No. 66). The market house, as seen at Wymondham and New Buckenham (No. 23), is now so embedded in the fabric of the shop at the corner of the High Street and Friday Market that it cannot be recognised from the outside.

Just to wander around the streets and to look at the town is a real pleasure. There is much to see, although it is sad that some buildings stand empty and appear even derelict. There are pubs in Friday Market and the Common Place and tea rooms are usually open in season. There is also the parish church, rebuilt after a disastrous fire in 1961, the Church of England shrine in Holt Road, built in 1931–37 and the Russian Orthodox chapel of St Seraphin of Sarov. This can be recognised by its onion dome in the converted railway station. If you are in Walsingham in the early spring the gardens of Abbey House are open to the public and the woods are filled with snowdrops. The extensive remains of the friary on the southern edge of the town are private and are closed to public view. (Little Walsingham main car park: NR22 6BN). A part of the pilgrim route was the Slipper Chapel, opened in 1934 as a Catholic Shrine, to the south in Houghton St Giles.

FURTHER READING

Longcroft, A., Brown, S., Brown, M., Barr, D. and Hinton, I. (eds), 2015, *A Study of Historic Buildings in a Medieval Pilgrimage Centre,* Norfolk Historic Buildings Group Journal 6.

MEDIEVAL TOWNS

INTRODUCTION

In 1066 Norfolk had two of England's most important urban centres: Norwich and Thetford. Both started life as small Anglo-Saxon settlements, growing to become thriving and wealthy towns with churches, marketplaces, defensive ditches and industries (including pottery production).

Anglo-Saxon Norwich probably had two marketplaces, on Magdalen Street and at Tombland. Town defensive ditches have been discovered during excavations both north and south of the River Wensum. In places the riverbank was consolidated with brushwood and revetments, supporting trade along the river. After the Norman Conquest, houses and churches were demolished to make way for a royal castle (No. 28) and new cathedral (No. 34). The city did not reduce in size, though, instead it expanded westwards with the foundation of a new borough for Norman settlers. This planned expansion had its own newly created marketplace, which remains the marketplace today. New town defences were added from the late thirteenth century (No. 49) and by the Tudor period it was without doubt England's second city. The city's wealth can be identified in the large number of surviving medieval churches and merchants' houses.

Thetford did not fare so well. Despite briefly being the seat of the Bishop of East Anglia (1071–94) and acquiring a large castle (No. 12), competition from Norwich, King's Lynn and Bury St Edmunds saw its importance wane.

During the medieval period, Norwich and Thetford were joined in the county's urban landscape by expanding rural settlements, new planned settlements, numerous small market towns (No. 66) and coastal ports. Lynn and Yarmouth are recorded in the Domesday Book, when they were both fishing and trading settlements. Lynn developed on the east bank of the River Ouse, in the area between the Purfleet and Millfleet and at South Lynn. Herbert de Losinga, Bishop of Norwich, founded St Margaret's church and the adjacent Saturday marketplace around 1100 (after which the settlement was called 'Bishop's Lynn'; it became King's Lynn after the dissolution of the monasteries). The developing town expanded north of the Purfleet, as formalised in around 1150 by Bishop Turbe, who created the Tuesday marketplace and planned streets on 'New Land'. The twelfth-century river frontage followed the line of King, Queen, Nelson and Bridge Streets, as evidenced by the survival of one twelfth-century house on King Street and a second in Queen Street, which was tragically pulled down in 1977. Over following centuries, the riverbank was consolidated and moved westwards in stages, to form the quayside we can see today.

By 1066 Yarmouth had developed on the sand spit that had blocked the Great Estuary. Bishop de Losinga established the priory and church of St Nicholas and in 1208 the town received a charter from King John. The marketplace and distinctive street pattern may have been established at this time: long curving streets follow the line of the spit with numerous cross streets ('The Rows') linking them. 'The Rows' are only about 1.5m wide and were lined with high-density housing – many were lost during Second World War bombing, but a few remain, so look out for Market Row and Sewell's Row on the west side of the marketplace. Great Yarmouth's town defences are impressive (No. 57), and there are good sections surviving in King's Lynn (No. 54). Despite the importance of Lynn and Yarmouth, other coastal settlements also had important roles in coastal and international trade, with Blakeney, Wiveton and Cley (No. 41) among the best documented.

It was not just the large centres that saw Norman town planning – a few small towns were entirely new creations, planted and planned in one go by powerful nobles. Castle Acre and New Buckenham retain their rectilinear medieval street patterns (Nos 26 and 23), whereas there are hints of similar organisation at Castle Rising (No. 24). Other towns controlled by manorial lords had less structured plans and probably developed over time: market centres like Aylsham, Swaffham and Harleston have streets that con-verge on marketplaces, for example. Over many centuries some medieval marketplaces had buildings built upon them, meaning we are only left with parts of their original open space; examples include Dereham, Holt, Swaffham and Worstead (No. 38).

We are lucky that so many medieval buildings survive in Norfolk's towns. Perhaps the most prominent are large municipal buildings alongside marketplaces: the Guildhall in Norwich and Trinity Guildhall in King's Lynn (Nos 50 and 55). Visually striking are the houses and warehouses of merchants, each of which has its own detailed and intriguing story to tell. Four twelfth-century stone examples survive – the Music House in King Street and beneath the magistrates' court in Norwich, the Tolhouse in Great Yarmouth and within Nos 28–32 King Street at King's Lynn – and others are known from archaeological investigations. King's Lynn and Norwich have wonderful collections of timber-framed buildings and brick and stone undercrofts, a selection of which are included here (Nos 51–53 and 56).

FURTHER READING

Atkin, M., 1993, *Norwich: History and Guide* (Alan Sutton).

Ayers, B., 2009, *Norwich: Archaeology of a Fine City* (Amberley).

Gouch, M., 2017, *Historic Great Yarmouth* (Great Yarmouth Local History and Archaeological Society).

Meeres, F., 1998, *A History of Norwich* (Phillimore).

Richards, P., 1990, *King's Lynn* (Phillimore).

Turner, H.L., 1971, *Town Defences in England and Wales*, pp.126–144 (John Baker).

49. NORWICH CITY WALLS AND COW TOWER

Norwich's city walls enclosed the largest area of any medieval town defences in Britain. With a length of about 4km, they were longer than those of London. Built from the 1280s to the 1340s, they demonstrated the confidence and wealth of the ruling class in one of the country's most important cities. They provided both a defensive and economic barrier, controlling the movement of merchants while protecting against attack and disease. The city remained largely within these confines until the nineteenth century.

Surviving sections of the wall and some of its towers are visible at Carrow Bridge, beside Carrow Hill, at the southern end of Ber Street, from St Stephen's roundabout to Chapelfield Gardens, beside Grapes Hill and Barn Road, west of Oak Street, south of Baker's Road and Magpie Road, at the northern end of Magdalen Street, and at the junction of Bull Close and Silver Roads. The wall between these sections followed Queens Road, Chapelfield Road and Grapes Hill (south of the River Wensum) and (north of the river) Bull Close Road. To the north-west and east the Wensum provided an effective barrier, so walls were not built alongside the river between Carrow Bridge and Barrack Street, nor between Barn Road and Bakers Road. Instead, a gate was built at Bishop Bridge (c.1340), with Cow Tower defending a tight bend in the river. There were twelve gates, all of which were demolished between 1791 and 1810 to improve traffic movements.

The walls stand up to 6m high and are built of flint, with battlements and brick dressings around arrow loops and tower windows. Brick arches on the inside supported the wall walk. There were many towers, including the well-preserved 12m-tall Black Tower at the top of Carrow Hill and the Boom Towers at Carrow Bridge. A chain was slung across the river between the Boom Towers to control the movement of boats and so tolls could be imposed on goods coming into the city by water. Richard Spynk, a Norwich merchant, paid for much of the wall's construction; he also made provision for thirty catapults and four large crossbows.

Cow Tower is an early artillery tower, built in the late fourteenth century to house a small garrison. It is 14.6m and three storeys high and has impressive early brick internal and external facings (both with many 'putlog' or scaffolding holes), a flint rubble core and knapped flint plinth. It is circular in plan, except for a projecting stair turret next to the entrance. Small guns could be fired from the loops, with larger guns fitted on the roof platform and fired through battlements. The last time the walls were defended (and the gates were closed) was during Kett's Rebellion (No. 64).

Norwich's late Anglo-Saxon defensive ditches were constructed before the Norman Conquest; these have been discovered during excavations north and south of the Wensum and are now entirely infilled. They were replaced by a ditch, bank and timber palisade constructed further from the city centre and enclosing a larger

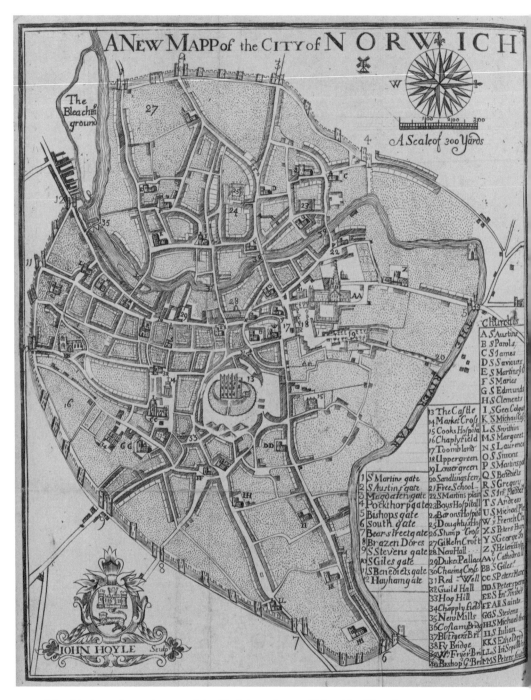

Norwich city walls are shown on John Hoyle's 1728 map of Norwich. All twelve gates are numbered, and Cow Tower is illustrated. (Norfolk Record Office [RYE 9 vol. 1.])

area in 1252–53. The late thirteenth- and fourteenth-century wall was then built on top of the 1250s bank. Excavations have shown the accompanying ditch was over 18m wide and up to 8.3m deep.

Surviving walls can be viewed from adjacent roads and paths. A riverside path links Cow Tower, Bishop Bridge and the Boom Towers. The section beside Carrow Hill, where there are paths inside and outside the wall and which includes the Black and Wilderness Towers, is particularly worth visiting. The only section of wall still standing to its full height is at the junction of Ber Street and Bracondale.

Above left: *The Black Tower and brick arches on the inside of the city walls, beside Carrow Hill, Norwich. (David Robertson)*

Above right: *Cow Tower, a late fourteenth-century artillery tower next to the River Wensum, Norwich. (David Robertson)*

Left: *The sixteenth-century eastern chamber of Norwich Guildhall. (David Robertson)*

Below: *The south facade of Norwich Guildhall, including the porch of 1861. (David Robertson)*

50. NORWICH GUILDHALL

The Guildhall is the largest medieval municipal building constructed outside London. It served as Norwich's administrative centre until 1938, when it was replaced by the current City Hall. It was a magistrates' court until the 1980s, since when it has had several uses, including a tourist information centre, café, jewellery shop and escape rooms.

The main three-storey block was built in 1407–13 by John and Thomas Marwe to replace the previous tollhouse. This is constructed of carefully knapped flint with limestone dressings. Three facades are original, but the south front was clad in brick in the early eighteenth century until it was replaced by the current flint in 1835. Originally there were two towers on the west side, but these collapsed in 1508. The sixteenth-century south-west door was added in 1857 after it was taken from a house in London Street.

In 1511 the eastern part of the building collapsed, to be replaced by the existing eastern chamber by 1535. The elaborate flint and stone lozenge and triangular chequer-work upper section of the chamber's eastern elevation is one of the building's most striking features. The clock turret above is dedicated to Norwich Mayor Henry Woodcock (1789–1879) and was added by Robert Kerr in 1850.

The south elevation includes an elaborate three-storey flint and limestone porch reminiscent of a church tower. The porch was rebuilt by Thomas Barry in 1861, who at the same time added the three-bay wings on either side.

Inside features associated with the Guildhall's use as both a city hall and a court survive on the ground and first floors. The eastern first-floor chamber has decorated wooden panelling (installed 1534–37), wooden seating, a timber ceiling and reused fifteenth-century stained glass. The only surviving part of the earlier tollhouse is a fourteenth-century brick undercroft, which lies beneath the eastern part of the Guildhall. At its western end are three large fourteenth-century barrel-vaulted brick chambers.

The Guildhall is located on Gaol Hill, on the north side of Norwich Market Place. (NR2 1JS)

51. NORWICH BRIDEWELL

The Bridewell was built in the fourteenth century as a private merchant's house and was later home to William Appleyard, the first Mayor of Norwich (in 1403–04 and 1405). It was bought by the City of Norwich in 1583 and converted into a prison and house of correction in 1585. In 1828 it was sold and subsequently used a tobacco and snuff factory, leather warehouse and a shoe factory. It was given to the city as a museum of trade and industry in the 1920s.

The building's most dramatic feature is its two-storey northern facade. This is made of beautifully knapped flint with stone dressings and is recognised as one of the finest examples of medieval flint work in the country. With its brick arch, the doorway to the east is eighteenth century, possibly part of work that saw the windows renewed in 1786 by Thomas Dove (following a fire in 1751).

The building is now made up of four ranges around a central garden. The eastern range would have been the medieval hall, from which two fourteenth-century archways remain. Its western elevation looks over the garden and is faced in eighteenth-century brick, as is the facade of the north range. The western range has nineteenth-century elements, including a shop front of 1828.

Beneath the northern and eastern ranges is the largest medieval undercroft so far discovered in Norwich. Built of brick with brick ribs and dating from the early fourteenth century, it represents one of the earliest uses of brick in the city. The eastern section has two sets of six bays (divided by a middle pier) while the northern section has five bays. The undercroft was originally entered directly from the street rather than the house, making it the only example in Norwich known to have been constructed with street-only access. It would have been used for storage until the building became a prison.

The Bridewell is open to the public as the Museum of Norwich, which tells the story of the city from the medieval period onwards (see the Norfolk Museums Service website for opening times). It is located in Bridewell Alley, between Lobster Lane and St Andrew's Street, next to St Andrew's church. The museum offers guided tours of the undercroft. (NR2 1AQ)

The medieval northern flint facade of the Bridewell, Norwich. (David Robertson)

52. NORWICH STRANGERS' HALL

Strangers' Hall combines a medieval merchant's house with stories of mayors and asylum seekers. It was used as a private home from at least the early fourteenth century through to the mid-eighteenth century, when it became lodgings for judges visiting the city to preside over court cases. Leonard Bolingbroke bought the property in 1899, opened it to the public as a museum and then presented it to the City of Norwich in 1922.

The medieval Great Hall is one of the most impressive parts of the building. It was built in the mid-fifteenth century for William Barley, a wealthy city cloth merchant, who would have used it for eating and entertaining. At the east end of the hall were his offices, each entered through a stone arched doorway. His private chambers were on the first floor above.

The earliest surviving section is the under-croft, which lies beneath the western part of the hall and a room to the north. This was built for an earlier house, probably in the 1320s for Ralph de Middleton. It has three vaulted bays; the wall piers and ribs are of stone, and the infill is brick.

Around 1500, Thomas Cawse, a mercer and mayor of Norwich, added a western range

The garden front of the Great Hall at Strangers' Hall, Norwich. Nicholas Sotherton's vaulted bay window is on the left, with Francis Cock's staircase bay on the right. (JulesFoto)

and stable courtyard. These were enlarged for Nicholas Sotherton, another mayor whose arms can be seen in the large fireplace in one of the western rooms. In the mid-sixteenth century Sotherton encouraged 'strangers' to settle in Norwich and, as a result, his house acquired its current name. The 'strangers' were Protestant refugee weavers from the Low Countries who had fled persecution by their Spanish Catholic rulers.

To the north of the hall is a front courtyard. The stairs and vaulted porch that connect the hall and this courtyard were added in around 1530 by Nicholas Sotherton. He also commissioned the hall's crown post roof and the high vaulted bay window that overlooks the garden to the south.

In 1627 Francis Cock, grocer and mayor, added the main staircase in the hall and the bay that contains it. He also remodelled the street range, which includes early sixteenth-century flint work on the ground floor and a timber-framed, jettied first floor. Sir Joseph Paine, a hosier, mayor and strong supporter of the restoration of monarchy after the English Civil Wars, lived at Strangers Hall in the 1650s and '60s. He added fireplaces in the west wing that carry the date 1659.

> *Strangers' Hall is now a museum of medieval and post medieval urban life (see the Norfolk Museums Service website for opening times). It is in Charing Cross, to the north of the city centre, in the Norwich Lanes. (NR2 4AL)*

FURTHER READING

Norfolk Museums Service, 1980, *Strangers Hall Museum* (Norfolk Museums Service).

53. NORWICH ELM HILL

Elm Hill is one of Norwich's most famous landmarks and has been described as the city's 'most picturesque street' (Pevsner and Wilson, 1997, p.295). In 1507 a fire destroyed all but four buildings: the churches of St Peter Hungate, St Simon & St Jude and Blackfriars and the Briton's Arms. The street was soon rebuilt and a good number of fine late medieval houses survive. This section focuses on the pre- and immediately post-fire timber-framed buildings, but the street's seventeenth- and eighteenth-century houses are also worthy of notice.

The Briton's Arms is the only house to have survived the 1507 fire. It is timber-framed with jetties on both upper floors. The arcading on the second floor is distinctive and unusual. The south elevation's medieval door is partly visible from the road. In the early fifteenth century the building was home to a community of religious women. It is now a coffee house and restaurant. St Peter Hungate stands next to the Briton's Arms. Its squat square tower is the most distinctive feature; Thomas Ingham paid for this to be built in 1431. John and Margaret Paston funded the nave, which was constructed after 1458.

The timber-framed Briton's Arms, with the sixteenth-century 12–16 Elm Hill behind, Norwich. (David Robertson)

Opposite is the east end of the Blackfriars' church. This building dates to 1440–70 and, as the only friary church left in England, is perhaps the most important on the street. The Blackfriars arrived in Norwich in 1226 and acquired land on St Andrew's Plan after 1307. Of their first church, only the undercroft and parts of Beckett's chapel remain (the latter just behind a gate leading off Elm Hill); the majority was lost to fire in 1417. At the dissolution of the monasteries, the City of Norwich bought the site, converting it over time into the events venue it is today.

Nos 12–16 Elm Hill has a jetty over brick infill on the ground floor. The central wooden door has a small window covered by a grille (a 'wicket') and hides a passage that leads to the property's rear courtyard. It also allowed access to quays along the river to the north.

Nos 21–27 sits on a sloping corner plot, so has a wedge-shaped ground floor and horizontal jetty above. The studwork and brick herringbone nogging (or infill) on the first floor at the Strangers' Club (22–24) contrasts dramatically with the cream-rendered ground floor. The wooden lintel over their passageway carries the mark of the city's mercers.

Studwork, brick nogging and the rendered ground floor at 22–24 Elm Hill, Norwich. (David Robertson)

Pettus House (41–43) was rebuilt after 1507. No. 41 has a jettied upper floor with exposed studwork and a row of five two-light windows. Three of the windows have been infilled but their decorative tracery remains. The ground-floor shop front is nineteenth century. The adjacent passageway leads to Wright's Court and more sixteenth-century buildings.

Flint House (34–36) has a flint and brick ground floor with an overhanging upper storey. It dates to around 1540 but has many later Georgian features. Vents for the building's fifteenth-century barrel-vaulted undercroft can be seen at ground level. Some of the later houses also overlay fifteenth-century undercrofts (11–13, 20 and 28–30).

By the mid-nineteenth century these once prosperous houses were considered slums and in the 1920s Norwich City Council discussed their demolition to make way for industrial buildings. The Norwich Society led a campaign that highlighted the importance of the street's buildings. From 1927 onwards this resulted in extensive restorations and the preservation of the beautiful street we have today. The Norwich Society's successful campaign is an early example of urban conservation and paved the way for the introduction of Building Preservation Orders in 1932. Today Elm Hill's beauty has wide appeal, which is reflected in its appearance in television programmes and films, including *Stardust* (2007) and *Jingle Jangle* (2020).

Linking Princes Street and Wensum Street, Elm Hill is located to the west of the cathedral and east of St Andrew's and Blackfriars' Hall. (NR3 1HN)

54. KING'S LYNN TOWN DEFENCES

The medieval importance of King's Lynn was reflected in its town defences and the considerable area they contained. The earliest records describe four timber towers at key entrance points to the town in the twelfth and thirteenth centuries. Licences and instructions for building and repairing masonry walls, earth banks and a moat were issued between 1266 and 1403. These were constructed to the north, east and west of the town, often following the line of old sea banks; the rivers Ouse, Gaywood (Fisher Fleet) and Nar provided protection on the west, north and south. Earthwork extensions to the north and south were added in 1643–45 during the English Civil Wars, along with elaborate polygonal-shaped outworks (some of which were alongside the medieval walls).

South Gate is the best surviving part of the town defences. Most of it dates to 1437 and can be attributed to Robert Hetanger, a London mason. In 1520 Nicholas and Thomas Harmer were contracted to undertake unspecified works on the gatehouse; it was remodelled in the nineteenth century and restored in 1982–85. The building is of three storeys with battlements and corner turrets. The south front is faced with

King's Lynn's town defences are shown on the 'Groundplat of Kings Lyn' by Henry Bell c.1670. The south and east gates are numbered '10' and '11' and the Civil War polygonal-shaped outworks are prominent. (Norfolk Museums Service [Lynn Museum, King's Lynn])

South Gate, King's Lynn, from the south. (John Fielding)

limestone, while the other three elevations are brick. One carriageway of London Road still passes beneath the large central pointed arch; the two side lower pedestrian arches were added in the nineteenth century. Originally there were rooms either side of the arch on the ground and first floors. Much of the bridge to the south is nineteenth century but it does include elements of a medieval stone predecessor.

It is unlikely the entire defensive bank was topped by a wall; instead it is thought flint, stone and brick walls only stood for short distances either side of each of the gates. Sections of wall survive in The Walks, Wyatt Street/Littleport Terrace and Kettlewell Lane. The East Gate on Gaywood Road (between Kettlewell Lane and Littleport Terrace) was built in the 1440s but demolished in 1800; part of the bridge associated with this can be seen underneath the modern road bridge. Brick arches north of the junction of St Ann's Road and North Street may have been part of a north gate and a later gun battery.

Guannock Gate contains medieval fabric but was largely rebuilt in the nineteenth century as part of landscaping The Walks. This public park was established in 1713 and contains a surviving section of town bank, one of the Civil War outworks and Red Mount Chapel, a pilgrimage chapel built in 1485. There is an impressive section of the town bank to the south of The Walks, alongside Windsor Terrace between Extons and Goodwins Roads.

At the southern end of London Road, adjacent to Southgates roundabout, South Gate still marks the southern entrance to the town (PE30 5SX). The Walks is east of the town centre (PE30 1NT) with Littleport Terrace and Kettlewell Lane to the north (PE30 1PP).

From left to right: the late nineteenth-century Town Hall, the porch of 1624, Trinity Guildhall (1421–28) and the gaol of 1784, King's Lynn. (David Robertson)

The Assembly Rooms of 1766–68, behind Trinity Guildhall, King's Lynn. (David Robertson)

55. KING'S LYNN TRINITY GUILDHALL, GAOL AND TOWN HALL

This complex of civic buildings typifies the commercial success of King's Lynn and political power of merchant families in the medieval and post-medieval periods. The oldest surviving part is the central Guildhall, which was built for the Guild of the Holy Trinity 1421–28. This guild was medieval Lynn's leading merchant organisation and, following the granting of a royal charter in 1204, controlled political life within the town. The Guildhall is a brick building with a grand front of flint and limestone in chequerboard pattern that faces Saturday marketplace. The huge upper window lights a massive hall that occupies the whole upper floor. Four small ground-floor windows light a stone undercroft, but the central two windows were originally doors.

The upper hall is accessed through an elaborate porch, entrance hall and staircase located to the west and built in 1624. The porch's chequerboard facade matches that of the Guildhall. Its central doorway has Doric columns and an elaborate pediment, above which are a large window and a decorative panel with the arms of Elizabeth I. The curved gable was added in 1664 and features the arms of Charles II.

Behind and beside the Guildhall, not visible from the street, are assembly rooms (1766–68) and a courthouse (1767). During the eighteenth and nineteenth centuries the main hall and assembly rooms were used for exclusive banquets, balls and concerts for Lynn's social elite.

East of the Guildhall is the gaol. This yellow brick building was designed by William Tuck, built in 1784 and replaced the undercroft as King's Lynn's main prison. Rustication around the door, a panel containing chains and sundial in the parapet are perhaps the most striking external features. Four eighteenth-century cells survive, but most date to 1937. To the north-west of the Guildhall is the Town Hall of 1895. Its front also features flint and stone chequer-boarding and is dominated by numerous windows. The Gothic-revival style successfully complements the facade of the Guildhall.

The Guildhall, gaol and Town Hall are located on the Saturday marketplace and Queen Street. The gaol and undercroft house Stories of Lynn, a museum and borough archive (see their website for opening times). Tours of the Guildhall, assembly room and courthouse are available on selected days. (PE30 5DQ)

Left: *The late fifteenth-century timber-framed southern warehouse at Hanse House, St Margaret's Lane, King's Lynn. (David Robertson)*

Below: *Hanse House, King's Lynn, from the south-west. The two late fifteenth-century warehouses are visible, linked by the short western wing and the white-rendered St Margaret's House on the east. St Margaret's church is to the north-east. (John Fielding)*

56. KING'S LYNN HANSE HOUSE

Hanse House is England's only surviving Hanseatic warehouse complex and symbolises the important role Norfolk's ports played in medieval international trade. The Hanseatic League was a confederation of German merchant guilds and towns that developed in the late twelfth century and controlled Baltic and much North Sea trade until the sixteenth century. Originally focused on Lübeck and Hamburg, the league had trading posts as far apart as Novgorod (Russia), Bergen (Norway) and London. It often came into conflict with nation states, including England. The Anglo-Hanseatic war of the 1470s was concluded by the Treaty of Utrecht (1474).

The League was granted rights in Lynn in 1271 and was subsequently involved in importing goods such as furs, beeswax, fish, cereals and timber, while exporting wool, skins, cloth, salt and cereals and other commodities. The Treaty of Utrecht gave them the right to establish a trading depot in the town, leading to the construction of Hanse House on land purchased for them by Edward IV.

Hanse House is made up of two long, parallel, late fifteenth-century warehouses, eastern and western ranges that connect these, and a sequence of western extensions. The southern warehouse is timber-framed and brick, with a deep jetty on St Margaret's Lane (the underbuilt brickwork is eighteenth century renewed in the 1970s). The northern warehouse is entirely of brick. Originally both warehouses were adjacent to the River Ouse but as land was reclaimed from the river both were extended westwards. The short sixteenth-century western wing between them is built of brick and has an elaborate roof. The extensions west of the cross-wing are seventeenth and eighteenth century.

In 1751 the warehouse complex was sold by the Hanseatic League to Edward Everard, a Lynn merchant. He converted the medieval eastern wing into St Margaret's House, a fine Georgian dwelling. This stuccoed brick, two-storey house fronts on to St Margaret's Place and looks out on to St Margaret's church. The whole complex was restored in the 1970s as offices for Norfolk County Council.

Hanse House can be seen from St Margaret's Place, St Margaret's Lane and South Quay. Although now privately owned, some sections are publicly accessible: part is a restaurant and wine bar, while others are an event and conference venue. King's Lynn is a member of the modern Hanse, a network of towns that once belonged to or had associations with the Hanseatic League, and holds an annual Hanse Festival. (PE30 5GN)

Above: *The southern section of Great Yarmouth town wall along Mariners' Road with its brick-lined arrow slits and a tower. (Peter Wade-Martins)*

Below: *The south-east tower beside Blackfriars Road. A section of the wall has recently been repaired. (John Fielding)*

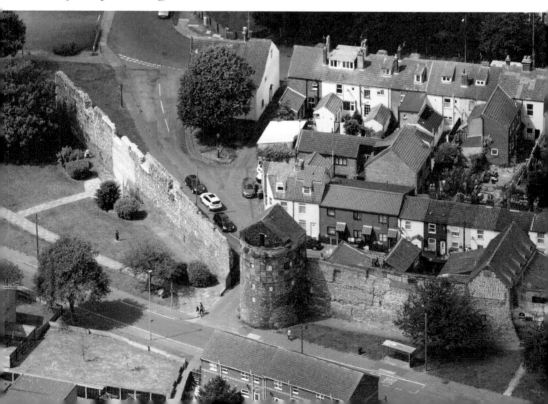

57. GREAT YARMOUTH TOWN WALL

Great Yarmouth grew up at the mouth of the River Yare (yare-mouth) as a very successful fishing port on the long sand spit that accumulated across the mouth of what had been in Roman times a great inland estuary. Breydon Water is now all that is left of that estuary. In times of conflict the town was vulnerable from invasion by sea, and it had considerable strategic importance as a coastal port facing the Low Countries. In 1261 King Henry III gave the burgesses of the town permission to enclose it with a wall and a ditch 'so long as the said burgesses shall well and faithfully behave themselves towards us and our heirs'. Over 130 years all 2,046m of the wall were completed. The ditch in front of the wall has long been filled in, but about two-thirds of the wall and eleven of the original eighteen D-shaped or circular towers or turrets remain, making it one of the most complete medieval town walls in England. There were ten gates, but sadly none survive. The wall enclosed the town on three sides and the fourth was open to the river where great chains on the south side could be pulled out of the water to block hostile ships. The bridge, not built until 1427, was defended by a gatehouse on the opposite bank. In 1596 an order was issued that all gates should be kept locked between 6 p.m. and 6 a.m..

The interior face of the town wall on Deneside with arrow slits, which were blocked when an earth bank was piled against the inside face in the sixteenth century to take cannon located at the new higher gun ports. Between the gun ports are blocked openings for small arms fire. (Peter Wade-Martins)

In places the wall survives up to 7m high. Its construction was relatively uniform with flint and mortar faced with knapped flints. Inside, there were brick arches supporting a wall walk, and arrow slits were located under the arches.

With the introduction of cannon, the wall was strengthened between 1545 and under the threat of the Armada in 1587–88 with a great earth bank to the rear. The low-level arrow slits were filled in and replaced with gunports for cannon on top of the new earth banks. Where the wall is still high enough, the gun ports can be seen faced with brick or dressed stone. At the south end where the wall reached the river a large earth mound, called the South Mount, was erected to locate cannon that could fend off hostile ships sailing in from the sea. It was probably during this period of refurbishment that the brick and flint chequerboard panelling, particularly obvious on the Blackfriars and south-east towers, was added.

Great Yarmouth was never attacked, although it did have to defend itself against Kett's Rebellion in 1549 (No. 64). The guns were removed in the 1680s, and the town gates were demolished for road widening in 1776–1837. In the eighteenth and nineteenth centuries the wall became heavily obscured by new houses built up against it, and the sections that are best seen now are those in the south-east corner in the area of Blackfriars' Road where there has been extensive post-war slum clearance.

With or without a guide, start the walk near the metal recycling centre at the south end of South Quay (at the site of the old south gate) and follow Mariners Road eastwards and then turn north along Blackfriars Road. Parts of this end of town were heavily bombed during the war and the gaps then filled in the 1960s with rather unattractive blocks of flats. As you walk north the wall becomes less easy to see where it is still hidden in yards and behind houses, but beyond Regent Road a fine section has been left exposed under the Market Gates Shopping Centre (1973–79). It is also obvious on the north side of the churchyard. The last section then crosses Northgate Street, where it terminates with a tower close to the River Bure. (Mariners Road as a starting point: NR30 3BZ)

FURTHER READING

Gooch, M., 2017, *Historic Great Yarmouth* (Great Yarmouth Local History and Archaeological Society).

Milligan, K.R., 1977, *Great Yarmouth Town Wall* (Great Yarmouth and District Archaeological Society). Out of print.

THE MEDIEVAL COUNTRYSIDE

INTRODUCTION

In 1066 the Norman conquerors found in Norfolk a countryside already prosperous and more populous than any other part of England. A recorded total of 27,000 individuals at Domesday indicates that there was an actual population of about 150,000. The 726 vills can be equated mostly to modern ecclesiastical parishes. Settlements remained where they were founded near their Middle Saxon centres (p. 69), but from the late eleventh century there was a gradual shift towards greens and commons, such as at Hales (No. 61). Trade was supported in this prosperous countryside by a network of market centres such as Wymondham (No. 66) between 8 and 16km apart.

This period of growth came to an end by about 1300 as the climate gradually deteriorated with periods of high rainfall, colder temperatures and severe storms. As the climate became wetter in the fourteenth and fifteenth centuries, so the heavy clay soils became increasingly difficult to cultivate and to drain. In the Broads water levels rose by up to a metre (No. 62). Then there was the Black Death in 1347–52, followed by further outbreaks in 1361, 1369, 1375 and 1391, reducing the national population by between 20 and 40 per cent. The Peasants' Revolt of 1381, which started in Essex, was the culmination of the unrest exacerbated by the heavy demands of the Poll Tax. The revolt was put down ruthlessly by Bishop Despenser at the Battle of North Walsham. In the fourteenth century, as the population declined, thirty churches were abandoned and gradually more land was taken out of the plough. As areas of grassland increased, sheep numbers grew and the wool trade flourished. The larger landowners then had the surplus income to invest in some of our finest fifteenth-century churches and their furnishings as at Worstead (No. 38), Salle (No. 39), St Peter Mancroft (No. 40) and Ranworth (No. 42). As more common land was fenced off for sheep, so social unrest grew, resulting in Kett's Rebellion of 1549 (No. 64). This was also put down as ruthlessly as the Peasants' Revolt had been 168 years earlier.

About a hundred churches stand, or used to stand, within the sites of deserted medieval villages. The earthworks of these deserted sites can be seen frequently on aerial photographs taken by the RAF in 1946 after the Second World War, but much of this evidence was later ploughed away between the 1950s and the 1970s with increased farm mechanisation encouraged by generous farm improvement grants from the government. We can be thankful that has now been stopped. A few good examples of the earthworks of deserted medieval villages with their streets and property boundaries are still visible, as at Godwick (No. 58) and Houghton (No. 59).

The late medieval countryside tells a story of population decline and village desertion from the more marginal lands, while at the same time the wealthy were able to spend huge sums on some of our finest churches.

FURTHER READING

Davison, A., 1996, *Deserted Villages in Norfolk* (Poppyland).

Williamson, T., 1993, *The Origins of Norfolk* (Manchester University Press).

58. GODWICK DESERTED MEDIEVAL VILLAGE

This multi-period set of earthworks is of the greatest interest for landscape historians. The site of Godwick's deserted village lies on the central Norfolk boulder clay plateau where heavy wet soils were never easy to cultivate. Making a living was hard and these areas were the first to decline following the Black Death. The Domesday population of Godwick was already small, and in the fourteenth century the numbers of taxpayers only just reached double figures. There were fewer than ten households in 1428. A survey of 1508 listed eleven out of the eighteen house plots on the north side of the street as void, and a survey of 1588 mentions further empty plots. By the time a map of Godwick was drawn in 1596 only three houses remained.

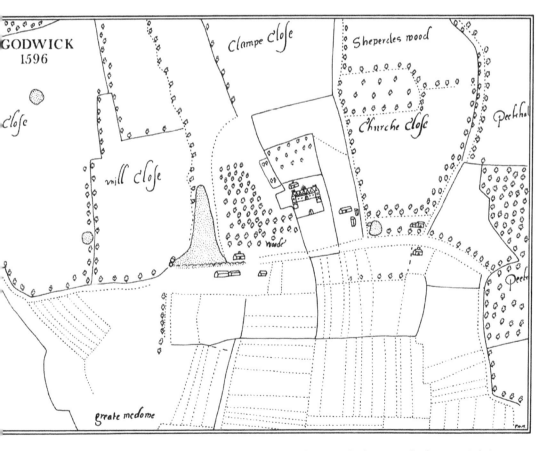

Redrawn extract of the map of Godwick dated 1596 looking south showing Chief Justice Coke's mansion set back from the village street with just a few houses remaining, in addition to the church, mill pond and a wonderful little water mill on the east end of the mill pond dam. (Drawn by Peter Wade-Martins)

Above: *The earthworks of Godwick deserted village from the west with the ruined church tower beside the sunken village street cut through by later clay pits. The old street runs from A to B towards the nineteenth-century farm buildings in the distance. (Mike Page)*

Left: *The ruined church tower rebuilt as a garden folly in the seventeenth century. (David Robertson)*

Godwick has some of the best village earthworks in the county. The main street is clear as a hollow way that was a part of a longer road that ran between Tittleshall and Whissonsett. Two other streets ran south from the main street, and the church stood in the angle of these roads. Running along both sides of the main street are the earthworks of the house plots, or tofts, where the property divisions show as shallow banks or ditches, and it is possible now to count seven along the north side and a further four, as well as the churchyard, on the opposite side. The church was depicted on the 1596 map but with a ruined tower that was partly rebuilt as a folly in the early seventeenth century, while the nave and chancel are now just visible as a raised area of ground. The 1596 map shows the village street continuing to the east along a mill dam with a mill pond to the south and a charming watermill at the far end, all now sadly lost under modern farm buildings.

Not long before and soon after the production of the 1596 map there were significant changes to the village. By 1586 the Drury family built a large house with gabled wings and a walled north-facing courtyard. Sir Edward Coke (1552–1634) then bought this 'Old Hall' as his Norfolk home and the Coke family were based here until they inherited Holkham manor (No. 87). As Chief Justice, he led the trials of Sir Walter Raleigh and the Gunpowder Plot conspirators, including Guy Fawkes. When he was imprisoned in the Tower of London in 1621 he wrote that he hoped he would be able to spend his last days at Godwick. Around the hall there were new enclosures, presumably for orchards and gardens, which replaced the old village house plots. Coke built the Great Barn in around 1597 across the line of the old street, and it is one of the most important and elaborate buildings of its type in Norfolk. In the eighteenth and nineteenth centuries the village area was peppered with 'marl' or clay pits for spreading marl as a fertiliser on the land. The Old Hall was replaced by the current Godwick Hall in 1843–46 and, after being gutted by fire, its remains were demolished in 1961. The Great Barn survives and is used today as an events venue.

There is a public footpath across the site as well as permissive access to many of the earthworks and church tower. A fine set of information panels starting in the Great Barn car park was installed in 2019. (PE32 2RJ)

FURTHER READING

Cushion, B. and Davison, A., 2003, *Earthworks of Norfolk,* East Anglian Archaeology 104, pp.38–40.

Cushion, B., Davison, A., Fenner, G., Goldsmith, R., Knight, J., Virgoe, N., Wade, K. and Wade-Martins, P., 1982, *Some Deserted Village Sites in Norfolk,* East Anglian Archaeology 14, pp.59–67.

Davison, A., 2007. 'Investigations at Godwick and Beeston St Andrew', *Norfolk Archaeology* XLV, pp.141–154.

Godwick Lost Village, 2019, *The Lost Village of Godwick,* www.lostvillageofgodwick.co.uk.

59. HOUGHTON DESERTED MEDIEVAL VILLAGE

Unlike Godwick, Houghton was a relatively successful community that contributed £6 to the Lay Subsidy tax in 1334, the second highest in its Hundred. The village in 1578–89 had eighty-two adults in twenty households, so it was still moderately prosperous even after the Black Death. In 1676 there were eighty communicants attending church. So, where did they live?

The village has disappeared, but a good set of earthworks lie in the park northeast of the hall where the sinuous line of a hollow way, with about a dozen house plots outlined by boundary banks on either side, is cut by the north drive. Exactly *when* this site was deserted is unclear, although we do know that it had gone by 1719 when a map was made of the park and the surrounding area.

About 600m to south of these earthworks, the church now stands entirely by itself with little sign of any village. But in 1719 there was another area of settlement here that was forcibly cleared in the eighteenth century by the landowner, Sir Robert Walpole, to extend his park around his new hall (No. 86).

There is legal access to the church, and access elsewhere in the park depends on advertised opening hours to the hall. (PE31 6SX)

The earthworks of Houghton deserted medieval village lie to either side of the north drive to Houghton Hall. They are not easy to see from the air and are best appreciated on the ground with the help of the site survey on page 185. (John Fielding)

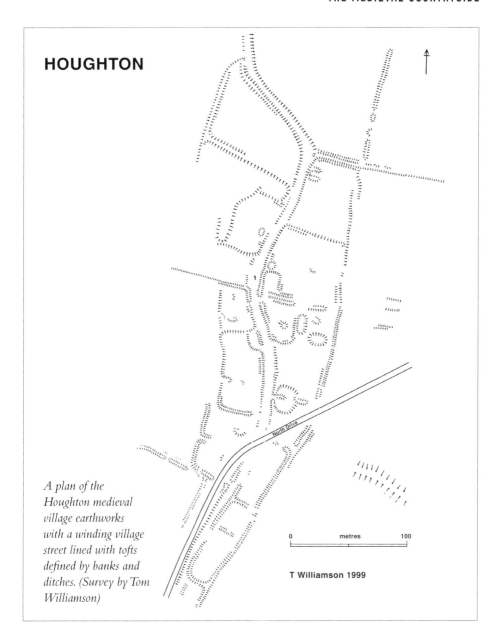

HOUGHTON

A plan of the Houghton medieval village earthworks with a winding village street lined with tofts defined by banks and ditches. (Survey by Tom Williamson)

North Drive

0   metres   100

T Williamson 1999

FURTHER READING

Cushion, B. and Davison, A., 2003, *Earthworks of Norfolk*, East Anglian Archaeology 104, pp.48–51.

Williamson, T., 1998, *The Archaeology of the Landscape Park. Garden Design in Norfolk, England, c.1680–1840*, British Archaeological Reports British Series 268, pp.55–59.

Yaxley, D., 1984, *Survey of the Houghton Estate by Joseph Hill, 1800 (*Norfolk Record Society).

60. RIDGE AND FURROW AT HILGAY

Like the earthworks of deserted medieval villages, relic medieval fields are hard to find. Traditionally, the best evidence is in the form of ridge and furrow. The individual ridges correspond to the narrow cultivation strips that were grouped together into blocks or 'furlongs'. The width of the strips is usually between 5 and 9m, and they were shared out around the villagers and individually cultivated. In Norfolk cultivation was mostly with horses rather than oxen. Tenants held their strips throughout the 'open fields' of the parish. The furrows formed the boundaries between the strips and provided drainage. In the Midlands the survival of ridge and furrow is still common, but in East Anglia it is rare, and we are not sure why.

In Norfolk the most convincing examples are entirely confined to a narrow strip along the fen edge from Babingley in the north down to Stradsett and Hilgay in the south. The most extensive areas were in Stradsett, although many of these have been ploughed away since the Second World War. Some still survive in pasture to the west of Stradsett Hall.

A rare survival of medieval ridge and furrow fields from the south on the slope between Hilgay village and the A10 bypass. (John Fielding)

In Hilgay there is a fine set running along a west-facing slope between the Hilgay bypass and the village. At the south end there is a furlong running at right angles to the others. These furlongs often ran in different directions according to the slope and drainage. In the Hilgay group the ridges are between 6.5 and 13m wide, with most of them being between 7 and 9m wide. The group is continuous for about 1.5km and covers an area of *c*.40ha.

The one question that has not yet been answered satisfactorily is why it is only along the fen edge that convincing examples of these fields can still be found. We know from old maps that there were strip fields elsewhere in the county, so was it the method of ploughing that was different or have they really all mostly been ploughed away? This is a matter of lively unresolved debate among landscape and agricultural historians, and it does remain a fascinating question.

This block of ridge and furrow lies on the east side of the A10 between the road and Hilgay village, and it is crossed by a public footpath that runs between the A10 and the road running south from the village as shown on the OS Explorer series map of the area. (PE38 0LB)

FURTHER READING

Liddiard, R., 1999, 'The distribution of ridge and furrow in East Anglia: ploughing practice and subsequent land use', *The Agricultural History Review* 47, pp.1–6.

Silvester, R.J., 1989, 'Ridge and furrow in Norfolk', *Norfolk Archaeology* 40, pp.286–296.

61. HALES GREEN

Hales Green from the south-east: possibly the largest surviving village green in Norfolk. (John Fielding)

Until the wholesale enclosure of commons in the eighteenth and early nineteenth centuries, old village greens were still the focus of settlement that could go back to the eleventh century. Previously, the village was centred on the parish church, which was frequently left isolated when settlement moved to the greens. Hales is unusual in that it still has an exceptionally large unenclosed green, roughly triangular some 1,500m north to south and 450m at its wider southern end. There are also big unenclosed greens at Mulbarton, south of Norwich, and at Brisley to the north-west of Dereham. Green-side settlement at Hales began probably in the late eleventh or twelfth centuries and it eventually left the church standing isolated almost 1km away to the east. We know this because there was an extensive field-walking project between 1980 and 1985, mainly by Alan Davison, who was a keen fieldworker and documentary historian. He was part of a group that collected and recorded pottery sherds of different dates from all over the parish. These pottery scatters demonstrate that green-side settlement here reached its peak, as was often the case, in the thirteenth and fourteenth centuries followed by a slow decline, so today there are only a handful of houses or farms remaining around the green.

Hales Green is a very pleasant public open space in which to walk, and it is worth looking out for the many the pits and ponds dug mainly around the edges of the green at various times to provide a source of clay probably for house building. Similar clay pits can be seen around Brisley Green.

There is open public access to the green. (NR14 6FN)

FURTHER READING

Barringer, C., 2005, 'Heaths and Commons' in Ashwin, T and Davison, A. (eds), *An Historical Atlas of Norfolk*, pp.84–85 (Phillimore).

Davison, A., 1990, *The Evolution of Settlement in Three Parishes in South-east Norfolk*, East Anglian Archaeology 49.

62. THE BROADS

No other human activity in the Middle Ages caused greater landscape change in Norfolk than the digging of vast pits, or turbaries, for the extraction of peat as a fuel. As the climate deteriorated, these pits gradually filled with water to create the 'the seemingly timeless world of marshes, fens, rivers and lakes' we know today (Williamson, 1997, p.1). Many people who are not familiar with Norfolk believe that the Broads represent the typical Norfolk landscape, but this remarkable wetland with 200km of navigable waterways is confined just to the valleys of the Waveney, Wensum and Bure and their tributaries. These waterways, with their sailing wherries and eighteenth- and nineteenth-century wind-powered drainage mills, created scenes immortalised by nineteenth-century artists of the Norwich School, including Cotman, Crome, Stannard and Stark. Some are on display in Norwich Castle Museum (No. 28).

In the Roman period the lower reaches of the valleys formed one great saltwater estuary that was open to the sea. Then, in the Anglo-Saxon period the long sand spit on which Great Yarmouth now stands gradually blocked the estuary, leaving just a narrow exit to the sea. Further upstream in the valleys the peat became accessible for exploitation as the land dried out in the early Middle Ages.

Hickling Broad from the south-east. (John Fielding)

The origins of these broad stretches of open fresh water remained a mystery until the 1950s, when a team of ecologists, historians and archaeologists made a significant discovery. Soil samples from boreholes sunk by Dr Joyce Lambert into the sediments in the Broads showed that these wide pits, averaging 3–4m deep, had vertical sides and were clearly human-made. C.T. Smith found good documentary evidence in the Register of St Benet's Abbey (No. 47) for peat digging from the twelfth century. The accounts of Norwich Cathedral Priory show that turves were the main source of fuel in their kitchens until the first half of the fourteenth century. Some manorial documents from the thirteenth and fourteenth centuries also show strong evidence for peat extraction. But digging came to an end as the climate deteriorated and water levels rose by up to a metre. The last mention of turves being used in the Norwich Cathedral Priory was in 1419. Thereafter the documents just talk about 'fuel' or faggots. At its height, extraction had been on a massive scale before the turbaries were abandoned.

Downstream, the silted up old Roman estuary became grazing marshes where the windmills, like those at Berney Arms (No. 98) and Horsey (No. 74), predominate. For ecologists these areas of open water, dykes and grazing marshes form the most important surviving freshwater habitat in lowland England. The story of how the grazing marshes were saved by ecologists from deeper draining and intensive arable farming is covered in No. 98.

The best way to see the Broads is by boat. Cruisers can be hired at places including Wroxham, and the Norfolk Wildlife Trust run educational boat trips on Hickling Broad. (Hickling Broad car park: NR12 0YJ)

FURTHER READING

George, M., 1992, *The Land Use, Ecology and Conservation of Broadland* (Packard Publishing).

Lambert, H.M., Jennings, J.N., Smith, C.T., Green C. and Hutchinson, J.N., 1961, *The Making of the Broads: A Reconsideration of their Origin in the Light of New Evidence* (Royal Geographical Society Research Series 3).

Linsell, S., 1990, *Hickling Broad and its Wildlife* (Terence Dalton).

Malster, R. 1993, *The Broads* (Phillimore).

Malster, R. 2003, *The Norfolk and Suffolk Broads* (Phillimore).

Swan, M., 1992, *The Battle for the Broads* (Terence Dalton).

Wade-Martins, S., 2015, *The Conservation Movement in Norfolk* (Boydell).

Williamson, T., 1997, *The Norfolk Broads: A Landscape History* (Manchester University Press).

63. THETFORD WARREN LODGE

From the late twelfth to early twentieth century the Norfolk and Suffolk Brecks were renowned for their rabbit warrens. These were large areas defined by boundary banks used primarily for the farming, protection and trapping of rabbits. There were at least twenty-six warrens, of which fourteen were in Norfolk. The meat they produced went to local markets, Cambridge colleges and London, while fur was sent to Brandon, Thetford, Swaffham, mainland Europe and later South America for processing. The warrens were initially established by monasteries or important landowners, including Thetford Priory, Bury St Edmunds Abbey and the Duchy of Lancaster. Most functioned until at least the eighteenth century, with the last closing in 1940.

In the medieval and post-medieval periods there were rabbit warrens all over the country, often in areas of land considered poor for arable farming. However, the Brecks warren landscape is among the best preserved. Boundary banks survive well, as do a few of the warren lodges that were home to the warreners and their families. Lodges also served as a defence against poachers and were used to store equipment and carcasses.

The fifteenth-century Thetford Warren Lodge. (David Robertson)

Thetford Warren Lodge is one of two Brecks' lodges with walls standing to their original height (the other is Mildenhall, Suffolk). Reminiscent of a small castle keep, it was probably constructed by Thetford Priory in the fifteenth century. It is rectangular, two-storey and built of flint with brick, tile and limestone dressings. The ground floor served as a store, with the upper floor providing living accommodation (including a garderobe in the north-west corner). Two attached wings were lost in a fire in 1935.

At their most extensive, Thetford Warren's perimeter banks measured around 16km long and enclosed over 1,000ha. They survive best on the western side. To the north of the B1107 they extend from the road to the marshes alongside the Little Ouse. In places there is more than one bank, in some cases up to five. Multiple banks like these may have been used to funnel rabbits into nets and traps. Selected sections are faced with flints, something that is not found at any other Brecks' warren. To discourage rabbits from escaping from warrens, the perimeter banks were topped with gorse and the animals would have been fed by the warrener.

Managed by English Heritage, Thetford Warren Lodge is located to the south of (and signposted from) the B1107 between Thetford and Brandon. (IP24 3NE)

FURTHER READING

Mason A. and Parry. J., 2010, *The Warrens of Breckland: A Survey by the Breckland Society* (The Breckland Society).

THE SIXTEENTH TO NINETEENTH CENTURIES

INTRODUCTION

As Norfolk entered the Tudor period in 1485 the larger landowners and merchants had money to spare and the dissolution of the monasteries in the 1530s provided the opportunity for the wealthy to extend their landownership. Many of Norfolk's great estates began to be built up at this time with families such as the Pastons of Oxnead, the Bacons of Stiffkey and the Hobarts of Blickling (No. 85) buying up monastic land. A new class of gentry was emerging who were building their manor houses of brick with their stepped gables, elaborate chimneys and mullioned windows.

Changes in society that involved the decline of the feudal system governed by the payment in kind and services to a feudal overlord and its replacement by a system based on money whereby a tenant paid rent to a landlord can be traced back to the Black Death (1348). The fifteenth and sixteenth centuries saw this decline intensify as community-based arable farming of individual strips within open arable fields, as at Hilgay (No. 60), was replaced by enclosures, often for sheep pastures, by a commercially minded elite. The discontent over this change could sometimes result in riots and the throwing down of fences, which reached a climax in Kett's rebellion in 1549 (No. 64).

The Civil War of the 1640s passed much of Norfolk by, with the majority supporting the parliamentary side. Links with the Low Countries meant that firstly Protestantism and later Puritanism were strong, and only in the northwest of the county did the royalists have much support, taking over King's Lynn for a short time in 1643. The strength of feeling against the established Anglican Church is clearly seen in the widespread destruction of statues, stained glass and wall paintings across the county, most vividly described at Norwich Cathedral (No. 34).

The county soon recovered from any dislocation of trade and commerce and continued to prosper. Market towns flourished as the building of market houses (No. 66) shows. Landowners such as Charles 'Turnip' Townshend (1674–1738) of Raynham, the Secretary of State to Queen Anne and George I, were experimenting with new crops and increasing the output of their estates. This intensification was made famous a generation later by Thomas William Coke of Holkham (1754–1842) (Nos 70 and 87). Townshend's close neighbour, Robert Walpole, became England's first Prime Minister (No. 86), and a fourth remarkable Norfolk man was, of course, Horatio Nelson (No. 71).

To understand Norfolk's eighteenth-century landscape, there can be no better place to begin than with Faden's map of Norfolk of 1797. Drawn at a scale of about one inch to the mile (a slightly smaller scale than the modern OS 1:50,000 map), it provides a detailed picture of the county at the end of the eighteenth century. Of particular importance are the numerous areas of 'commons, heaths and wastes' that are shown covering in total about 64,750ha. Of the 465 sites identified as 'commons' on the map, most were enclosed as part of agricultural improvement, and they disappeared over the next thirty years. While commons were mostly on the wetter clays, the areas labelled as 'heaths' were more usually on the gravelly, drier soils. Enclosure of commons usually involved an Enclosure Act that would be initiated by the local landowner. Where there was no dominant landowner, commons were more likely to remain open. This may explain why the large commons at Brisley, Hales (No. 61) and Mulbarton still survive.

The real impetus for farming change came with the years of scarcity during the Napoleonic wars (1796–1815) when the pressure for the enclosure of both open fields and commons had a huge impact on the landscape. Squared fields with straight enclosure roads driven across previous heaths and commons were created. Enclosure was often only a first step in increasing output. Poor heathy acid soils would need marling with alkali-rich clay dug from marl pits, many of which survive as landmarks within the fields today. Increased grain production led to the building of brick barns on the newly enclosed lands. Beside them were the cattle yards where cattle, bought from drovers from the north at the great cattle fairs at Norwich, were fattened and increasingly valued for their meat, but also for the manure that could be spread on the fields to raise output.

By the end of the eighteenth century the basis of the county's wealth was changing as machines powered by water, wind and steam replaced human muscle. Norfolk ceased to be a centre for the hand-production of cloth and instead became a producer of food, particularly grain, for an industrialised nation. The old centres of spinning and weaving, such as Worstead (No. 38), stagnated.

The 'Golden Years' of British Agriculture (between 1840 and 1880) were times of prosperity that not only encouraged enclosure and farm building, but also the development of new techniques by the large capitalist farmers. Entrepreneurs built lavish corn halls such as at Diss (No. 76) where farmers could do business with local corn merchants.

To be productive, wetlands needed draining. The first enclosure act for Norfolk was for 'draining, improving and inclosing common at Stokesby' in Broadland in 1720. Wind pumps began to appear across the Broadland marshes, with forty-seven being shown on Faden's map of 1797. This allowed these wetlands to be used for summer grazing. A new road was built across the marshes from Acle to Yarmouth in the 1820s, now the busy A47. Drainage of the Fens had been started by the Duke of Bedford in the seventeenth century, but more pumps were constantly needed as the peat shrank. Faden's map shows forty-six windmills across the Ouse Washes, all of which had to be replaced by steam in the nineteenth century. Along the east and south coast of the Wash Faden's map shows the embankments that had been thrown up to keep the sea off grazing marshes between Walpole Cross Keys and North Wooton, dated between 1774 and 1791.

It is from this period that the landed wealth of Norfolk has left its most obvious mark on the landscape in the form of mansions and parks clearly marked on Faden's map, often with the name of the landowner beside them. The landed magnates such as Lord Leicester at Holkham (No. 87) and the Walpoles at Houghton (No. 86) built remarkable houses within large parks on which they employed some of the most famous landscape designers of the time. 'Capability' Brown designed parks at Kimberley, Langley and Melton Constable between 1750 and 1770, with Humphrey Repton producing a large number of 'Red Books' showing possible developments for at least twenty other Norfolk parks between the 1780s and the 1820s such as Sheringham (No. 88), but not all of these were carried out. By the 1770s the landscaped park was the accepted setting for the houses of the fashionable and indicated that the elite could afford to be surrounded by non-productive land. Although gentry houses and parks are shown across the county, those on the more densely populated and fertile lands around Norwich are mainly smaller than those out to the west. Many parks were designed by their owners, their gardeners and their land agents. Trees were planted, lakes dug and roads diverted around them. Sheltered from the world within their belts of trees, their owners could indulge their tastes for field sports and experiment in new farming and animal breeding techniques. Much of the wealth that supported these lifestyles came from the improved agriculture, and with it increased rental income from their huge estates.

The new farming methods relied heavily on cheap seasonal labour, which brought its own problems as unemployed workers sought help from a Poor Law system based on individual parishes. The solution was seen to be the building of huge often prison-like buildings as workhouses, such as Gressenhall (No. 72) and later Pulham Market (No. 73), which aimed at being an unattractive option for the destitute.

A central feature of several Norfolk market towns is the market house or cross. Market houses in New Buckenham, North Walsham and Wymondham, were all built after disastrous town fires in the seventeenth century, while that at Swaffham was built in the eighteenth century.

The period since 1600 saw the function of the many market towns change from being mainly centres of commerce to being manufacturing hubs in their own right. Gradually new factory-based industries such as maltings, breweries, iron foundries and shoemaking were established. More than fifty maltings supplied nearly forty breweries across nineteenth-century Norfolk. Thetford was the home of Burrells, a major steam engine producer, while iron foundries in other towns produced agricultural machinery for both a local and an international market. In Norwich the Norwich Yarn Company's mill beside the river was built in 1839 (No. 84), but the city was already becoming a major centre of shoemaking rather than textile manufacture. Surplus labour moved from the countryside to the expanding towns, wages slowly began to rise and the most acute problems of poverty were reduced. However, with no state social security, fear of the workhouse was never far away.

The improvement of transport helped the industrial development of the county. The North Walsham and Dilham Canal (No. 81) built in the 1830s and designed to carry agricultural goods was never an economic success, but the building of a railway network was one of the great achievements of the period. Not only did it connect many small communities with their local town, but also provided much-needed employment. The railways also allowed for the cheaper transport of coal inland and thus helped the expansion of foundries and agricultural implement makers in the market towns. Corn mills, both water and wind-powered, were established. Gradually, gasworks, as at Fakenham (No. 80), piped water and sewage systems were introduced.

The railway also encouraged the growth of the tourist industry. Great Yarmouth added tourism to its already thriving fishing and port activities (No. 83). While Cromer was already becoming fashionable before the railway, tourism expanded after its arrival in 1877 with new hotels and a golf course. Some of the more well-heeled visitors grumbled about the lowering of social standards as travel became cheaper. New Hunstanton was created as a resort on the Wash by the Le Strange family, who invested in the branch-line extension from King's Lynn in 1867. A second area of development also encouraged by the railways was in the Broads. By 1891 there were thirty-seven companies offering boats for hire.

The eighteenth century saw the gradual growth of Atlantic-facing ports such as Glasgow, Liverpool and Bristol away from the East Anglian North Sea-facing towns. Nonetheless, the fine eighteenth-century mansions around the Tuesday Market and the Custom House (No. 67) in King's Lynn, show that its days as an important port were far from over, with grain leaving the productive farmlands of Norfolk and wine and luxury goods coming in from the Continent. The rich merchants of King's Lynn ran the town like a 'city state' and were seen as 'urban lords' rather than traders.

Great Yarmouth too continued to be important for both coastal and European trade as well as being a fishing port and assembly point for Nelson's Baltic fleet. Norfolk's most famous son is remembered there as well as at his birthplace of Burnham Thorpe (No. 71).

Norwich remained an important market, financial, provincial and cathedral city with wealthy and cultured citizens able to support the building of independent chapels, fine houses, a theatre, a public library, two hospitals and assembly rooms, while banks and financial institutions built impressive offices to assure their customers of their commercial stability (No. 90).

FURTHER READING

Ayers, B., 1994, *Book of Norwich* (Batsford/English Heritage).

Barringer, J.C., 1980, 'Introduction' *Faden's Map of Norfolk* (Larks Press).

Ketton-Cremer, R.W., 1969, *Norfolk in the Civil War* (Faber and Faber).

Macnair, A. and Williamson, T., 2010, *William Faden and Norfolk's 18th-Century Landscape* (WINDgather).

Meeres, F., 1998, *A History of Norwich* (Phillimore).

O'dell, A., 2020, *Norfolk Market Towns and their Industrial Development in the Nineteenth Century* (Norfolk Industrial Archaeology Society).

Richards, P., 1990, *King's Lynn* (Phillimore).

Wade-Martins, S. and Williamson, T., 1999, *Roots of Change, Farming and Landscape in East Anglia c.1700–1870* (British Agricultural History Society).

Wade-Martins, S. and Williamson, T., 2008, *The Countryside of East Anglia: Changing Landscapes 1870–1950* (Boydell).

Wade-Martins, S., 2002, *Changing Agriculture in Georgian and Victorian Norfolk* (Poppyland).

Yaxley, D. and Virgoe, N., 1978, *The Manor House* (Boydell).

64. KETT'S OAK

Kett's oak, recognised in the Tree Council's list as one of Britain's 'fifty grandest trees', stands beside the B1172 on the parish boundary between Hethersett and Wymondham. It is a reminder of the last major rebellion against economic and social hardship in Norfolk, which took place in 1549, and the oak has assumed symbolic significance over the centuries. The railings were first replaced in 1870 by supporters of the early Agricultural Labourers' Union, who were again active when there was work to preserve the tree in 1933. It has remained a place of pilgrimage for political radicals ever since.

Estimates of the number involved in Kett's rebellion vary, but well over 10,000 people camped on Mousehold Heath outside Norwich for seven weeks. Their aim was to petition the Lord Protector Somerset, the head of the young Edward VI's Council, listing twenty-nine grievances. It was sent to Somerset, but ignored. Instead the rebellion was put down by troops under the Earl of Warwick. The final conflict saw over 3,500 dead, the burning of much of Norwich and the execution of the rebellion's leaders.

The causes of unrest were complex and not confined to Norfolk, although the most serious conflict was here. The immediate flashpoint was enclosure of the open fields and commons for sheep by the large farmers and landowners. This involved the eviction of tenants, loss of commoning rights and the reduction of land in arable for food crops. This meant less labour was needed and there was a fear of food shortages. Some of the sheep farms were very large indeed, with the Fermoys of East Barsham running as many as 17,000 sheep. Economic distress was compounded by inflation as the coinage was debased to help pay for ill-fated Scottish wars. The rebels soon received support from the Norwich poor, where a decline in sales for the traditional woollen weaves such as worsted (No. 38) were causing unemployment and distress.

This rumbling discontent found as its leader the charismatic Robert Kett and his brother William. We know very little about them except that they were themselves landowners in Wymondham. Robert was a tanner and William a butcher in the town. Robert himself had enclosed for sheep, but as the unrest spread he took down his own fences before leading an ever-increasing band of rebels from Wymondham to Hethersett, breaking down fences on the way. Tradition has it that on the parish boundary beside the oak tree he addressed his followers. His supporters included both landless labourers and small dispossessed farmers from more than fifty villages. Their aim was to march to Norwich, gathering more men as they went and to camp outside the city until their demands were met. Provisions were sent to the camp from their home parishes, which also provided arrows for the final conflict. Kett set up his administrative headquarters on Mousehold Heath at St Michael's chapel; the focal point of the camp, where discussions took place.

Decisions were then made at the nearby 'Oak of Reformation'. This oak has long-since disappeared, although the ruins of St Michael's chapel are in the wildlife area overlooking the city and managed by the Friends of Kett's Heights. It is remarkable that an orderly camp was maintained for seven weeks and this testifies to Kett's administrative skills.

The final battle against the Earl of Warwick was fought at 'Dussendale', the site of which is disputed. Suggestions range from Sprowston, to the north of the city, or to the east in Postwick, where the name 'Dussings Deale' appears on a map of 1718. After their defeat, William and Robert Kett were taken to London for trial and then brought back to Norfolk for execution; Robert was hanged from the ramparts on Norwich Castle and William from the tower of Wymondham Abbey.

In 1949, on the 400th anniversary of the rebellion, a plaque to Robert Kett 'in reparation and honour to a notable and courageous leader' was unveiled at the entrance to Norwich Castle Museum (No. 28).

Kett's Oak beside the B1172 at the parish boundary between Wymondham and Hethersett. (David Robertson)

According to Rutledge (2005, p. 103):

Kett's rebellion remains a paradox. Apparently spontaneous, its organisation and rapid spread suggest prior planning. Led by a man who was himself an encloser and minor manorial lord, it could claim with more than usual justification to uphold government policy. But such a rising had no future. In an age which treated peaceful protest as rebellion, the camps either had to disband or be destroyed.

(Kett's Oak: NR9 3DJ; St Michael's Chapel: NR1 4AZ)

FURTHER READING

Hoare, A., 2016, *On the Trail of Kett's Rebellion* (Barker's Print). This describes the various sites associated with Kett in Norfolk.

Jary, L.R., 2018, *Kett 1549. Rewriting the Rebellion* (Poppyland).

Land, S., 1977, *Kett's Rebellion: The Norfolk Rising of 1549* (Boydell).

Rutledge, E., 2005, 'Kett's Rebellion 1549' in Ashwin, T. and Davison, A. (eds), *An Historical Atlas of Norfolk*, pp.103–104 (Phillimore).

Yaxley, S. (ed.), 1987, *The Commoyson in Norfolk 1549 by Nicholas Sotherton* (Larks Press).

For an imaginative recreation of these events the novel *Tombland* by C.J. Sansom (2018) is a good read.

65. WAXHAM BARN

Not far behind the sand dunes of the receding eastern coast of Norfolk stand the remains of a sixteenth-century manorial complex. The barn's importance lies in its position within the complex close to the church and the hall, its exceptional size, and the quality of the workmanship. It was compulsory purchased by the Norfolk County Council because of its poor state of repair, culminating in the collapse of part of the roof in the great gale of 1987. It is now managed by the Norfolk Historic Buildings Trust and open to the public.

Waxham was regarded of strategic importance at the time the complex was built in the 1580s. The area was identified as a possible landing place for an invading army and the site is shown as a fortified manor on maps drawn at the time. The Woodhouse family are first mentioned at Waxham in 1504 but their greatest wealth was accumulated in the 1540s and '50s when they were buying up monastic lands as they came on the market, acquiring neighbouring Ingham in 1538, Hickling in 1542 and Broomholm in 1546. Not only did these purchases bring land, but their buildings were also a quarry of materials for the family's building project at Waxham. The grandeur of the barn and the high status of the house demonstrate clearly the wealth of the family at the time.

Waxham Hall itself has been altered many times over the centuries, but the sixteenth-century wing of an original courtyard house surrounded on three sides by a flint boundary wall still stands with an impressive stone gateway to the north. Beyond the house are earthworks that are evidence for earlier moats and fishponds.

To the south and beyond huge asbestos farm buildings is the great Waxham barn, dated by tree-ring evidence to 1583–84. It is one of the largest in the county, comparable only with those at Godwick (No. 58) and Paston, built by Norfolk's other two most influential families, the Cokes and the Pastons. Their size reflects the great wealth of these Norfolk magnates and were built to store their own produce as well as to impress. Internally, Waxham is 53.75m long, 8.5m wide and 11.5m high. It is built of flint with brick dressings around the window openings. Reused ashlar is used in the three original cart entrances to the south and on the buttresses along the side walls. Those at the corners are angle buttresses, a technique found in medieval buildings that was probably used here so that stone salvaged from monastic sites did not need to be recut. The north wall and gable ends, which were visible from the house and its approaches, are decorated with a diaper pattern formed of brick headers. Ventilation slits around the building are also edged with brick. The roof is thatched and supported by twenty massive roof trusses. It is unusual, but similar to that at Godwick and Paston in that it is composed of two different types of trusses that alternate along the building. Perhaps the same group of craftsmen were involved at all three sites. During the eighteenth or nineteenth century opposing cart entrances were cut through the north wall and wings enclosing a livestock yard were built at either end.

Left: *The manorial complex at Waxham from the south-west. To the north (top of the picture) are what remains of the original wall, still with its central gatehouse, that surrounded the hall. The barn in the foreground is now divided from the hall by twentieth-century sheds, and the church is to the right. (John Fielding)*

Below: *The fifteenth-century thatched Waxham barn with its nineteenth-century side wings surrounding yards on both sides. (John Fielding)*

A café occupies the south-east wing and the barn can be hired for private functions. It is open when the café is operating. There is a display explaining its history and a guidebook for sale in the café. (Car park: NR12 0EA)

FURTHER READING

Heywood, S., and Ayton, J., 1994, 'Waxham Great Barn', *The Annual*, pp.24–33.

66. WYMONDHAM MARKET HOUSE

One of the many joys of exploring Norfolk is the number of market towns often with an open marketplace where grand Jacobean and Georgian residences built for the wealthy townspeople stand beside humbler dwellings and buildings often retaining Victorian shop fronts. Impressive inns with arched carriage entrances dating from the coaching age dominate some marketplaces. Many have nineteenth-century corn halls (No. 76) and all have their individual character. Records of 174 markets, some of which only flourished for a short time, can be traced to the period before the Black Death in 1349. Many disappeared, with only thirty-one remaining in the seventeenth century. By the nineteenth century there were just fifteen about 16km apart from each other. Eight kilometres was about as far as traders would want to travel with their animals and goods for sale.

Wymondham's Friday market was established by a charter from King John in 1204. The charming octagonal timber-framed building, called the Market Cross, dominates the triangular marketplace, standing at the upper end. There was probably a market house here from the Middle Ages. In 1389 the prior of Wymondham recorded that various miracles were said to have happened by the cross in the public highway. This may have been destroyed at the Reformation or in the 1615 town fire that gutted the whole centre of the town, which was then almost completely rebuilt. The streets radiating from the marketplace are still lined with some fine

Wymondham marketplace with the market house in its centre. (John Fielding)

The octagonal timber-framed market house, built in 1617–18, now used as a tourist information centre. (Peter Wade-Martins)

The mid-fifteenth-century Green Dragon public house with three of its four original shop windows. (Peter Wade-Martins)

timber-framed and jettied seventeenth-century houses. Only the Green Dragon pub, opposite the chapel of St Thomas Becket in Church Street, survives from before the fire. Dating from the mid-fifteenth century, it retains four arched shop windows, like those at Walsingham (No. 48).

The new Wymondham market house was constructed in 1617–18. The upper floor is supported on eight posts with a middle post connected to the outer ones by a spider's web of arched braces in the roof. Below the upper room is the open area supported by wooden pillars. Arched braces support the upper floor decorated with original carvings containing representations of spindle wheels, spoons and carpentry tools; a reminder that Wymondham was the centre of spoon and brush making. The windows were replaced in 1863 when the exterior plaster was removed to reveal the timber studwork. The outer stair was replaced in 1989.

The upper room was probably used for sessions of the market court, which were held every Tuesday where offences against the rules of the market were heard. Market tolls and stall holders' fees would be collected. It was very much the centre of the community, with royal proclamations read there, laws published and criminals punished. As the market declined in importance with the coming of the railway, the purpose of the upper room changed and it became a reading room from about 1870 to 1912. It now contains the town's tourist information centre.

The upper room is open during tourist information centre hours. 'A walk around old Wymondham', obtained from the tourist information centre, is an excellent walking guide to the historic centre of the town and Wymondham Abbey. (NR18 0YY)

FURTHER READING

Barringer, C., 2005, 'Markets and Fairs in the 18th and 19th centuries' in Ashwin, T. and Davison, A. (eds), *An Historical Atlas of Norfolk*, pp.138–139 (Phillimore).

Wymondham Heritage Society, 2018, *The Wymondham Market Cross 400th Anniversary,* (Wymondham Heritage Society).

67. THE CUSTOM HOUSE, KING'S LYNN

The Custom House, beside Purfleet Quay in King's Lynn, was built as a merchants' exchange in 1683 and has been described as 'one of the most perfect classical buildings in provincial England' (Pevsner and Wilson, 1999, p.111). Designed by local architect Henry Bell (1647–1711), it was inspired by both Dutch and London buildings of the period. Its resemblance to the old Town Hall in Amsterdam as depicted by seventeenth-century Dutch painters is striking. Originally the ground floor had open arcades similar to market houses such as at Wymondham (No. 66). It now houses the town's tourist information centre.

While Norfolk's great country houses were designed by nationally famous architects, local men were responsible for work in the major towns. Henry Bell was the son of a wealthy King's Lynn merchant who after a Cambridge education and undertaking the Grand Tour took up architecture as a serious pastime. It was unusual for an architect to come, not from the aristocratic or gentry class, but from a mercantile background. His first commission was outside Norfolk in Northampton, where he was responsible for re-planning and building the town after a disastrous fire in 1675. He was much influenced by the baroque architecture of Wren and Vanburgh and designed several buildings in King's Lynn.

The elegant custom house in King's Lynn overlooking the Purfleet. (David Robertson)

The Duke's Head public house on the Tuesday Market was probably also his work and was built for the merchant John Turner, for whom he also designed a fourteen-bay classical house on the opposite side of the market that was destroyed by fire in 1768. A later Norfolk commission was the rebuilding of North Runcton church, where he was a trustee, between 1703 and 1713.

The Custom House is open during tourist information centre hours. (PE30 1DU)

FURTHER READING

Richards, P., 1990, *King's Lynn*, p.65 (Phillimore).

Denver Sluice from the south. The Cut Off Channel comes in from the bottom right into the straight Relief Channel which flows north to Kings Lynn. The River Great Ouse comes in from the bottom left then curves to the left before meandering north to the sea roughly parallel with the Relief Channel. The two seventeenth-century cuts, the Old Bedford River and the New Bedford River, feed into the Great Ouse from the left just beyond Denver Sluice. (John Fielding)

Looking north along the Ouse Washes between the two Bedford Rivers. (John Fielding)

68. DENVER SLUICE AND THE DRAINING OF THE PEAT FENS

The Norfolk fens are divided between the siltlands bordering the Wash, or Marshland as this area became known, and the peat fens further inland to the south. To understand the modern-day drainage of the eastern peat fens it is important to understand the significance of Denver Sluice, first built in 1653. This sluice represents the culmination of various fenland drainage schemes that go back to the 1630s. At Denver the waters of the Great Ouse divide between the original course of the river and a new cut, the Relief Channel, which was dug between 1954 and 1959 parallel with the river for 17km. This joins the Ouse lower down just before King's Lynn so that the two together can deliver fenland flood water into the Wash.

Flowing into the Relief Channel at Denver is the Cut Off Channel, completed in 1964, which starts near Mildenhall. Over a distance of 43km it intercepts the waters of the Lark, the Little Ouse and the Wissey and conveys them into the Relief Channel. The Cut Off Channel was cleverly modified in 1972 under a water transfer scheme so that the flow could be reversed in dry weather away from Denver. Then, with the help of pumping stations, a tunnel and a pipeline, the water feeds into the upper reaches of the Essex river system and into reservoirs serving Chelmsford and Colchester – a distance of 145km.

At Denver there are also the outflows of two long straight cuts that feed into the Great Ouse just below the Sluice. These are known as the Old Bedford River (opened in 1637) and the New Bedford River (opened in 1651) and were a part of the original drainage scheme designed by the great Dutch engineer Sir Cornelius Vermuyden to take water out of the low-lying peat fen to the south.

Until the seventeenth century the southern peat fens were a land of water and grassland used for cattle grazing, fishing and fowling. It was reliably reported that people often walked about on stilts! However, the seventeenth century was a time of great enthusiasm for agricultural improvement where marginal land everywhere was being reclaimed and brought under the plough. The possible drainage of these fens offered a spectacular challenge because it would be so expensive. This was the age of the 'Adventurers', who were willing to risk their capital in ventures such as this, and the 'Undertakers', who were contracted to carry out the work.

The first significant move came in 1630 when a group of landowners near Thorney and Whittlesey approached the Duke of Bedford to provide the money to drain an area of 76,000ha, which later became known as the Bedford Level. This was an enormous undertaking that few people other than the Duke could afford. The key part of the scheme as advocated by Vermuyden was to bypass the meandering Great Ouse by digging a long straight cut, which became known as the Old Bedford River, from the upper reaches of the Ouse near Earith down to re-join the river at Denver. This was completed in 1637. In 1650 Vermuyden was asked to dig a second, wider, cut parallel with the first, known as the New Bedford River or the Hundred Foot Drain because of its width. This was intended to be the main channel for the waters of the Great Ouse. Denver Sluice stopped the heavy flow of water coming down the New Bedford River from then flowing up the old course of the Great Ouse when tides lower down were high. The area between the two Bedford Rivers, known as the Ouse Washes, was designed to be washlands that acted as a reservoir to hold water at times of heavy rain. Great banks were constructed on the outer sides of the two Bedford Rivers to keep the waters of the washlands from spreading over the surrounding land.

Neither Vermuyden nor any of the other early engineers foresaw the consequences of these cuts. As the peat began to dry out it shrank rapidly, thus making it impossible for the water to flow off the fields into the new cuts. The better the drainage, the more rapidly the peat wasted. What had seemed like a promising enterprise in 1652 had become a tragedy within fifty years.

The solution to the problem was to introduce pumping engines to lift the water from the field dykes into the drains and then into the rivers. The only satisfactory source of power to drive these engines was wind, and it was the introduction of wind pumps that saved the peat fens from re-flooding. Scoop wheels lifted the water from one level to the next, and by 1725 four-sailed wind pumps had become commonplace. On William Faden's map of Norfolk of 1797 they are shown all along the banks of the Great Ouse upstream of Denver Sluice. Sadly, none survive in Norfolk today, but there is one at the National Trust's Wicken Fen reserve in Cambridgeshire. They were always wooden and were never replaced by brick tower mills, as in the Broads, because the riverbanks were not sufficiently stable to take their weight.

The continued lowering of the peat left riverbanks, which were standing on the peat, liable to collapse. Overspill became a problem and the peat under the banks became so porous that much of the water soaked out again. So the banks had to be strengthened. By the beginning of the nineteenth century the peat had sunk so much that wind pumps were no longer adequate either. Substantial areas of the peatland were liable to serious flooding once again. So, a 30hp steam engine was installed in 1820 5km south of Denver Sluice and others followed, all using Newcastle coal brought in on the waterways.

In Deeping Fen in Lincolnshire the power of these new steam pumps was demonstrated when a 60 and an 80hp pump working together, designed by Joseph Glynn, replaced forty-four wind pumps in draining 10,000ha in 1825. The steam pumps were massive beam engines in brick sheds and boiler rooms with their tall brick chimneys. Gradually wind pumps were replaced by coal-fired pumping stations with even more efficient centrifugal pumps replacing scoop wheels. The last great stretch of open water was Whittlesea Mere in Cambridgeshire covering 880ha, which was drained in 1851 in three weeks of continuous pumping. It was then kept dry even though the land surface dropped by up to 2m over the next seven years. Oil engines were introduced from 1913, but from 1948 electrically driven pumps took over.

While peat fen drainage has now been stabilised, the sad side of the success story is that many waterlogged archaeological sites buried for centuries or thousands of years in the peats are now being exposed on the surface and blown away in peatland dust storms. Also:

'… we bear witness to perhaps the greatest single ecological catastrophe that ever occurred in England. Consider too, that the process of "improvement" also swept away vast, undocumented and untold expanses of rich wildlife habitat around and beyond the core of the Fens. The scale of destruction is almost beyond comprehension.' (Rotheram, 2013, p.185)

On the positive side, there are plans to restore some of the few remaining peatlands. At the RSPB's Lakenheath Fen Nature Reserve in Suffolk there are ambitious plans to restore an extensive area as a part of a wider Wet Fens Partnership scheme. Between 1996 and 2002, 200ha of arable farmland was converted back into reed beds and meadows by water management and the planting of a third of a million reeds. So, in a small way at least some of the peatland drainage may yet go full circle.

The complex of sluices at Denver are visible from the road, and there are guided tours advertised. The Norfolk section of the Ouse Washes can be viewed from the Welney Wetland Centre at PE38 0AZ.

FURTHER READING

Astbury, A.K., 1957, *The Black Fens* (Golden Head Press).

Darby, H.C., 1968, *The Draining of the Fens* (Cambridge University Press).

Darby, H.C., 1983, *The Changing Fenland* (Cambridge University Press).

Godwin, H., 1978, *Fenland: Its Ancient Past and Uncertain Future* (Cambridge University Press).

Rotheram, I.D., 2013, *The Lost Fens: England's Greatest Ecological Disaster* (History Press).

Summers, S., 1973, *The Great Ouse: The History of a River Navigation* (David and Charles).

Above: *Happisburgh lighthouse and lighthouse keepers' cottages built in 1791. (Peter Wade-Martins)*

Left: *The spiral stairway running around the interior of the lighthouse. (Peter Wade-Martins)*

69. HAPPISBURGH LIGHTHOUSE

The Norfolk coast may not appear to present a danger for shipping since it has no rocky shoreline, but 14km out to sea from Happisburgh are Happisburgh Sands. In 1789 during severe winter storms seventy ships and 600 men were lost off this section of the coast. This led to the appointment by Trinity House of Captain Joseph Hoddard to carry out a survey of the shoals off 'Hasborough Gatt and the Newarp Bank' with a view to establishing a floating lighthouse. As a result, two floating lights, and two lighthouses (the high' and 'low') were built on land at Happisburgh in 1791, lit by red patent lamps and reflectors that could be seen 24 to 27km offshore in fine weather. The two lights could be used to guide vessels around the southern end of the sands. Faden's map of Norfolk of 1797 shows coal-fired lighthouses at Cromer, Happisburgh, Winterton and Caister-on-Sea with smoke billowing from them. However, this did not prevent one of England's worst naval disasters when in 1801, HMS *Invincible*, on its way to join Nelson's fleet in the Baltic, became grounded and sunk with the loss of 400 of its crew of 595.

During the nineteenth century, the intensity of the lights was improved several times. In 1863 new lamps were installed, but the prisms are still in use. In 1865 gas replaced oil lamps. Uniquely, the gas was manufactured on site from coal and stored in gas holders behind the lighthouse. In 1883 the low light was threatened by coastal erosion and had to be demolished. Shortly afterwards, to distinguish the high light from that at Winterton, it was painted with three distinctive red bands. Gas was replaced by paraffin in 1910, followed by acetylene and finally electricity in 1947. At the base of the lighthouse are two square, simple classical lighthouse keepers' houses with passageways to the tower.

Threatened with closure in 1988, the lighthouse was taken over by an independent trust and it remains operational.

The lighthouse is open to the public on advertised days. (NR12 0PY)

FURTHER READING

Denton, T. and Leach, N., 2010, *Lighthouses of England: The South East* (Foxglove Media).

70. THE GREAT BARN, HOLKHAM

The Great Barn at Holkham from the south-west. (Susanna Wade-Martins)

The Great Barn in Holkham Park was built by Thomas William Coke, later the first Earl of Leicester of Holkham, between 1784 and 1792 as a showpiece to be visited by his guests attending the annual sheep shearings. This was an annual three-day event attended by leading farmers and aristocracy to promote improved farming techniques. The barn was the work of Samuel Wyatt, a country house architect who was employed by the estate at the time designing park lodges, farmhouses and farm buildings. Wyatt enjoyed trying new techniques and layouts and the Great Barn was no exception. Welsh slates were used on the original sill openings as well as on the roof rather than the locally available clay tiles. Instead of the more usual E-plan for farm buildings with a long barn and cattle sheds in the arms enclosing yards, here the barn is at a controlling central point in the middle surrounded by cattle yards. The building itself is cased in yellow bricks in a simple classical style with two porches under porticos, thus breaking away from the local vernacular, and instead more in keeping with the hall. The hall (No. 87), built by Thomas William's predecessor, another Thomas, was designed as a 'Temple to the arts', while the barn was seen as a temple to improved agriculture. Great patriotic landlords, such as Coke, were custodians not only of the arts, but also of agriculture. Before the trees surrounding the barn grew up it was visible from the house, and the link between the two was one that would have been made by Coke's contemporaries. It was the produce of farming that supported the great house and all it stood for. The Great Barn was a symbol of the improved agriculture of the time, as Ironbridge and Coalbrookdale in Shropshire were for industrial change.

The barn is not open but can be approached from walking routes within the park. (NR23 1RT)

FURTHER READING

Hiskey, C., 2016, *Holkham: The Social and Architectural History of a Great English Country House*, pp.296–297 (Unicorn Press).

Wade-Martins, S., 2009, *Coke of Norfolk*, pp.102–103 (Boydell).

71. THE NELSON MONUMENT, GREAT YARMOUTH

The number of Norfolk pubs with the name 'Nelson' or 'The Norfolk Hero', is an indication of how much the memory of Nelson has long been revered in the county. Born in the parsonage in Burnham Thorpe in 1758, he first went to sea as a midshipman in the *Raisnable* under his uncle, Captain Suckling, in 1771. By 1778 he was commanding his own ship, the *Agamemnon*. In 1793, aged 34, he held a farewell party for his neighbours in the pub in Burnham Thorpe, then called The Plough, before he left Norfolk to take up his first command as rear admiral and join the war against Napoleon. On arriving in Great Yarmouth, returning overland via Hamburg from the Mediterranean in November 1800, he was greeted as a returning hero and sworn in as a freeman of the borough proclaiming, 'I am a Norfolk man and glory in being so.' The following year Yarmouth Roads was the assembly point for the Baltic fleet, and Nelson was again in the town. Returning there after a successful expedition, he visited the naval hospital where sailors wounded in the Battle of Copenhagen were recovering. Yarmouth therefore felt a close association with Nelson and, after his death on HMS *Victory* at Trafalgar in 1805 and the final defeat of Napoleon at Waterloo in 1815, a group of local dignitaries began raising the money to erect a monument to him. Suggestions included a memorial in Norwich Cathedral, on Castle Hill and at the junction of the Newmarket and Ipswich roads on the edge of the old city. Finally, a site on the Denes, south of the naval hospital at Great Yarmouth, was agreed, the land given by Yarmouth Corporation.

The 'Naval Pillar' in Great Yarmouth from the south-east. (John Fielding)

Grecian Victories support the globe with Britannia above on top of the 'Naval Pillar'. (Peter Wade-Martins)

The monument was designed by the Norwich architect and a leading protagonist of the Greek Revival, William Wilkins. In 1817 he had submitted designs for a 'Waterloo Monument' in London that was never built, but his interest in Greek architecture is fully illustrated in the 'Naval Pillar' at Yarmouth, built between 1817 and 1819. On the sides of the square capital of the Doric column, the names of the four most famous of Nelson's victories (Trafalgar, Aboukir, St Vincent and Copenhagen) are inscribed. Above, six draped Grecian Victories support on their heads a drum surmounted by a globe inscribed with Nelson's motto *Palmam Qui Meruit Ferat* (Let him who has merited take the palm) and a statue of Britannia. The monument is 44m high and 217 steps wind their way up the interior of the pillar to a small observation platform on the top. It is a pity that it is now surrounded by a sad-looking industrial estate.

Nelson is also remembered in his birthplace of Burnham Thorpe, where his father was parson and he was born. The parsonage has since been rebuilt, but the pub, now called The Lord Nelson, still stands.

The column was restored for the bicentenary of the battle of Trafalgar in 2005 and is open to the public on a limited basis. (NR30 3PS)

FURTHER READING

Lewis, C., 2005, *Nelson I Am Myself a Norfolk Man* (Poppyland).
Pocock, T., 1994, *Horatio Nelson*, second edition (Pimlico).

There are many good biographies of Nelson available, but these two books emphasise his Norfolk connections.

72. GRESSENHALL UNION WORKHOUSE

By the late eighteenth century the system of poor relief based on a poor rate levied by individual parishes was in crisis. A rise in population and economic dislocation meant that these rudimentary methods of helping the poor were no longer able to cope. In Norfolk the collapse of hand spinning and weaving meant an important source of employment was disappearing, and there was a surplus of labour in the countryside. Although new farming techniques were labour intensive, work was seasonal. Because of the shortage of employment, work was often casual and low paid, frequently well below a living wage. Various solutions were tried. In some parishes a dole to support wages was given, while elsewhere parishes grouped together in 'corporations' to build 'houses of industry'. Those who were unable to make ends meet would only be helped if they moved into them. Loans were available for the building work and it was claimed that this 'indoor relief' was a far cheaper solution than helping people in their own homes ('outdoor relief'). Six Corporation Houses of Industry, mostly in the east of the county, were built by 1805, reflecting the scale of rural near-destitution in these relatively highly populated areas.

The front of the Mitford and Launditch Union workhouse at Gressenhall from the south-east with the chapel to the left and long residential wings to the right. (John Fielding)

The House of Industry at Gressenhall was built at a cost of £15,000 on former common land for the Mitford and Launditch Hundreds and opened in 1776. Inmates worked on a 50-acre (20ha) farm providing food for the paupers. The plan of the original building was H-plan with a seven-bay range with a central three-bay classical pediment topped with clock, cupula and bell to summon paupers from the fields. To the east, an L-plan range, originally fronted by an open arcade that was later enclosed, housed paupers in small, single-cell family units.

The 1834 Poor Law Amendment Act enforced a national system of workhouses administered through Unions of parishes. Outdoor relief was abolished and conditions in the workhouse were harsh. Families were split and housed in different wings, and men and women had access to separate exercise yards. New buildings, work rooms and a perimeter wall were built at Gressenhall including, in 1868, a chapel designed by the Norwich architect R.M. Phipson. Gradually the system became less harsh. Aged married couples were housed together in a separate cottage range, now Cherry Tree Cottage. In 1930 the workhouse became a 'Public Assistance Institution' and in 1976 it was transferred to the Norfolk Museums Service, where part of it forms Gressenhall Farm and Workhouse Museum.

The museum is open from March to October: see the Norfolk Museums Service website for details. (Car park: NR20 4BT)

FURTHER READING

Digby, A., 1978, *Paupers' Palaces* (Routledge).

Dymond, D., 2005, 'Workhouses before 1834' in Ashwin T. and Davison, A. (eds), *An Historical Atlas of Norfolk*, pp.146–147 (Phillimore).

Pope, S., 2006, *Gressenhall Farm and Workhouse* (Poppyland).

73. PULHAM MARKET WORKHOUSE

The 1834 Poor Law Amendment Act was passed as a cost-cutting measure to reduce the expenditure on poor relief. Unlike the earlier systems, it was highly centralised under a Poor Law Board in London. Norfolk was divided into eighteen poor law 'Unions' each administered by Boards of Guardians, closely monitored from London. Twelve new workhouses were built and others, such as Gressenhall (No. 72), were enlarged. Standardised plans for the new buildings were produced by the Board, emphasising an element of control that made claiming poor relief an unpleasant experience. Workhouses such as Pulham Market were arranged around a central hub with wings accommodating different 'classes' of pauper. High walls divided the yards between the four radiating wings. Children, men and women, including married couples, were separated. Pulham Market Workhouse, serving Depwade Union, was designed by the Norwich architect William Thorold along the lines recommended by London to hold 400 paupers at a cost of nearly £10,000. He was also responsible for designing workhouses at Thetford, Kenninghall, Rockland All Saints, Hindringham and Great Snoring.

The Depwade Union workhouse at Pulham Market from the north-west. The two remaining gun turrets are visible at the two rear corners of the perimeter wall. (John Fielding)

Most have been demolished but at Pulham Market the original layout and many of the buildings remain. The whole was surrounded by a high wall, since partly demolished, with gun turrets at the corners. The Board of Guardians had to justify this extra expense to London, writing that it was necessary to protect the workhouse from attacks by the local poor infuriated by the end of outdoor relief forcing the destitute to move into this prison-like building if they needed help. Two policemen had to be employed in summer 1837 to protect the building while it was being completed.

The building now stands by the busy A140 and can be seen from the road. It is partly converted to flats and partly a hotel. Park at the garden centre beside the site for a stroll around the exterior of the buildings. (IP21 4YJ)

FURTHER READING

Digby, A., 1978, *Paupers' Palaces* (Routledge).

Digby, A., 2005, 'Poor Law Unions and Workhouses, 1834–1930' in Ashwin T. and Davison, T., *An Historical Atlas of Norfolk*, pp.148–149 (Phillimore).

Wade-Martins, S., 1988, *Norfolk: A Changing Countryside*, pp.57–58 (Phillimore).

74. HORSEY WIND PUMP AND DRAINAGE OF THE BROADLAND MARSHES

The large area of marshland to the west of Great Yarmouth formed when the main rivers through the area (the Bure, Yare and Thurne) were blocked by the sand spit on which the town now stands. Less extensive are the marshes along the Thurne between Horsey and Waxham. Embanking of the marshes began in the Middle Ages, and isolated grazing farms were established on higher patches of ground. At that time the only form of drainage was long serpentine dykes following the lines of earlier natural creeks.

It was not until the eighteenth century that the use of wind pumps to raise water from the new dykes into the rivers using a scoop wheel began. Initially the pumps were wooden structures, but by the mid century more substantial brick tower mills were built. The earliest dated examples are at Oby (1753) and Brograve, near Hickling (1773). By the time of Faden's map of Norfolk, published in 1797, there were forty-seven mills across the Broadland marshes. The early mills had canvas 'common' sails that had to be spread across the wooden frames of the sails

Horsey windpump, dated 1912, from the south, built to lift water from the dyke in the foreground into the staithe connecting with Horsey Mere beyond. (John Fielding)

by hand. The caps to which the sails were attached had to be turned into the wind using a tail pole. The fantail, invented in 1745, ensured that the sails could be turned automatically into the wind, and in 1807 William Cubitt's patent sails fitted with automatically adjusting shutters compensated for wind speed. From 1851, the invention of the centrifugal, or 'turbine', pump began to replace the scoop wheel. This was a vertical screw that raised water by centrifugal force, driven through bevel pinions off the driving wheel on the main mill shaft. This meant that mills were able to drain a much larger area. In a steady wind the turbine could lift half as much water again as the scoop wheel. However, they were more difficult to manufacture and maintain, and scoop wheels remained popular. During the 1920s there were still thirty wind pumps working in the Halvergate area (No. 98), but the last stopped working in 1953 as diesel, and later electric, pumps replaced wind power.

The present mill at Horsey is one of the last to be built and so contained all the latest technology. It is probably the fourth on the site and was constructed by the local millwright Dan England of Ludham. It replaced the Black Mill, which had been built between 1797 and 1826, but the cap blew off in 1895. Although it was replaced two years later, it was clear that the structure was unstable and the new mill on the footprint of the old was built in 1905. It was last used in 1943 when it was struck by lightning, and, like so many other mills at the time, it was replaced by a diesel pump. The Horsey estate was acquired by the National Trust in 1948 and there have been several periods of restoration since then, the latest being completed in 2019.

Other mills that have been, or are due to be, restored include the Stracey Arms wind pump on the A47, Hardley Mill at Langley near Chedgrave and Thurne Mill, where there is a wind energy museum.

It is now possible to climb Horsey Mill, admire its beautifully restored machinery and walk out onto the gallery around the cap, where there are fine views across the marshes. Check the National Trust website for opening times. (Car park: NR29 4EE)

FURTHER READING

Earl. S., 1993, 'Windpumps' in Wade-Martins, P. (ed.), *An Historical Atlas of Norfolk*, pp.164–165 (Norfolk Museums Service).

Macnair, A. and Williamson, T., 2010, *William Faden and Norfolk's 18th-Century Landscape* (WINDgather).

Maltster, R., 2003, *The Norfolk and Suffolk Broads* (Phillimore).

Yardy, A. and Scott, M., 2005, 'Windmills' in Ashwin, T. and Davison, A. (eds), *An Historical Atlas of Norfolk*, pp.172–173 (Phillimore).

75. WELLS SEA BANK AND RECLAMATION OF THE COASTAL MARSHES

Those who choose to walk the distance from Wells town to the beach along the top of the mile-long bank will be aware of the contrast between the landscape of water and salt marshes to the right (east) and the green fields to the left (west). This earthwork marks the final phase of marsh drainage along this section of the coast, which began at the end of the seventeenth century in Holkham parish to the west to create summer grazing pastures. It is also part of the wider history of post-medieval land reclamation along Norfolk's north and west coasts.

In 1840 a report by the civil engineer J.M. Rendle proposed the construction of a bank that would both protect the northern marshes between Holkham and Wells from the sea and keep the channel through to the port at Wells free of encroachment by the sand dunes. However, it was very expensive, and it was not until 1852

Wells sea bank from the south-east with salt marshes to the right and the reclaimed pasture to the left. (Mike Page)

that work commenced on a less ambitious scheme, with the building of the main bank beginning in 1857. The total cost was £18,700 (double the original estimate). The newly reclaimed land to the west of the bank was divided into rectilinear fields that were steam ploughed and cultivated before being laid down to pasture in the 1880s. Although there was a major breach in 1862 and again in the 1970s, the advancing sand dunes have been held back and the main channel kept open for shipping. The bank remains a vital part of Norfolk's coastal defences.

There is a car park at the north end of the bank from where it is possible to walk along the bank into Wells. (Car park: NR23 1DR)

FURTHER READING

Hiskey, C., 2016, *Holkham: The Social, Architectural and Landscape History of a Great English Country House*, pp.444–447 (Unicorn Press).

76. DISS CORN HALL

The 'golden years' of agricultural prosperity in the middle of the nineteenth century spawned a unique type of building: the corn hall. Corn halls were built in many of Norfolk's market towns such as Fakenham (1854–55), Dereham (1856–57), Swaffham (1858) and Attleborough (1863). However, by far the grandest was constructed in Diss in 1854. King's Lynn and Norwich also had their halls, that at King's Lynn built in 1854 and Norwich in 1861.

Diss' medieval wealth came from the manufacture of linen from the locally grown flax and hemp, but by the nineteenth century corn was more important. Farmers would come in to do business at the corn hall and banks, while their families would frequent the various shops behind their elaborate shop fronts around the central triangle.

All these halls were commercial ventures and served two purposes. Firstly, they provided a venue for the sale of corn. The various grain merchants had desks within the large hall to which farmers would bring samples of grain on market day with which to bargain. The decline of the halls can be dated to the growth of a national grain market after the Second World War, although that at Diss was one of the last to close in the 1990s. They also served as venues for local entertainment, such as bazaars, sales of work, Friendly Society dinners, concerts and exhibitions. Some, as at Diss, also contained reading rooms and libraries.

Diss corn hall with its elaborate classical front and the new arts centre behind. (John Fielding)

One of the corn merchant's desks used in the corn hall. (Peter Wade-Martins)

Prior to the building of a hall, grain merchants would do business in local pubs, but in 1854 Thomas Lombe Taylor, Lord of the Manor of Diss and part owner of the local brewery, announced that he would be building a corn hall, which he would then hand to trustees to manage. It was designed by George Atkins of Diss and built on Market Hill, in accordance with Taylor's wishes, by local workmen. It is a striking classical building and a copy of the Ilisus temple in Athens with a central portico carried on Ionic columns. The central hall is still impressive with giant Doric pilasters and, like Dereham, it originally had a glass roof. *The London Illustrated News* reported that: 'The building is not only admirably adapted to its purpose, but beautiful in the harmony of its proportions and ornamentation.'

In 2010 a programme of work to restore the corn hall as an arts and events centre was included in a major town centre improvement scheme. With the help of both local support and a major lottery grant, this project included the regeneration of the surrounding shopping streets. The Heritage Triangle project, completed in 2017, has rejuvenated the area as a bustling centre with shops, cafés and leisure facilities. Useful panels provide information about the history of the various shops and businesses. The corn hall is now restored to its former glory and remains at the centre of the social and cultural life of Diss. A new wing contains exhibition galleries and a café as well as an interactive display on the history of Diss and the hall. The original trading room has been completely restored and is used for concerts and events as well as the town's council chamber.

The corn hall, café and galleries are open from 10 a.m. until 4 p.m. six days a week. (IP22 4LB)

FURTHER READING

Diss Heritage Triangle Trust, 2018, *Traders of the Triangle and their Shops* (Diss Heritage Triangle Trust).
Howkins, A., 2013, 'Diss Corn Hall', *Rural History Today* 25, pp.2–4.

77. LETHERINGSETT WATERMILL

Letheringsett may seem an unlikely place to see an impressive complex of industrial buildings in such a rural setting. Here we find not only a large watermill, but also, next door, a maltings and brewery (No. 78), both relying for their existence on locally produced wheat and barley.

Descending to the west of Holt, the A148 road takes a sharp bend across the River Glaven. To the left, before crossing the river, is a water mill, the only one still grinding flour in the county. Five hundred and eighty water mills are mentioned in Domesday Book, one of them at Letheringsett. Between sixty and seventy are shown on Faden's map of 1797, and they played a crucial role in the county's economy, grinding not only flour, but also animal feed, bone for fertilisers and pounding rags for paper. A mill on this site is mentioned in various documents from the Middle Ages to the eighteenth century.

The triple-gable four-storey watermill and millpond, built in 1804, from the west. (Peter Wade-Martins)

The mill stones in modern wooden casings on the upper floor. (Peter Wade-Martins)

The present building was erected by Richard Rous in 1804 and consists of a triple-gable, four-storey building capable of housing four sets of millstones. It is an example of the more sophisticated type of mill being built at that time. The less efficient undershot wheels were being replaced with either overshot or breast-shot wheels. Here the wheel fed by a mill pond can either operate as an undershot, or, by lifting a sluice to raise the water level to halfway up the wheel, operate as a more efficient breast-shot wheel. The mill went out of use in 1946 and lay derelict until the 1980s, when it was restored and has been milling since 1986. Designed to house four working grinding stones, there are now two producing about 3.5 tons of flour a week.

The mill and shop are open most days except Sundays during the summer months. (NR25 7YB)

78. LETHERINGSETT MALTINGS

An advertisement in the local paper for 12 August 1780 announcing the sale of a 'Brewing Office, large Malt House with convenient buildings thereto belonging with a Publick House adjoining' attracted the eye of the ambitious Coltishall maltster and brewer William Hardy I (1732–1811). Anxious to extend his business, he bought the business along with a small farm and moved to Letheringsett in 1781.

A brewery and malt house are mentioned in a deed of 1749, but when William took over, he immediately set about reorganising the brewery. In 1797 he passed over the management of the site to his son William Hardy II (1770–1842) and it was during his time that the business flourished and output was at its peak, enabling him to buy neighbouring Letheringsett Hall in 1803 and the water mill (No. 77) in 1826. Elsewhere, malt houses and breweries were moving into the towns as these businesses became larger, capital intensive and more mechanised, but William's business acumen meant he saw the advantage of bucking the trend and remaining near the source of his main raw material, barley for malting, and convenient for supplying the tied pubs that formed the bulk of the brewery's trade. Mid century it was producing about 2,100 barrels a year compared with the larger Norwich firms with an annual output of between 5,000 and 10,000 barrels. A hundred pubs were 'tied' to Letheringsett at some point between 1781 and 1895, when the business was sold to Morgans brewery in Norwich.

After William's death in 1842, family involvement in the business declined until the final sale of the complex to Morgans. By 1936 the brewery building itself was occupied by a bus company but it burnt down that year and was then demolished. Although the brewery buildings have gone, the tun house and the associated maltings, with the malt house with two impressive kilns with revolving cowls fronting the road, survived and remained derelict until recently.

With their architectural embellishments, the malt kilns would be the first to be seen and admired by travellers coming down the road from Holt and before crossing the elegant brick bridge, erected by William Hardy II in 1818. The present kilns were rebuilt after a fire in 1827, although the long malt house survived and probably pre-dates William Hardy's purchase of the site. A plaque with the initials WH and the date 1814 remains on one exterior wall of the tun house where the great casks were housed for maturing and conditioning the beer. Many of the other buildings within the complex were converted to housing between 2013 and 2015 and are hidden behind high walls and gates, but the size and scale of the original operation is still clear. The main long north–south building was the malt house, probably built before 1780 with steeping tanks housed at the southern end and enlarged in 1814. Here the barley was soaked before being spread across the two levels of malting floors along the length of the malt house building. Careful control of the temperature and humidity was needed, which explains the range of window openings at two levels in the long walls that are typical of malt houses. The barley was kept turned with wooden

The malt kilns, built 1827, dominate the bend in the busy A148 Holt to Fakenham road. The malt kilns face the road, while the long malthouses with two levels of malting floors stretch back behind. To the right around a courtyard are stables and cartsheds. The only remaining brewery building is the hipped roof tun house for storing full barrels on the right-hand side. (John Fielding)

shovels until the grain started to sprout. It was then placed on the floor of perforated tiles above the furnace in the kilns, where it would be roasted. The whole range of malt house and kilns is 45m long. Under the malt house ran a tunnel carrying water from the river that powered a water wheel for the malt mill under the kilns. Other buildings around the yard included open cart sheds, storage buildings and a stable block. The size and architectural significance of these buildings, as well as the complex arrangements of sluices, mill pond and tunnels to turn the water wheel to power the malt mill, was emphasised in a report to North Norfolk District Council in 1996. This described them as 'arguably the most important industrial complex in Norfolk'.

The whole complex has been converted to housing, but the unique architecture of this rural industrial group can be appreciated by driving round to the car park of the King's Head, a fine late-Georgian gault brick building of 1808, and walking back towards the road. (NR25 7YB)

FURTHER READING

Bird, M., 2020, *Mary Hardy and Her World Vol. 2: Barley, Beer and the Working Year*, pp.227–394. (Burnham Press).

Durst, D., 2004, 'Letheringsett: Industrial Archaeology in a Rural Setting, part 4', *Journal of the Norfolk Industrial Archaeology Society* 7, pp.5–40.

79. BILLINGFORD WINDMILL

The milling of grain as well as other seeds has always been an important rural industry and Billingford is the only Norfolk windmill that retains its original machinery. Many of the suitable sites for watermills were already occupied by Domesday (1086). However, it is not until the thirteenth century that there are references to windmills in the county, and an open trestle, or 'post' mill is shown on the great brass on the tombstone of Adam de Walsokne and his wife dated 1349 in St Margaret's Minster, King's Lynn. These early mills were wooden and the whole structure turned into the wind on a post. In the eighteenth century brick mills were constructed where only the cap turned the mill machinery inside. Faden's map of 1797 was the first county map to depict windmills and shows 256 across the county. This was probably a time when numbers were at their highest. Windmill technology, which had been improved in the eighteenth century (No. 74), coincided with a period of agricultural prosperity when most of the cereals eaten were home-produced rather than imported. From the 1870s milling began to be concentrated in ports. Only eleven were working in 1937.

The last windmill to work was that at Billingford, 5km to the east of Diss. Closing in 1956, it was the first to be acquired by the Norfolk Windmill Trust in 1965. The present brick tower mill was built in 1860 after a 'flour mill, nearly new' was blown down. The mound on which this post mill stood can still be seen to the south-west of the present mill. The builder was the miller, G. Goddard, whose name and date are carved into the brick-work, but only visible in low light. The mill has five storeys with a Norfolk-style, boat-shaped wooden cap and a six-bladed fan tail to turn the sails into the wind. The boat-shaped cap was introduced by the England family of millwrights from Ludham and is found across central and eastern Norfolk and Suffolk. Mills in the west of the county have domed ogee-type caps in common with the traditional styles of Lincolnshire. The cap is designed to turn on wheels running along a metal track around the top of the brick wall and the fantail ensures that the sails are always facing into the wind. Most windmills

Billingford windmill, built 1860. (Mike Page)

were worked by four sails. They are carried on wooden stocks and are fitted with shutters that can be adjusted depending of the strength of the wind. The tension of the shutter mechanism is set by a weight on a chain. The force of the wind opens the shutters as it increases and the weight closes them as the wind decreases. All the machinery is driven off the wind shaft in the cap. Power is transferred via the 'headwheel' and 'wallower' to the vertical main shaft running down the centre of the building, from which the milling machinery is powered. The millstones are on the second floor. The bottom stone is fixed while the upper stone turns to grind the grain fed between the two stones through hoppers. The flour then runs out through a chute to where it is bagged.

> Billingford is the only Norfolk windmill that retains its original machinery. It has recently been repaired and should soon be milling and producing flour again. It stands on Billingford Common and can be seen from the Angles Way long-distance footpath. (IP21 4ND)

FURTHER READING

Apling, A., 1984, *Norfolk Corn Windmills* (Norfolk Windmills Trust).

Ling, J., 2015, *Windmills of Norfolk* (Amberley).

Rix, A., no date, *Billingford Windmill* (Norfolk Windmills Trust).

Yardy, A. and Scott, M., 2005, 'Windmills' in Ashwin, T. and Davison, A. (eds), *An Historical Atlas of Norfolk*, pp.172–173. (Phillimore).

80. FAKENHAM GASWORKS

The processing and producing of coal gas for sale was invented by William Murdoch in 1792. The subsequent spread of local gasworks across the country in the first half of the nineteenth century providing gas for municipal and household use must have transformed urban life as streets and houses could be lit at night. By 1830 Norfolk's three major centres had gasworks, with most smaller market towns following by 1850. The change to natural gas in the late 1960s meant that most of these premises with their characteristic gasholders beside them disappeared, with the last closing in 1981.

Fakenham gasworks opened in 1846, the town was lit by gas lamps later that year, and at its peak it was providing power for 500 households. The works were closed in 1965. The present buildings date from 1907–10 and are a rare example of a small gasworks relying on manually operated Victorian technology. As larger gasworks closed, they were demolished, and it soon became clear that Fakenham was the only one left in England and Wales. (The National Gas Museum in Leicester is housed in an ornate gatehouse, all that remains of a large urban enterprise.) As a result of the determination and hard work of a local committee, the Fakenham Museum of Gas and Local History was opened in 1987.

Aerial view of Fakenham gasworks showing the remaining gas holder to the left and the retort house with its brick chimney in the centre. Close to the retort house is a black tower in which the crude gas was passed through water to remove tar and ammonia. (John Fielding)

Inside the retort house. (Peter Wade-Martins)

Coal gas, commonly called town gas, was a mixture of inflammable gases (methane, carbon monoxide and hydrogen). It was produced by heating coal in sealed ovens called retorts. At Fakenham two underground furnaces heated fourteen retorts arranged in two settings. They are 2.9m long with doors at the front and pipes carrying away the crude gas. The stoker would charge the retorts by shovelling in coal using a long-handled shovel, then closing and sealing the door. When fully 'cooked' the hot coal residue (now mostly carbon and known as coke) was removed and the retorts restocked. This was hot, heavy and dirty work in an environment containing many toxic substances and explosive gases. The heated coal gave off volatile components (the flammable gases) as well tar, ammonia and hydrogen sulphide. The crude gas was passed through water causing the tar and ammonia to condense out. Hydrogen sulphide was removed by a chemical process in cast-iron boxes called purifiers. The cleaned gas was then stored in gasholders. Of the two at Fakenham when it closed, one remains. The by-products of coke, tar, ammonia and sulphur found ready markets. All the equipment for the manufacture and cleaning process survives at Fakenham and the whole sequence is clearly displayed.

The museum is open from Easter to October. Check their website for opening times. As well as the gasworks themselves there is a fine display of domestic gas appliances dating from Victorian times to the 1960s. The 'Further Reading' booklets listed below are all available at the museum. (NR21 9AY)

FURTHER READING

Anon, no date, *Fakenham Museum of Gas and Local History. Museum Guide* (Fakenham Museum of Gas and Local History).

Anon, no date, *History of Fakenham Museum of Gas and Local History* (Fakenham Museum).

Bridges, E.M., no date. *A History of Fakenham Museum of Gas and Local History Museum Guide.* (Fakenham Museum of Gas and Local History).

81. NORTH WALSHAM AND DILHAM CANAL

The earliest canals in Britain were built in the 1760s, connecting the coal-producing areas with markets in the fast-growing industrial towns and ports. Although they were slow, they were cheaper than road transport and suitable for heavy goods such as coal or delicate wares such as pottery. These busy canals could produce large profits for their owners and encouraged others to speculate on less viable routes. In an agricultural county such as Norfolk there was little incentive to build canals, but in 1812 an Act was passed authorising the construction of a canal 14.5km long connecting mills along the valley of the River Ant down to staithes at Wayford Bridge in Smallburgh. Until the canal was built, Wayford Bridge was as far as wherries could go upstream from Yarmouth, but the canal provided a direct water-borne connection from Yarmouth to four flour mills and two mills at Antingham grinding bones for fertiliser, as well as other agricultural goods. There were offshoots along Tyler's Cut to staithes at Dilham and East Ruston. Shares were sold and the canal finally opened in 1826. Lord Suffield, who owned the Antingham mills, was a major shareholder. The route required six locks to cope with the 18m drop along its length. They were built to accommodate Norfolk wherries, capable of carrying 18–20 tons of goods with a draught of 0.9m. Tolls were collected at Tonnage Bridge, where there was a wharf and a cottage.

Below left: *A stretch of the North Walsham and Dilham canal north of Tonnage Bridge, from the north, with in the foreground a branch of the canal leading to East Ruston Staithe. (John Fielding)*

Below right: *Lock walls at Honing Lock. (Peter Wade-Martins)*

Ebridge Mill, mill pond and canal lock to the left under restoration. (John Fielding)

The restored lock and lock gates at Bacton Wood. (Peter Wade-Martins)

The canal was never a financial success. Tolls were too high to attract the coal trade and there was only a sparse population along its route. The most northerly 2.25km to Antingham above Swafield were abandoned in 1893. Trade declined steadily, and in 1912 a breach in the canal bank at the northern end washed away several of the staithes. The mill owners, Edward Cubitt and George Walker, as the North Walsham Canal Company, bought the canal in 1922 and dredged the lower portions, but its last commercial use was in 1934.

At the southern end, the lock walls at Honing (TG331270) and Briggate (TG315274) are still standing, but the mill at Briggate was burnt down in 1975. The next mill upstream at Ebridge (TG311297), owned by Cubitt and Walker, was still partly water-powered in 1937. The water wheel was removed in 1966 and the mill has been skilfully converted to residential use overlooking the recently dredged and cleared mill pond. The lock and lock gates have been partly rebuilt by the North Walsham and Dilham Canal Trust, adding to the interest of this beautiful and now tranquil area that a century and half ago must have been busy with wherries loading and unloading bone fertiliser, flour, animal feed and grain. Much of the northern stretch is in private hands, but work is taking place to renovate this section of the canal as well. The mill pond at Antingham (TG264325) survives and a stream from it following the old canal flows through the gardens of the old mill (now called Antingham Lodge). The most northerly of the canal bridges is Bradfield Bridge (TG286319), and the next bridge is on the B1145 south of Swafield (TG286319). Here the canal terminated after 1893 and there is a small canal basin on either side of the bridge. Between here and the next bridge at Royston (TG297313) the canal runs along an embankment with a footpath beside it. At Bacton Wood ((TG299306) the canal lock and lock gates and quay have been fully restored and the owners hope to open the canal for water traffic up as far as Swafield and to start Bacton Wood Mill working as a water mill again.

While the northern part of the canal was abandoned above Swafield Bridge in 1893, there are several pleasant walks along the rest of the canal shown on the O.S. Explorer Map 252. From Tonnage Bridge (TG347260) for 3km up to Honing Lock there is a footpath that connects to Weavers Way. From Ebridge Mill (TG311297) there is a mixture of public and permissive footpaths that provide access up to Swafield Bridge (TG286319) and links to the Paston Way. Boat trips run from Ebridge Mill (for details see the North Walsham and Dilham Canal Trust website). Another way to see the canal is to canoe upstream (canoes can be hired at Wayford Bridge: TG349248) as far as Honing lock, a distance of just over 3.2km.

FURTHER READING

Boyes, J. and Ronald, R., 1977, *The Canals of Eastern England* (David and Charles).

82. EAST DEREHAM STATION AND THE COMING OF THE RAILWAYS

Norfolk, with its lack of heavy industry and large centres of population, was one of the last counties to see a railway network established. The Yarmouth to Norwich Railway was opened in 1844 and the Norwich to Brandon in 1845, providing a link on to London. Lines linking the major market towns of Dereham, Fakenham and Wymondham to Norwich and King's Lynn were all built by 1850, with stations along their route connecting previously remote villages to the major centres. This left much of the north coast without a railway, but in 1862 a line reached Hunstanton from King's Lynn and in 1877 Cromer and Sheringham were linked to Norwich. A Broadland line was opened from Norwich to North Walsham via Wroxham in 1874, providing routes to the major holiday resorts.

East Dereham's position in the middle of the county made it an important railway junction with trains to Norwich via Wymondham, King's Lynn via Swaffham, and Wells via Fakenham. Trains to London went via Wymondham and Brandon. Dereham station was opened in 1846 for freight and 1847 for passengers. Built of brick with stone dressings, it is a charming Tudor-style building with a restored

East Dereham station opened in 1846. (Peter Wade-Martins)

waiting room and ticket office and is the headquarters of the Mid-Norfolk Railway Company, which has reopened the line as far as Wymondham to the south and has plans to extend north to County School, North Elmham. Situated on the edge of the town, a new industrial area and streets of terrace housing rapidly grew up around it. Much of the nearby marshalling yard is now under modern buildings but two sets of maltings are evidence of the importance of the railway for the transport of agricultural produce.

The railway also provided for the import of industrial goods and raw materials as four iron foundries, agricultural implement makers, a steam sawmill, brewers, and a sack factory, established by the end of the nineteenth century, testify. Of equal importance was passenger transport, bringing people into East Dereham from neighbouring villages for market day. There were several trains to Norwich via Wymondham every day with connections to London. The Rev. Armstrong, vicar of Dereham, never ceased to wonder at the speed with which he could get to and from London. In 1863 he caught a train from London at 8 a.m., reaching his desk in Dereham by 3 p.m. 'It is only by such practical examples that we understand what wonderful things railways are and how time and space are annihilated by them' (quoted from his diaries in Wade-Martins, S., 2018, *A Vicar in Victorian Norfolk*, p. 195 (Boydell)).

The last British Rail passenger train left Dereham station in 1969, while goods traffic was carried for another twenty years. The ownership of the line from North Elmham to Wymondham was transferred to the Mid-Norfolk Railway Company in 1997.

The Mid-Norfolk Railway Company now run trains regularly, often with steam-powered engines, between Dereham and Wymondham at weekends during the summer. (NR19 1DF)

FURTHER READING

Gordon, D., 1977, *Regional History of the Railways of Great Britain Vol. 5 East Anglia.* (David and Charles).

Joby, R., 2005, 'Railways' in Ashwin, T. and Davison, A. (eds), *An Historical Atlas of Norfolk,* 152 (Phillimore).

83. GREAT YARMOUTH, MARINE PARADE

The development of Norfolk's tourist industry began in the eighteenth century when the wealthy leisured classes sought out the picturesque Norfolk coast for the health-giving sea air and bathing. Yarmouth was one of the first destinations to be discovered, and had become a fashionable bathing place and health resort by the middle of the eighteenth century, when there was a bath house near the sea front.

Yarmouth stands on the sand spit between the River Yare and the sea and faces both ways. The old town is crowded along narrow rows surrounded by the medieval town wall (No. 57) facing the riverside harbour, while the seaside resort sprang up on the eastern side facing out to sea. Further south, towards the sandy tip of the spit were the Denes where the Nelson Monument was built (No. 71) and on which local fishermen beached their open boats (a favourite subject for Norwich school painters) and set sail for inshore catches.

The southern part of Great Yarmouth Marine Parade. The landward side is lined with large nineteenth- and early twentieth-century shops, grand houses and hotels. The Wellington Pier and Winter Gardens are in the foreground. (John Fielding)

Postcard of 1908 looking north along Marine Parade with trams running along the landward side, bathing machines along the shore and the original Britannia Pier in the distance. (Postcard courtesy of Mike Page)

The main approach for visitors was by road and this route was made easier with the construction of the Acle Straight across the marshes in 1820. Yarmouth was discovered by Charles Dickens in the 1840s when he set scenes in *David Copperfield* there. He described it as 'The finest place in the Universe', and no doubt there actually were those such as Mr Peggotty who lived in upturned boats on the sands.

The real era of expansion of the resort came with the arrival of the railways in 1844 and the Bank Holiday Act of 1871. The Victoria Building Company constructed 'large and elegant mansions for the accommodation of the higher class of sea bather' on the sea front. Kimberley Terrace and the houses round Albert Square opposite Wellington Pier are good examples of their work. The Wellington and Britannia Piers were built in the 1850s (The Britannia was rebuilt in art nouveau style in 1901 and the entrance to the Wellington Pier in 1926.) and the town was described in 1854 as having achieved 'great celebrity as a bathing place'. The heyday of the resort was in the Edwardian period. The glass and iron Winter Gardens, now due to be restored, was purchased from Torquay by Yarmouth Corporation in 1903 and re-erected beside the Wellington Pier. Elaborate gardens were laid out alongside. At this time Yarmouth was described as the 'brightest and merryest resort in the kingdom', with two theatres, dancing in the Winter Gardens, the assembly rooms (built in 1863), golf and sandy beaches.

A ¾-mile long Marine Parade, linking the piers, was first constructed in 1857 and many of the buildings associated with the Victorian and Edwardian resort still stand along its length. In 1877 it was widened by 20m and new hotels, boarding houses and private houses built. The present Hollywood cinema was originally an aquarium opened in 1876. As well as tanks and ponds for a variety of fish, alligators and seals there was a reading room and a roller-skating rink on the roof. The tourist information centre is on the parade in a building built in 1861 as a sailors' home for shipwrecked mariners. The Hippodrome circus with its fine art nouveau terracotta facade was designed by R.S. Cockrill and built in the 1900s. It still contains the original circus ring. The Gem cinema, now the Windmill theatre, opened in 1908 as the first cinema in the town.

Although the glory days of the seaside resort are past, the flavour of this period can still be sensed in a walk along the Marine Parade on a sunny winter's afternoon. (NR30 2EH to NR30 3JG)

FURTHER READING

Gooch, M., 2017, *Historic Great Yarmouth* (Great Yarmouth Local History and Archaeological Society).

84. ST JAMES' MILL, WHITEFRIARS, NORWICH

It is perhaps surprising that a building described by Ian Nairn and quoted by Pevsner and Wilson (1997) as 'the noblest of all English Industrial Revolution mills' should be found in a city far from the industrial heartlands. Yet, until the nineteenth century Norwich's major industry had been textiles with its origins in the plentiful supply of wool from the surrounding countryside and new skills learned from seventeenth-century immigrants (the 'strangers') fleeing religious persecution in Europe. In the eighteenth century it supported a skilled labour force of about 100,000 outworkers in and around Norwich, engaged in hand spinning and weaving. With the introduction of firstly water-powered and later steam-powered machinery to the north and west of Britain after 1780, Norwich fell on hard times. With little scope for harnessing enough waterpower to run machinery, and no ready source of coal, textile manufacture declined. Discontent among the unemployed led to riots and partly explained the strong support for the Chartist movement in the city in the 1830s. Some efforts to modernise were made and the jacquard machine, a French invention that used punched cards to create the pattern, was introduced. It was only by concentrating on the upper end of the market such as the manufacture of silk crepes and the hand-finished Norwich shawls that the industry survived, but on a very much smaller scale employing only 6,000 workers by 1900.

The imposing St James' Mill, Norwich, built in 1839, from Whitefriars Bridge. (John Fielding)

By the 1820s the city weavers were relying on yarn bought in from Yorkshire and elsewhere, and so the local banker, director of the Norwich Union and mayor of Norwich at the time, Samuel Bignold, set up the Norwich Yarn Company in 1833 as a joint stock venture. The first mill was built at the east end of St Edmunds church in Fishergate. At the annual meeting in 1836 it was evident that the mill could not produce more than one-third of the yarn required by Norwich weavers and so it was agreed that a further mill, twice the size, should be built at St James by Whitefriars' Bridge. It was completed in 1839, was steam-powered and cost £30,000 to build. Its riverside site meant coal could be brought in by water. Originally there were six buildings in this complex including two weaving sheds, two engine sheds (of which only one survives), a boiler house and a 30m chimney. The firm was never a success and the six floors of the building were let out to different manufacturers who ran about sixty-five spinning frames and 500 looms there, employing 1,000 people in 1850. However, they could not compete with the Yorkshire producers and the Yarn Company was wound up by the end of 1851. The building is now let as offices.

The building itself is of brick, wedge shaped in plan and six stories high. The parapet along the roof line rises to meet a dome at one end. Its design is variously attributed to Norwich architects John Brown and Richard Parkinson.

The mill is visible from Whitefriar's Bridge and is occasionally open on Heritage Open Days.

FURTHER READING

Meeres, F. 1998, *A History of Norwich*, pp.140–141 (Phillimore).

GREAT HOUSES

85. BLICKLING HALL AND PARK

The view of the south front of Blickling Hall from the Aylsham to Saxthorpe road is breathtaking, but the history of the house goes back further than the impressive Jacobean building. An earlier moated house is associated with many famous names. From 1432 the property was owned by Sir Thomas Fastolfe, made famous by Shakespeare, and in 1459 it was bought by the Boleyn family. Tradition suggests that Anne Boleyn, the ill-fated second wife of Henry VIII, was born here. In 1619 the estate was purchased by Henry Hobart of a minor Norfolk gentry family, who had made his fortune in a legal career and owned houses in both London and Norwich. In 1746 a later John Hobart was created the first Earl of Buckinghamshire.

The house that stands within the moat of the earlier building is an extravagant display of Henry Hobart's success. The south and east wings were built between 1619 and 1626 to the design of Robert Lyminge, also the architect of Hatfield House in Hertfordshire, of which the south front at Blickling with its shaped gables and corner turrets is reminiscent.

Blickling Hall from the south-east. The south front was completed in 1620. The formal gardens to the right were redesigned in the 1930s. The lake can be seen in the distance. (Mike Page)

The first-floor long gallery, designed for walking and taking exercise, particularly in inclement weather, is the most spectacular room in the house. The ceiling is a masterpiece of plasterwork with twenty-six 'emblems' representing the Christian virtues that could be contemplated while walking in the room. It was converted into a library in 1745 with new Victorian bookcases and a chimney piece inserted in the 1860s. The house remained largely unaltered until the 1760s when the Norwich architects Thomas and William Ivory (No. 44), worked here rebuilding the west front in Jacobean style. The remodelling of the north front is almost indistinguishable from the Jacobean work. Inside the house, the staircase was moved and new suites of rooms created.

Later, Lord Suffield of Gunton inherited the estate through marriage. Finally, it passed to the Lothian family, and the eighth Marquis took up residence in 1850. Major works were undertaken to make the house more comfortable. A heating system was installed and many of the bedrooms redecorated. The west wing was rebuilt behind its Jacobean front. The 11th marquis, Phillip Kerr, inherited in 1932. To protect Blickling for future generations, he devised the Country Houses Scheme whereby in place of death duties, houses and their contents could be left to the National Trust intact with their estate income as an endowment. The bill was enacted by Parliament in 1937, and Blickling was the first property to benefit, passing to the National Trust in 1941.

The gardens and park at Blickling have a beauty all of their own that has evolved over the centuries. In the grounds a temple, very like that at Holkham (No. 87), was built in 1738, and the orangery was designed by Samuel Wyatt (1737–1897) in the 1780s. Its similarity to the vinery he designed at Holkham is obvious. A pyramidal mausoleum for the second Duke of Buckinghamshire was designed by the London architect Joseph Banomi (1739–1808) and built in 1793.

The park was extended during the eighteenth century to cover 32ha by 1790, the whole being surrounded by woodland. The lake was also remodelled and a high Gothic tower designed by the Ivory brothers was built on the south-western edge of the park from which the park, house and gardens could be admired.

The Blickling Hall opening times are on the National Trust website. Car parks on the edge of the park in various places provide access to the park. (Car Park for the hall: NR11 6PA)

FURTHER READING

Dallas, P., Last, R. and Williamson, T. 2013, *Norfolk Gardens and Designed Landscapes*, (WINDgather Press).

Maddison, J., 1987, *Blickling Hall* (National Trust guidebook).

86. HOUGHTON HALL AND NEW HOUGHTON VILLAGE

Robert Walpole, generally regarded as England's first Prime Minister, dominated politics from 1722 for the following twenty years. He survived the financial disaster of the South Sea Bubble, selling his shares before the bubble burst, and used his wealth to build one of Norfolk's finest houses on his estates at Houghton. Designed chiefly by Colen Campbell (1676–1729), an outstanding figure of eighteenth-century architecture, the new hall stands close to the site of the previous house. Built between 1722 and 1735, Houghton is the first Norfolk house to be built in the newly fashionable style of the sixteenth-century Italian architect Palladio and patronised by the Whigs as a faithful version of classical architecture. (A more florid baroque was favoured by the Tories). Palladio's designs were based on classical temples and obeyed strict rules of proportion and symmetry. With the service rooms below, the principal rooms were raised up a full storey above the ground with fine views across the estate along carefully arranged avenues and vistas through the park. The interior survives very much as it was intended by the foremost designer, William Kent. Like many other country houses, Houghton was not a family home so much as a place to entertain and impress political supporters.

Houghton Hall from the south-west with the formal gardens in the foreground. The avenue as it approaches the house can be seen at the top right. (John Fielding)

The village of New Houghton created outside the park. (John Fielding)

The park too was impressive, covering c.400ha. The garden and some of the avenues were linked to the old hall, but much of what remains was designed by Walpole alongside Charles Bridgeman, popular at the time for his formal geometric designs. Although there have been changes since, many of his avenues and vistas survive. Bridgeman's work involved the demolition of what remained of the old village to the south of the hall, leaving the church isolated and a fixed point in a changing landscape and isolated in the park.

A visitor to the almost-completed hall reported in 1731 that Sir Robert had removed 'about twenty houses to a considerable distance', creating the village of New Houghton on either side of the road to the south, just beyond the park and hidden from the house by a belt of trees. Their plain standardised design, in contrast to the ornate hall, emphasised the suppression of any individuality among its deferential inhabitants. It is one of the earliest 'model' villages in England.

The house and gardens are open on specific days during the summer. Check the hall website for details. (PE31 6SX)

FURTHER READING

Dallas, P., Last, R. and Williamson, T., 2013, *Norfolk Gardens and Designed Landscapes*, pp.221–223 (WINDgather).

Edwards, D. and Williamson, T., 2000, *Norfolk Country Houses from the Air*, pp.44–47 (Sutton).

87. HOLKHAM HALL, PARK AND MONUMENT

Begun in 1734, just as Houghton Hall was finished, Holkham Hall took nearly thirty years to build and is a perfect example of the Palladian style of architecture. It was never conceived as a home, but rather as a 'Temple to the arts' inspired by the owner Thomas Coke's 'Grand Tour' of Italy (1712–18), where he met the architect and interior designer William Kent. The final design was the work of Coke himself, Kent, the Palladian architect Lord Burlingham and the Norwich architect Matthew Brettingham, who drew the early drawings and supervised the work.

While the exterior is severe in its rigid Palladian symmetrical correctness, the interior is lavish. The north-facing entrance is through a magnificent basilica-like marble hall with pillars modelled on the temple of Fortuna Virilis in Rome. It is a fine example of the Palladian maxim of applying Roman temple features to domestic buildings. Unusually, the formal entrance is at ground-floor level, with steps sweeping up to the principal floor of the main block containing the public rooms. The west range is entirely occupied by a long statue gallery to house the works brought back from Italy by Thomas Coke. Much of the eastern side contains his library. From the moment visitors entered the house they knew that this was the creation of a man of culture with impeccable classical taste.

This taste was also reflected in the park, originally much smaller than the present one amounting to about 15ha. Formal vistas, a miniature classical temple and triumphal arch were erected. The park was extended from the 1770s by its new owner, the spokesman for 'improved agriculture' Thomas William Coke, to create the largest park in Norfolk at 1,200ha. The lake was given an informal twist, islands were created, and more clumps were planted. Unlike many other parks, much of the land beyond the immediate vicinity of the house remained arable.

THE MONUMENT

The boundary of the original park to the north was marked by a lodge designed by William Kent in line with the centre of the house and the obelisk on the hill beyond. In 1845 the lodge was demolished and replaced by a monument to Thomas William Coke. It consists of a fluted column 40m high, surmounted by a wheat sheaf. This is supported on a capital decorated, not with acanthus leaves as in a true classical design, but by those of a turnip, the fodder crop that made possible the keeping of larger sheep flocks through the winter to manure light Norfolk soils. Bas-reliefs illustrating the main aspects of the 'Norfolk' system of agriculture promoted by Coke were commissioned from the sculptor John Henning the younger. Representations of agricultural implements and pedigree stock were placed on the four corners with strap lines associated with Coke under them: 'Breeding in all its branches' under the

Above left: *Holkham Hall from the north-west with nineteenth-century parterres to the south and the lake is in the foreground (Mike Page)*

Above right: *The impressive monument to Thomas William Coke, which stands central to the house on the edge of the north lawn. It was disliked by his daughter, Elizabeth, who thought the wheat sheaf on the top looked like an 'ugly pot plant'. (Peter Wade-Martins)*

Right: *The bas-relief on the south face of the monument showing Thomas William Coke in the centre at the annual Holkham sheep shearing. (Peter Wade-Martins)*

Devon Ox, and 'Small in size, but great in value' under the Southdown sheep. Under the plough are the words, 'The improvement of agriculture' and under the seed drill is the Whig motto 'Live and let live'. A long inscription on the north face eulogises Coke's agricultural and political achievements.

Check opening times of the hall on its website. The park is open for walking at all times. (NR23 1AB)

FURTHER READING

Dallas, P., Last, R. and Williamson, T., 2013, *Norfolk Gardens and Designed Landscapes*, pp.206–311 (WINDgather).
Edwards, D. and Williamson, T., 2000, *Norfolk Country Houses from the Air*, pp.47–50 (Sutton).
Hiskey, C., 2016, *Holkham: The Social and Architectural History of a Great English Country House* (Unicorn Press).
Wade-Martins, S., 2009, *Coke of Norfolk* (Boydell).

88. SHERINGHAM PARK

Sheringham Park is one of the most well-known and extensive of the landscapes designed by the Norfolk landscape designer Humphrey Repton (1752–1818). It was his favourite and his final commission. In it he combined forces with his son, John Adey Repton (1775–1830), who designed the house. All was conceived as one. The new owner, Abbott Upcher, bought the land from the Flower family and although there had been some planting of trees on the surrounding hills by Cook Flower, the only house was a farmhouse. It took several years to agree the site for the house with the new owner, and it was finally sited facing south, sheltered from the sea, on the landward side of a wooded hill.

Work on the project began in 1811 and the Reptons produced an attractive 'red book' typical of the type produced by Humphrey for other estates, showing both the landscape as it existed with the proposed changes hidden under a flap. This was not only his last 'red book', but also the most ambitious and it was produced in a larger format than his earlier ones. An illustration shows the scene looking north towards the sea before the house was built. Workmen with picks and shovels are working on what was to be the drive to the new house. Lift the flap and underneath is shown the new house nestled at the foot of the hill with the now-completed fine carriageway leading down to it. Other illustrations show designs for picturesque thatched lodges and a hilltop temple.

Sheringham Hall, begun in 1813, from the south with the house sheltered from the sea by a wooded hillside to the north. (John Fielding)

Unusually, Repton recommended that the parkland be limited to about 35ha and planted with a scattering of freestanding trees. Rather than enclosing the park with a belt of trees, thus isolating it from the surrounding landscape, there were to be views across arable fields. Repton wrote that the changing of the colours of the fields through the seasons would create more interest than extensive green grass. Upchers' religious and philanthropic fervour may be sensed in the suggestion in the red book that one day a month the poor should be admitted to the woods to pick up dead sticks for firing.

Sheringham Park is now famous for its collection of rhododendrons begun in the 1850s, but continued well into the twentieth century.

Since 1987 Sheringham Park has been owned by the National Trust. The park is open to the public, but the house and the recently restored kitchen gardens are let and are private. (Car park: NR26 8TL)

FURTHER READING

Bate, S., Savage, R. and Williamson, T., 2018, *Humphrey Repton in Norfolk*, pp.145–149 (Norfolk Gardens Trust).

Dallas, P., Last, R. and Williamson, T. 2013, *Norfolk Gardens and Designed Landscapes*, pp.406–410 (WINDgather).

89. SANDRINGHAM HOUSE AND GARDENS

Sandringham House is one of the few late-nineteenth-century large country houses to be built in the county. The estate of 2,800ha was bought by Edward, Prince of Wales (later King Edward VII) in 1862 at a cost of £220,000 and his first aim was to rebuild the earlier house, but it was demolished 1868. Only the conservatory from the earlier house designed for the previous owner by the flamboyant architect S.S. Teulon was retained and converted into a billiard room. The new house by one of the royal family's favourite architects, A.J. Humbert (1822–98), was to be a mansion suited for the entertainment of guests visiting what was to be one of England's premier shooting estates. It was of red brick with Ketton stone dressings, numerous gables and two striking cupolas. A ballroom, built of the local carstone, was added in 1883 and described by Princess Alexandra as 'a great success and avoids pulling the hall to pieces each time there is a ball or anything'. Further alterations and additions were made after a fire in 1891. The house was approached via a straight drive from the north through elaborate wrought and cast-iron gates by the Norfolk architect and designer Thomas Jeckyll (1827–81) and built at the Norwich Iron Works of Barnard, Bishop and Barnard for the International Exhibition of 1862. They were

Sandringham House from the south-west. (John Fielding)

then presented as a wedding present to Prince Edward and Princess Alexandra. The open view across lawns from the gates to the house was altered to give more privacy in the 1940s by curving the drive and planting hedges. Formal gardens were created with a geometric pattern of box-hedged beds flanked by avenues of pleached limes.

Much of the rest of the park and garden layout is as planned in the nineteenth century and is an excellent example of a Victorian landscaped park, much of it planned by W.B. Thomas (1811–98). The central feature is the Upper Lake on the southern edge of the lawn. Along the northern bank is a 'Pulhamite' rock garden with a cascade to the lower lake. James Pulham (1820–98) invented a method of making artificial stone whose durability was guaranteed.

Across the public road is the 5.6ha (14-acre) walled kitchen garden with an elaborate arched entrance. With its glass houses and well-laid-out flower and vegetable beds it was one of the spectacular sights of the age in its Victorian and Edwardian heyday. Since then the glass houses have been demolished.

Both house and gardens reflect the glory days of empire, commerce and technology. Except for the walled garden, the grounds are open most of the year. (PE35 6EN)

FURTHER READING

Cathcart, H., 1964, *Sandringham: The Story of a Royal Home* (W.H. Allen).

Dallas, P., Last, R. and Williamson, T., 2013, *Norfolk Gardens and Designed Landscapes,* 362–366 (WINDgather).

Edwards, D., and Williamson, T., 2000, *Norfolk Country Houses from the Air,* pp.106–107 (Sutton).

Sandringham Guidebook, 1996 (Sandringham Estate Office).

THE TWENTIETH CENTURY

INTRODUCTION

There have been more changes in Norfolk in the twentieth century than in any previous 100 years and much of this is illustrated in its landscape and buildings.

The century opened with the countryside in decline. The population of most villages had decreased since 1850. Farming, particularly cereal farming, was suffering from cheap imports, and only those who could diversify into dairying or fresh fruit and vegetables were making profits at anything like the level possible before 1870. Landowners were having to accept lower rents and many of the owners of the great estates were relying on income from investments to keep up their lavish lifestyles. Some estates, particularly in the poor Breckland soils, were already being sold to those who had made fortunes elsewhere and for whom a grand house with good shooting was a badge of success. Proximity to the royal family at Sandringham (No. 89) and the legendary shooting there was a bonus.

Living conditions and wages for farm workers were far lower than those in the towns, which offered greater variety of employment. The population of the market towns, especially those with railway stations, iron foundries, maltings, and breweries, was rising. Weekly markets and services, such as banking, were flourishing. The largest and fastest-growing centre was, of course, Norwich where the opulent buildings put up by banks and insurance companies such as Norwich Union (No. 90) were an indication of the fact that, although agriculture was suffering, there was still plenty of landed and commercial wealth in the county.

The First World War provided a temporary boost for agriculture as foreign supplies of food were cut off. It also provided a way out of the drudgery of farm work for young men seeking the excitement of the battlefield. More than 100,000 Norfolk men served, but 12,000 never returned and the lists of names on village war memorials are a sad reminder of the devastation caused by war. For the first time since the Napoleonic Wars the strategic importance of Norfolk was recognised. Coastal batteries were established, and air power became significant. Zeppelins bombed Yarmouth, Sheringham, Dereham and King's Lynn. Thirty airfields were constructed, and Norwich companies such as Mann Egerton, Boulton and Paul, and Savages of King's Lynn were building aircraft.

As men returned from war, agricultural depression set in again and by the 1920s, Norfolk was one of the poorest counties in England. As rents for farmland declined, the great estates began selling, often to their tenants, changing the social fabric of the countryside. Elsewhere unemployment rose, particularly in the old industrial towns in the north of the country. To help alleviate poverty, provide work and to replace timber that had been felled for the war effort, a government scheme of afforestation began. The Forestry Commission was set up in 1919, and the largest lowland forest was created around Thetford (No. 93). By 1934 nearly 10,000 hectares had been planted, employing both local and north country labour. A new village for forestry workers was created at Santon Downham (Suffolk).

The story of the inter-war years is not all one of depression. The holiday industry, which had begun to develop in the nineteenth century, continued to grow and was to become an important source of income for the county. New amusements sprang up along Yarmouth's Marine Parade (No. 83). The arrival of the motor car allowed visitors to explore away from the railway lines. From the 1930s small chalets, often prefabricated by Boulton and Paul, appeared along Broadland rivers, particularly the River Thurne. While caravan parks along the coast north of Yarmouth were established from the 1950s, sailing on the Broads became popular with the number of boats to hire rising from 495 in 1931 to 2,445 in 1995, by which time half were motor cruisers.

In agriculture, new crops such as sugar beet were introduced, as well as an increasing emphasis on soft fruit and fresh vegetables. The Alley brothers in South Creake were running a wholly mechanised farm in the 1930s, but it was not until the 1950s that tractors generally replaced horses and transformed farming. Huge poultry sheds, often on wartime airfields, became a feature of the landscape after 1950.

The Second World War again saw Norfolk in the front line of invasion. Coastal batteries and pillboxes (No. 94) were built and the entire Norfolk coastline was festooned with barbed wire and mined. Forty-five airfields (Nos. 95 & 97) were established. The year 1942 saw devastating air raids on Norwich and Yarmouth, resulting in massive rebuilding of their central areas in the immediate post-war period. The strategic importance of Norfolk was maintained throughout the Cold War with several airbases, including West Raynham (No. 97), remaining operational until the 1980s.

The post-war years have seen some immense changes within the county. The pattern of employment evolved as the introduction of new and ever-larger machinery resulted in a huge decline in the amount of labour required on farms and in the increasing amalgamation of holdings. The greater use of fertilisers and herbicides meant productivity rose. Improved drainage meant areas such as the Halvergate Marshes (No. 98) could be transformed. Alongside these types of intensification, we see the increasing influence of the conservation movement with the foundation of the Norfolk Naturalists Trust (now the Norfolk Wildlife Trust) and the Norfolk Archaeological Trust, both in the 1920s.

For the first time agriculture was not the prime employer in villages. While farm workers had to look elsewhere for employment, a more affluent group of newcomers were moving in. As car ownership increased, so did the distances people were prepared to travel to work, and villages in easy reach of major towns grew with new housing development. Near the north coast second homes began to dominate and people of retirement age moved in. Many of the market towns retained small industries employing large numbers of people. In Dereham Metamic clocks, Jentiques furniture and Hobbies making fretwork kits employed 3,000 people between them, but from the 1970s there was a decline in these local companies with closures, amalgamations and takeovers. Production moved to China and the Far East. Market towns, like the surrounding villages, have become commuter and retirement centres.

Norwich, Thetford and King's Lynn also grew in the post-war years and there is much to celebrate in Norwich's modern architecture. In 1963 the University of East Anglia was founded and the Sainsbury Centre (No. 99) was added fifteen years later, establishing the city's importance as an artistic and cultural hub. Our survey of sites that illustrate the history of the county ends with the Forum housing the new Millennium Library (No. 100). But the story continues with the Stirling Prize for new architecture being awarded in 2019 to Norwich City Council's housing scheme in Goldsmiths Street near the centre of the city.

FURTHER READING

Douet, A., 2012, *Breaking New Ground: Agriculture in Norfolk 1914–1972* (Coldbath Books).

Wade-Martins, S. and Williamson, T., 2008, *The Countryside of East Anglia: Changing Landscapes 1870–1950* (Boydell).

90. NORWICH UNION HEADQUARTERS, SURREY STREET, NORWICH (NOW AVIVA)

Norwich can boast many monumental and ornate Victorian and Edwardian buildings that are the work of two Norwich architects, Edward Boardman and George Skipper. They illustrate the wealth that farming and landed estates was bringing into the city at that time, supporting a growing financial centre. They include banks, shops and offices and the rapidly expanding Norwich Union.

The work of the Norwich architect George John Skipper (1856–1948) was equal in quality to more famous London-based practices. His earlier work in Norwich includes the Arts and Crafts Royal Arcade (1899) and Jarrolds frontage at the corner of Gentleman's Walk and London Street (1903–05) as well as his own offices (now part of Jarrolds) next door. At the second-floor level of this ornate terracotta facade are six panels depicting scenes of builders and architects at work.

His masterpiece was the headquarters of Norwich Union (now Aviva) in Surrey Street. Built in 1903–04, it is described by Pevsner and Wilson as 'One of the country's most convinced Edwardian office buildings' (Pevsner and Wilson, 1997, p.308). The building inspires the kind of awe normally reserved for cathedrals, with its main hall using fifteen different marbles, elegant stained glass windows, classically inspired frescoes and intricately carved panelling.

The imposing headquarters of Norwich Union with a modern Aviva blocks of offices behind. (John Fielding)

It was as an exponent of Edwardian Baroque that Skipper realised his potential and this is clearly displayed in the building for Norwich Union (then called the Norwich Union Life Insurance Society). The origins of Norwich Union go back to the founding of the Norwich Fire Office in the 1790s. In 1808 Thomas Bignold set up a separate office for life insurance. He was followed by his son, Samuel (1791–1875) who was secretary of both the fire and life companies for nearly sixty years. Norwich was already an important banking and financial centre serving a wealthy landed and farming hinterland, and business continued to grow. In 1864 the firm took over the world's first insurance company, the Amicable Society, which had been founded by Bishop Talbot of Oxford (c.1659–1730). Statues of both Talbot and Bignold flank the entrance to Skipper's building, which took its inspiration from Amicable House in London's Fleet Street. Faced with buff Clipsham stone, the lower levels are heavily rusticated and the two statues occupy niches in large wings either side of the imposing entrance. Above is a huge Grecian portico with ionic columns under a pediment. The whole facade exudes solid reliability.

The interior hall is as spectacular as the exterior. On either side of the entrance steps in the outer hall are bronzes depicting Solice and Protection. Subtle references to insurance and its benefits appear in every part of the building. The main hall itself with its huge domed roof, forty marble pillars and marble-lined walls is breathtaking. The different types of marble used were all intended for Westminster Cathedral, but when they were not required there Skipper persuaded the Society to buy them for its offices. In the middle of the marble floor is the innovative heating and air conditioning system conceived by Skipper. A bronze pendant swings gently over a pillared construction from which warm air is wafted around the hall in the winter and cool air in the summer. The aim of all this grandeur was to reassure policy holders of the Society's strength and prosperity when they came in to pay their premiums at the rows of high-backed mahogany desks that filled the hall. Around this grand entrance were the strong room, the actuary's offices and typing rooms. A wide and equally grand staircase leads to a second floor where the boardroom, luncheon room and committee rooms, as well as solicitors' offices, were housed.

The hall is open to the public during office hours during the week and a short guidebook is available as well as displays on the history of the company.

FURTHER READING

Aviva, no date. *Surrey House* (Aviva).

Meeres, F., 1998, *A History of Norwich*, pp.194–195 (Phillimore).

91. EDITH CAVELL GRAVE AND MONUMENT

The execution of Norfolk-born nurse Edith Cavell by the German military in 1915 was used to great affect by British recruiting officers in their propaganda to persuade men to enlist in order to stop the 'barbaric judicial murder of innocent women'. Statues to her are to be found in Belgium and North America as well as across England, including near Trafalgar Square, and there is a memorial outside Norwich Cathedral on Tombland.

Born the daughter of the vicar of Swardeston in 1865, she began her education at Norwich High School before moving to boarding school elsewhere. Few careers were open to women at the time and she became a governess, working in Belgium from 1890 to 1895. She returned to England to care for her father and on his recovery, at the age of 30, decided to train as a nurse, working in several hospitals in the south of England. Ten years later, in 1907, she was recruited to become matron of a nursing school in Belgium, where she was responsible for the expansion of nursing training. When war broke out in 1914 her schools and hospitals were taken over by the Red Cross where soldiers from both sides were treated. It was at this time that she became part of an elaborate network helping British and Allied troops to escape to neutral Holland, often housing those escaping. This was against German military law and the suspicions of the occupying force were raised. On 3 August 1915

Edith Cavell monument on Tombland unveiled in 1918. (John Fielding)

she, along with others, was arrested. How far she was also involved in espionage is unclear, but the charge against her did not include spying. She admitted being instrumental in conveying sixty British and fifteen French soldiers as well as 100 French and Belgian civilians of military age across the border. It is always possible that some of these men were carrying messages for the Secret Intelligence Service. She, along with five others, was found guilty of 'war treason', a crime punishable by death under German law, and was executed by firing squad on 11 October 1915 at Tir National Shooting Range in Schaerbeck. News of her execution was greeted with horror and she soon became an icon of self-sacrifice in wartime and of the nursing profession.

After the war, her body was brought back for a memorial service at Westminster Abbey and finally to Norwich, where she is buried outside the east end of the cathedral. Her gravestone was restored to commemorate the centenary of her death in 2015. Her memorial in Tombland was unveiled by Queen Alexandra in October 1918 in front of huge crowds. It shows a grateful British soldier stretching up to place a wreath below her bust. (NR1 3NY)

FURTHER READING

Grant, S., 1995, *Edith Cavell 1865–1915* (Larks Press).
Souhami, D., 2010, *Edith Cavell* (Quercus).

92. BURSTON STRIKE SCHOOL

The story of the Burston Strike School is a unique example of rebellion against the education provided in the early twentieth century through the good offices of farmer- and parson-dominated managers only loosely controlled by an education committee of the county council. The strike was taken up by the trades union movement as a 'microcosm of the rural war ... between farm and field, the cottage and the big house' (Groves, 1949, p.152).

A school board for the parishes of Burston and Shrimpling was set up in Burston in 1875. Board members included the rectors of both parishes and three others. From the beginning it was difficult to recruit teachers, and in 1911 Mrs Higdon and her husband took over. No doubt there were some misgivings among the managers as the Higdons were known to have caused problems in their previous school. It is clear from the school log books that Mrs Higdon had no intention of changing her ways when she arrived at Burston. She complained about the state of the school and shortly after her arrival she sent a list of faults to the managers. These included serious leaks in the roof, the state of the stove (the bottom was worn out), the rails on the fire guard were out, there were holes in the hand basin, a leaking tank and faulty tap. In December 1912 she demanded that the managers came down to see the wet walls on which the boys were expected to hang their caps.

The single-room Burston Strike School opened in 1917. (Peter Wade-Martins)

As a result of her efforts, His Majesty's Inspectors' report of 1912 stated that the condition of the school was 'promising', there was a 'good tone' and the pupils were 'taking pride in their work'. Standards in arithmetic were high.

However, there were problems. As teachers, the Higdons were well aware of the deprivations suffered by pupils and their parents, and Tom Higdon particularly was involved in encouraging the labourers to join the Agricultural Labourers' Union and seek places on parish councils. He had a fierce temper and frequently caned pupils. The Higdons were seen as political agitators, and the school board was soon looking for excuses to sack them. In 1914 they were finally forced out over the case of two children who were caned. On 1 April 1914, when Edna

Detail showing some of the ninety stones commemorating donations by local Labour party branches and trades' unions. (Peter Wade-Martins)

Howard took over as temporary head, her first entry in the log book states that there were only six senior and nineteen infants in the school 'the rest being on strike'. Sixty-six children were on the green marching 'with banners'. This was the beginning of a protest that lasted for the next twenty years.

As the months wore on the children, supported by their parents, refused to attend school and eighteen parents were summoned to court for the non-attendance. The Higdons set about teaching the children in the open air on the green, before hiring a carpenter's shop. As news of this act of defiance spread, money came in from trades unions and co-operative branches all over the country. Marches continued all summer with 1,500 people one Sunday. Soon there was enough support for the building of the strike school to begin, and it opened in May 1917.

The single-room brick building stands alone on the green at Burston and many of the facing stones are inscribed with the names of the unions who donated them as well as prominent socialists such as Leo Tolstoy.

Whilst the vicar and other school managers had expected the strike to be 'a nine-day wonder', the strike school became instead an institution, not only providing a solid grounding in the three Rs and Christian beliefs, but also 'for the training of children in the principles of freedom and socialism' (Edwards, 1974). Described as 'The first Trades Union School in England', it received financial support from the trades union movement and was visited by many of the prominent socialists of the day.

Gradually over the years numbers dwindled and the school finally closed in 1939 when the remaining eleven children were readmitted to the county elementary school, and so this unique experiment in alternative education ended.

See the Burston Strike School website for details of opening times. (IP22 5TS)

FURTHER READING

Edwards, B., 1974, *The Burston Strike School* (Lawrence and Wishar).

Groves, R., 1949, *Sharpen the Sickle* (Porcupine Press).

Higdon, T.G., 1984 reprint, *The Burston School Strike* (Diss).

Scobie, D., 1991, *The School that Went on Strike* (Oxford University Press).

Zamoyska, B., 1985, *The Burston Rebellion* (BBC).

93. THETFORD FOREST

Covering nearly 19,000ha, Thetford Forest is the largest lowland pine forest in England. Although many of its numerous visitors consider it to be a natural landscape, it was in fact created during the first half of twentieth century and is now considered an important historic landscape in its own right.

During the First World War there was significant demand for timber in Britain, particularly for use in trenches on the Western Front and in coal mines. With less than 5 per cent of the country covered by woods, the shortfall in the availability of home-grown timber was readily apparent. To address this a government committee proposed the planting of around 72,000ha of trees over the next eighty years. In 1919 the Forestry Commission was created, tasked with promoting forestry across Britain and acquiring land for afforestation. A secondary purpose was to create jobs in rural areas suffering from high levels of unemployment after the war.

In 1922 the Forestry Commission started to plant trees in the Norfolk and Suffolk Brecks. The first purchase was near Swaffham, quickly followed by land at Elveden and Santon Downham (both in Suffolk). By the mid 1930s the Commission's Norfolk holdings included property at Lynford, Beachamwell, Methwold, Cockley Cley, Croxton, Didlington, Weeting, West Harling, Hockham and Feltwell. More than 80 per cent of this land was acquired from large estates, many of which were struggling financially after the First World War during a period of agricultural depression and newly introduced death duties.

Part of Thetford Forest, between Weeting and Mundford. The road on the right-hand side of the picture is the A1065. (Mike Page)

Most of the Thetford Forest was established within twenty years; indeed by 1945 few trees were being planted and most of the acquired land had been stocked. From mid 1960s onwards the cycle of large-scale felling and restocking commenced, and this continues today. Scots pine was initially the favoured species, as it is well suited to the Brecks' soils and climate and was already widely used in the area's plantations and hedges. Corsican pine, Douglas fir, European larch and broad-leaved trees were also planted and the first of these is now the forest's dominant species. Trees were planted by Forestry Commission staff and, between 1928 and 1939, by men who were brought to four Ministry of Labour camps from areas with high unemployment in the north and west. The Woman's Timber Corps was established in 1942, which saw many 'Lumber Jills' working across the forest during the final years of the Second World War.

Large-scale tree planting resulted in heaths, rabbit warrens (No. 63), agricultural land, woods, tree belts and several landscape parks disappearing. In the process numerous prehistoric and historic features were preserved, probably more extensively than would have been the case if the land had been in agricultural use. It is possible to explore the forest today and see round barrows, the sites of deserted villages, post-medieval flint mines, and banks that would have defined warren, parish, field and wood boundaries.

Much of Thetford Forest is open access land (as shown on Ordnance Survey Explorer map 229). There are many walking, cycling and horse-riding trails, including the Brecks Forest Way (between Thetford and Brandon), themed Brecks Heritage Trails, and those that radiate out from the High Lodge visitors centre (off the B1107 between Thetford and Brandon). Car parks include those at Lynford Arboretum, Lynford Stag, St Helen's picnic site and Great Hockham. (High Lodge: IP27 0AF)

FURTHER READING

Skipper, K. and Williamson, T. 1997, *Thetford Forest: Making a Landscape, 1922–1997* (Centre of East Anglian Studies).

94. SECOND WORLD WAR COASTAL DEFENCES

The evacuation of Dunkirk and the defeat of France in 1940 saw the English coast become a Second World War front line. The south coast was the most likely location for a German invasion, but East Anglia was potentially a place that could see alternative or diversionary landings. Fixed defences were therefore constructed rapidly along the entire Norfolk coast.

The coast was provided with an outer crust of defences intended to make landing enemy forces as difficult as possible. These included coastal batteries, military camps, pillboxes, trenches, concrete blocks that would have hindered the movement of tanks and other vehicles, on- and off-shore minefields, and barbed wire and scaffolding placed close to the shoreline. Pillboxes – concrete and brick buildings, many built to standard templates – survive on beaches, in marshes, in sand dunes and on cliff tops all along the coast. Some are relatively intact, but others have been damaged by the sea and people; one rests upside down on Happisburgh Beach, having fallen from an eroding cliff top. Although the minefields, scaffolding and barbed wire were cleared after the war, sections of scaffolding occasionally turn up on beaches.

Second World War pillbox on the cliff top, to the east of Beach Lane car park at Weybourne. Since the 1940s other associated structures have fallen from the cliff onto the beach, to be broken up by the sea; it will not be long before this one follows them. (David Robertson)

Nine coastal batteries were constructed in June 1940 and by 1942 there were fourteen. All housed searchlights and two guns, most of which had previously been used by the Royal Navy, and fired 100lb shells. The guns were attached to concrete bases and housed in gun houses, some of which survive in part at least (as at Brancaster). Originally the batteries were crewed by coast regiments of the Royal Artillery but from 1943 they were gradually handed over to the Home Guard or closed. By early 1945 only one at Great Yarmouth remained operational and it closed at the end of the war.

The coastal defences stood ahead of additional lines of defences inland. These concentrated on important infrastructure (including road and rail junctions, bridges and airfields) and a series of 'stop lines'. Stop lines were continuous arrangements of pillboxes, gun emplacements and ditches designed for local troops to slow down invading forces, giving Army reserves and the Navy time to mobilise and defeat the invaders. One of Norfolk's stop lines ran from Burnham Market to Beccles, via Fakenham and Norwich (line A).

Remains of Norfolk's defences can be seen along the coast. One section with multiple surviving features in the 4.5km stretch between Weybourne and Sheringham, where the Norfolk Coast Path follows the cliff top and passes pillboxes, a substantial anti-tank ditch and (on Skelding Hill) the site of the Sheringham battery. One of the pillboxes has been converted into a bird hide, another for overnight stays by its owner. Parking is available at Beach Lane Weybourne (NR25 7SR) and The Esplanade Sheringham (NR26 8LG).

FURTHER READING

Osbourne, M., 2008, *20th Century Defences in Norfolk* (Concrete Publications).

95. HETHEL AIRFIELD CHAPEL

Between 1942 and 1945 American military personal were stationed in large numbers in East Anglia, They included thousands of members of the United States Army Airforce (USAAF) on twenty-nine airfields across Norfolk. Many of the airfields now have memorials to USAAF crews; a few have museums that tell the story of the American 'Friendly Invasion'. At Hethel a group of buildings has been restored as a museum and memorial to the 389th Bomb Group (part of the 2nd Air Division), which was based here between June 1943 and May 1945.

The exhibitions are based in the chapel and gymnasium buildings and recently erected nissen huts. There is a Second World War wall painting of Christ on the Cross in the chapel and in the chaplain's rooms alongside there is a painted map of Europe. Displays include uniforms, combat records, artefacts and photographs.

Hethel was constructed as a heavy bomber base in 1940–41. By the time the 389th Bomb Group, nicknamed the 'Sky Scorpions', arrived it had three concrete runways, a perimeter track, three hangars and fifty 'hardstands' or dispersals. The latter were used to ensure aircraft were spaced out while parked, to reduce losses during air attacks or accidents. While based here, the Sky Scorpions flew B-24 Liberators on 321 missions, 307 of which were from this airfield, and lost more than 100 aircraft. The missions took them to North Africa, Crete, Italy, Austria, Romania, France and Germany.

After the USAAF left, Hethel became a Royal Air Force (RAF) fighter base and home to Spitfires and Mustangs. In 1946 two Polish squadrons were present. It then became a Personnel Transit Centre, playing a role in the demilitarisation of the United Kingdom.

Closed in 1948, the airfield was sold in 1964. In the mid 1960s Lotus Cars moved in and built factories and offices where many of the air force buildings once stood. They still use parts of runways and the perimeter track to test cars.

Second World War wall painting of Christ on the Cross in Hethel airfield chapel. (Ian Robertson)

Hethel airfield, with the chapel and gymnasium in the centre foreground (marked A) and the flying field behind the Lotus buildings in the centre. (John Fielding)

The museum holds open days (check their website for opening times). Follow signs for 'Lotus Cars' from the A11 Wymondham–Mulbarton junction or B1113 between Bracon Ash and Wreningham. At the northern end of Potash Lane turn right onto the track that leads to the exhibitions. Two hangars remain elsewhere on the airfield, one of which can be seen from St Thomas' Lane. (NR14 8EY)

FURTHER READING

Delve, K., 2005, *The Military Airfields of Britain: East Anglia – Norfolk and Suffolk*, pp.99–102 (Crowood Press).
McKenzie, R., 2004, *Ghost Fields of Norfolk*, pp.52–53 (Larks Press).

96. LANGHAM DOME

An unusual and striking building, Langham Dome was constructed in 1942 to train anti-aircraft gunners and support the defence of the United Kingdom against aerial attack and invasion. It was one of forty built across the country, of which only four are thought to survive. It was restored by the North Norfolk Historic Buildings Trust and the Friends of Langham Dome with support from the Heritage Lottery Fund in 2013–14, and since then has been open to the public.

The Dome Teacher is made of reinforced concrete, circular, about 12m in diameter and stands around 7.5m tall. After completing classroom lessons, trainee gunners moved inside the dome, where stop-frame films showing enemy aircraft were projected onto the interior walls. Trainees would use a dummy gun to try and shoot down the planes, while being subjected to the noise and sights of planes attacking, bullets being fired and bombs exploding. What was then brand-new technology is now considered the forerunner to modern computer simulators and games. Once a trainee's accuracy had improved, they would move on to artillery ranges at Stiffkey and Weybourne, where they would fire live ammunition at cloth targets pulled behind planes.

The dome was located on the periphery of Langham airfield, which opened in 1940. Under the control of Coastal Command, the squadrons based here were tasked with protecting friendly shipping, destroying enemy naval and merchant vessels, and meteorological reconnaissance. A wide range of units used the station, including Polish, Czechoslovakian, Australian and New Zealand squadrons. In April 1944 Langham's 'ANZAC' squadrons helped clear the English Channel of enemy shipping ahead of D-Day.

Concrete Dome Teacher built at Langham airfield in 1942. (David Robertson)

The site of Langham airfield, with the dome labelled A, now covered with turkey sheds. (John Fielding)

Langham's international flavour continued after the Second World War. In 1946 it became home to the Royal Netherlands School of Technical Training, as the United Kingdom supported post-war recovery in the Netherlands. From 1951 to 1957 the American Army used the base for anti-aircraft training, and trainees used the dome to shoot down radio-controlled targets launched from Weybourne.

The military use of the airfield ceased in 1958. Bernard Matthews Limited purchased the site in 1961, after which, as at many Second World War airfields, turkey sheds were constructed on some of the runways.

The dome (TF 995 418) sits alongside the road from Langham to Stiffkey (via Cockthorpe). Check the Langham Dome website for opening times. (NR25 7BP)

FURTHER READING

Delve, K., 2005, *The Military Airfields of Britain: East Anglia – Norfolk and Suffolk*, pp.125–128 (Crowood Press).
McKenzie, R., 2004, *Ghost Fields of Norfolk*, pp.54–57 (Larks Press).

97. WEST RAYNHAM COLD WAR AIRFIELD

Former RAF West Raynham is one of the most complete 1930s' Second World War and Cold War airfields in the county. Unusually, many of its technical and residential buildings can be seen by the public, as they are now within a business park and private houses. The flying field is now a solar farm.

Work started on the airfield in 1936 and, by the time it was opened in spring 1939, it had a large grass landing area with buildings on the western side, including the four large surviving hangars, accommodation blocks and a control tower. It started life as a bomber and training station, with fighter squadrons sharing the base from 1942. During the Second World War it was home to well-known aircraft, including Blenheims, Hampdens, Wellingtons, Mosquitos and Beaufighters. To defend against aerial and ground attacks, there were three anti-aircraft guns, machine guns and sixteen pillboxes (some of which survive), but these did not prevent the Luftwaffe bombing the station several times during 1940. In 1943 two concrete runways for possible use by very heavy bombers were added and later a new control tower was constructed, but the very heavy bombers never arrived. The restored tower, now a private residence, is one of only five of its type in the country to survive.

West Raynham Cold War airfield, much of which is now a business park and private housing, from the south-east. The 1930s' hangars, Cold War dome trainer and two control towers are on the edge of the flying field, which is now a solar farm. (John Fielding)

From the end of the Second World War until the early 1970s, the airfield was the RAF's leading Cold War operational and training fighter station. A wide range of fighters were tested and housed including the Kestrel, an experimental vertical take-off aircraft that led to the famous Harrier jump jet. In 1956 four Hunters were lost when thick fog across East Anglia prevented them landing (the four pilots ejected).

From 1965 to 1970 the site was home to Bloodhound surface-to-air missiles, then the United Kingdom's main air defence weapon, under the control of 14 Squadron. They returned in 1975 and, under the control of 85 Squadron, remained until the late 1980s. By the late 1980s, West Raynham was the only site with active Bloodhound launchers left in the country and decommissioned missiles were stored on the runways. From 1983 until the airfield's closure in 1994, it was also home to 66 Squadron, RAF Regiment, and their Rapier surface-to-air missiles. The dome trainer used to train Rapier crews survives. After closure, the site remained in the hands of the Ministry of Defence until it was sold for commercial, residential and agricultural use in 2006.

It is possible to explore the western part of the airfield by walking around the business park and residential streets. The owners of the second control tower have installed displays and hold open days. (NR21 7AJ)

FURTHER READING

Delve, K., 2005, *The Military Airfields of Britain: East Anglia – Norfolk and Suffolk*, pp.246–249 (Crowood Press).
McKenzie, R., 2004, *Ghost Fields of Norfolk*, pp.118–125 (Larks Press).

The second control tower at former RAF West Raynham. (David Robertson)

98. THE HALVERGATE MARSHES CONTROVERSY AND BERNEY ARMS WINDMILL

The role of Norfolk in the development of agriculture in Britain has long been recognised but in recent years initiatives in the county have led to a sea change in the national system of government grants to farmers with a recognition of the importance of conservation of wildlife and the traditional landscape.

The marshlands of east Norfolk represent some of the most important wetlands in Britain. They have been drained and grazed as the numerous old wind pumps testify, but until the mid-twentieth century there were no pumps sufficiently powerful to reduce water levels low enough to allow for arable farming. The traditional land use was to let the marshes by annual auction to farmers from further inland to graze their cattle during the summer months.

This was true on the extensive Halvergate marshes on the edge of the Yare, with the tall Berney Arms windmill pumping water off the area. The present Berney Arms mill was built in 1865 to replace an earlier one that also ground cement for the Reedham Cement Company. Chalk from the Whitlingham quarries near Norwich was brought by wherry to the mill. This use came to an end in 1883 but the mill continued to work as a drainage mill until 1948 when it was replaced by a diesel pump. The mill was taken over in 1951 as an historic monument by the Ministry of Works (now English Heritage).

Looking north across the River Yare to Berney Arms windmill and the Halvergate Marshes beyond. (Mike Page)

As advanced pumping machinery and corrugated PVC underground piping became available it was possible to drain more efficiently and convert grazing marshes to arable farming, thus reducing biodiversity and bringing irreparable change to the marshland landscape. As plans for widespread drainage of over 3,000ha at Halvergate became public in the early 1980s, opposition grew, involving particularly the conservation body Friends of the Earth under the local leadership of Andrew Lees. Finally, in 1985 using the powers available under Section 40 of the 1981 Wildlife and Countryside Act, the Broads Grazing Marshes Conservation Scheme was launched by the Broads Authority. The aim of this experimental project was to demonstrate how livestock farming and landscape conservation could be integrated. Management agreements were negotiated, and subsidies were offered to participating farmers who were required not to increase drainage and to keep livestock numbers low and farm in an environmentally friendly way. This highly successful experiment was the beginning of the designation of Environmentally Sensitive Areas (ESAs) on a national scale, which in turn has led to the various agri-environment schemes that have helped secure a future for some of our most fragile farmed landscapes all over the UK.

Berney Arms windmill is opened for pre-booked parties arranged with the local RSPB. It can only be reached by boat or rail. The best views of the marshes are either from the top of the windmill or from the Roman fort at Burgh Castle on the high ground to the east (No. 16). (NR31 9PZ)

FURTHER READING

Ewans, M., 1992, *The Battle for the Broads* (Terence Dalton).

George, M., 1992, *Landuse, Ecology and Conservation in Broadland* (Packard).

Wade-Martins, S., 2015, *The Conservation Movement in Norfolk* (Boydell).

99. THE SAINSBURY CENTRE

The Sainsbury Centre for Visual Arts opened in 1978, making it one of the first major public buildings designed by the architects Norman and Wendy Foster. At the time, Norman Foster was relatively unknown but has since become one of the most productive and recognisable architects of the late twentieth and early twenty-first century, responsible for buildings across the world.

The 1970s' structure is a large rectangular steel and glass box, measuring over 150m long and reminiscent of an aircraft hangar. The internal tubular steel frame is visible at either end but on the sides it is concealed under external plastic-coated aluminium panels and internal grilles and panels. Services, ventilation and blind control systems are housed in the 2m-wide space between the side wall's inner and outer panels; many are visible from inside. This was an innovative approach at the time of construction and helped to create the building's huge, flexible and functional interior.

The enormous internal space houses exhibitions, teaching facilities for the department of art history, cafés and a shop. The Centre's principal collection of world art and artefacts was donated by Sir Robert and Lady Lisa Sainsbury, who were both heavily involved in developing the Fosters' design. Foster has explained they 'shared the belief that the study of art should be an informal, pleasurable experience, not bound by the traditional enclosure of object and viewer'.

The large rectangular steel and glass box that is the 1970s' Sainsbury Centre (towards bottom left), within the University of East Anglia, Norwich. The curved glazed wall of the 1980s' Crescent Wing and 1960s' Ziggurats are also visible. (John Fielding)

By the late 1980s more space was needed to house the Centre's growing collections so Norman Foster was commissioned to design the Crescent Wing. This is immediately adjacent to the original building with its exhibition spaces below ground. All that is visible from outside is a curving glazed wall. Additional extensions were opened in 2006 and 2013–14.

The Centre is located on the western edge of the University of East Anglia, facing out across parkland and the University Broad. The University houses other important buildings, including the Ziggurats of Norfolk and Suffolk Terraces designed by Denys Lasdun in 1966–67.

The Sainsbury Centre is signposted on the University of East Anglia's campus and from the B1108 and A47. Buses stop close by on Chancellors Drive. Car parking can be accessed via University Drive (off the B1108) and Chancellors Drive. (NR4 7TJ)

100. NORWICH CENTRAL LIBRARY, TECHNOPOLIS AND THE FORUM

This is the story of a process, which started with a disaster and culminated in the building of the best-known, and possibly most enjoyed, piece of modern architecture in the county.

THE CENTRAL LIBRARY

At 7.31 a.m. on Monday, 1 August 1994 the first call was received by Norwich Fire Station to say that the Norwich Central Library was on fire. At 7.34 a.m. three fire engines were dispatched, followed in the coming hours by twelve more along with two hydraulic platforms, but they could not save the main part of the building. The Central Library, designed by the city architect David Percival, had been built in 1960–62 and opened by Queen Elizabeth, the Queen Mother, in 1963. It was much-admired as a piece of contemporary architecture, but fire had destroyed most of the structure and its contents above basement level except for parts of the high-level book stack. This included the lending library, the reference library, the American 2nd Air Division Memorial Library and much of the Norfolk Studies Library (originally established in 1880). The Norfolk Studies Library was made up of around 70,000 volumes, of which 26,000 were lost. It also had a collection of around 30,000 old photographs, of which about 15,000 were destroyed, including a number dating from the 1850s. Of the immensely important Colman Library of around 7,500 antiquarian books, pamphlets and papers of the greatest local and national interest, about 2,500 were destroyed. It was a catastrophe, and the leading article in the *Eastern Daily Press* the next day was headed 'Our heritage burned away'.

The county archives held in the Norfolk Record Office below stairs in the basement were, however, not burnt. Not a single Record Office document was lost, although some were damaged by water that had penetrated through ducts linked to the warm air heating system, which served the whole building.

The Record Office had a contingency disaster plan in place, so that the water-damaged documents could be quickly whisked away to be freeze-dried at the Harwell Atomic Energy Research Establishment. For the rest, there were frantic searches for suitable storage space, and Warmingers, the Norwich waste-paper merchants, generously offered their empty building on Ber Street in Norwich. So, it was possible to clear the strong room in an impressive ten days. The Record Office actually had a long-term relationship with Warmingers, who every now and then passed on documents, such as manorial records and estate maps, which had come to them as wastepaper. Their Ber Street building was large enough to take the lot. A temporary Record Office opened a year later after everything had been moved again to Gildengate House in Anglia Square.

On 26 April 1995 an independent report was released that showed the fire started in defective wiring in a bookcase, as a result of poor communication, inadequate inspection and maintenance by county council officers. The fault had been reported four days earlier, but it had not been corrected. The ventilation system could have fanned the flames, and the devastation was so complete that the building above basement level could not be saved. It was a loss deeply felt by the people of Norfolk.

TECHNOPOLIS

By May 1995 the city council were floating the idea of a 'Technopolis' to take its place. This would consist of a modern library, a hi-tech visitors' centre and a facility to put local businesses 'in the forefront of new information technology', much of it paid for by the Millennium Commission. By July Technopolis was to be 'A computer mini-city for Norwich' (*Eastern Daily Press*, 15 July 1995). Costing £79 million, it was to be a futuristic project to combine the latest information technology with entertainment, education, business and tourism, but despite strong promotion and after a very vigorous county-wide debate, the idea did not gain traction and died. It was rejected by many people who said that the computing aspects of the project would quickly become an outdated white elephant. On 17 May 1996 the Millennium Commission also rejected the grant application for Technopolis.

THE FORUM

After this rejection by the Millennium Commission, a scaled-down scheme for a new Norfolk and Norwich Millennium Library, designed by a leading firm of international architects, Sir Michael Hopkins and Partners, quickly become a welcome alternative. Michael Hopkins, with Norman Foster and others, had become leaders in the field of hi-tech architecture in Britain and had demonstrated that lightweight steel-and-glass structures could be energy efficient. The practice combined ultramodern techniques and traditional architecture. Their proposal, 60 per cent of the size of the previous design, was unveiled in March 1997; it was to be a U-shaped, three-storeyed structure faced with hand-made bricks with a mostly glass roof covering a central atrium and an all-glass front wall facing St Peter Mancroft church (No. 40). This £60 million version was approved by the Millennium Commission, which offered £30 million in June 1997, almost three years after the fire.

The Forum, Norwich, opened in 2001. (John Fielding)

First there had to be a six-month archaeological excavation on a part of the site nearest St Peter Mancroft, and that began in November 1998. Construction work started in June 1999, and the roof with glass and zinc panelling was being assembled by August 2000. The new building was formerly christened 'The Forum' in June 2001. It was to house the Millennium Library, including the old Norfolk Studies Library (renamed the Norfolk Heritage Centre), a tourist information centre, a new American Memorial Library, exhibitions, a shop, the Radio Norfolk and Look East studios, a restaurant and a coffee shop. Beneath all that would be a car park for 250 cars to generate income. Large-scale purchases, funded by an insurance settlement, combined with a successful public appeal, helped to replenish library stocks. The new Norfolk Heritage Centre now contains a freshly assembled comprehensive collection of printed material and old photographs telling the story of Norfolk and its people. The library was formally opened on the first of November 2001 and in April 2003 it received a Civic Trust award. 'The building had fulfilled its brief with a strength and quality that will stand the test of time' (*Eastern Daily Press*, 4 April 2003).

Meanwhile, the Heritage Lottery Fund announced that it would provide a separate £4.2 million grant towards a new £6.7 million Archive Centre for the Norfolk Record Office and the East Anglian Film Archive to be housed in a new building at County Hall on the outskirts of the city near Trowse.

We can all feel so thankful that the county archives survived, even if many of the irreplaceable items in the old Norfolk Studies Library were lost. After more than seven tumultuous years Norwich had gained a state-of-the-art Archive Centre and what has become one of the most popular public libraries in the UK, visited by 5,000 people a day.

The Forum is open 7 a.m. to midnight, the Heritage Centre 10 a.m. to 7 p.m.. This is a good place to study further the ninety-nine other places described in this book. (NR2 1TF)

Norwich Central Library engulfed in flames. The report in the Eastern Daily Press *on 2 August 1994 said: 'The blaze tore through the building at temperatures in excess of 1000 degrees centigrade reducing priceless relics from Norfolk's past into smouldering pieces of ash.' (Archant)*

ABOUT THE AUTHORS

DAVID ROBERTSON MA, MCIFA

David is an archaeologist, historian and geographer who has been studying Norfolk's archaeology and history for over 25 years. Between 2005 and May 2019 he worked for Norfolk County Council's Historic Environment Service; prior to that he was employed by archaeological contractors, including the Norfolk Archaeological Unit. Having run his own heritage consultancy business for two years, he is currently lead national historic environment adviser for Forestry Commission England (Forest Services).

PETER WADE-MARTINS BA, PHD, FSA, MCIFA

Peter is retired, having spent his life studying the archaeology of Norfolk, and has a strong interest in interpreting the landscape to a wider audience. He was County Archaeologist for Norfolk from 1973 to 1999 and then Director of the Norfolk Archaeological Trust until 2014, a career which is summarised in *A Life in Norfolk's Archaeology* (2017). While running the Trust he acquired a number of important monuments which were opened to the public with on-site interpretations schemes.

SUSANNA WADE-MARTINS MA, PHD, FSA

Susanna is a rural historian of the 18th and 19th centuries with a specific interest in buildings and landscape. She is an Honorary Research Associate of the School of History at the University of East Anglia. She has lectured widely on agricultural buildings and landscape history both locally and nationally and has worked for both English Heritage and the Scottish Royal Commission on Ancient and Historic Monuments on projects covering historic farm buildings.

ABOUT THE AERIAL PHOTOGRAPHERS

JOHN FIELDING

John has been an aviation nut since he was a child and never imagined that one day he'd be able to fly his own aircraft or that he'd be able to combine flying with his other great hobby: photography. He first went solo 43 years ago in a glider with the RAF cadets but didn't take up flying seriously until the 1980s. After a break for children, he returned to the air in 2009, and since then he has taken thousands of photographs throughout the UK; 2,700 aerial shots of Norfolk taken from both aircraft and drone can be viewed in his Flickr album.

MIKE PAGE

Mike's interest in flying started when he joined the Waveney Flying Group in 1960. Photography was his hobby and he started taking aerial pictures as he flew around East Anglia. His early photos were film images which he catalogued and stored until digital imagery became readily available. Mike now has what is believed to be the largest aerial photo collection of East Anglia containing almost 200,000 images, all available online. He has published 19 books of East Anglia plus several videos and DVDs. All proceeds from his photo sales and royalties from books are donated to local charities.

SELECTED INDEX